# Macroeconomic Modelling, Economic Policy and Methodology

Demonstrating that there are (superior) alternatives to the modern macroeconomic mainstream and its DSGE (dynamic stochastic general equilibrium) models, this book presents the cutting edge in macroeconomic modelling, economic policy and methodology from the perspective of heterodox economic thinking.

The first part of the book explores methodological issues, advocating for a stronger ethical consideration in macroeconomics and for the adoption of a strategy of pluralism to ensure that macroeconomic theory is capable of adapting to real-world issues. The second part highlights recent trends in empirical Stock-Flow Consistent models by collecting a group of the most well-developed empirical models of five different economies: the Danish, the Dutch, the French, the Italian and the Argentinian models. In all five cases, the models are used to discuss various policy aspects of the individual economies. Finally, the book explores issues of macroeconomic policy which are largely neglected by mainstream economists including financial (in)stability and macro imbalances. The book emphasizes the need for investigating sectoral balances, which are crucial elements for investigating imbalances from the heterodox perspective.

This book will be of significant interest to students and scholars of macroeconomics, economic modelling, economic methodology and heterodox economics more broadly.

**Mikael Randrup Byrialsen** is Associate Professor at the Aalborg University Business School, Denmark.

**Hamid Raza** is Associate Professor at the Aalborg University Business School, Denmark.

**Finn Olesen** is Professor at the Aalborg University Business School, Denmark.

**Routledge Frontiers of Political Economy**
Civil Society, the Third Sector and Social Enterprise

**Corporations, Accounting, Securities Laws, and the Extinction of Capitalism**
*Wm. Dennis Huber*

**Moral Discourse in the History of Economic Thought**
*Laurent Dobuzinskis*

**Economics and Art Theory**
*Edited by Stratos Myrogiannis and Constantinos Repapis*

**Capitalism and Agrarian Change**
Production and Reproduction in Indonesia
*Muchtar Habibi*

**Capitalist Agriculture and the Global Bee Crisis**
*Rebecca Ellis*

**China, Trust and Digital Supply Chains**
Dynamics of a Zero Trust World
*Warwick Powell*

**Macroeconomic Modelling, Economic Policy and Methodology**
Economics at the Edge
*Edited by Mikael Randrup Byrialsen, Hamid Raza and Finn Olesen*

***Economics, Anthropology and the Origin of Money as a Bargaining Counter***
*Patrick Spread*

***Bernard Schmitt's Quantum Macroeconomic Analysis***
*Alvaro Cencini*

For more information about this series, please visit: www.routledge.com/Routledge-Frontiers-of-Political-Economy/book-series/SE0345

# Macroeconomic Modelling, Economic Policy and Methodology

## Economics at the Edge

**Edited by**
**Mikael Randrup Byrialsen, Hamid Raza and Finn Olesen**

Routledge
Taylor & Francis Group
LONDON AND NEW YORK

First published 2023
by Routledge
4 Park Square, Milton Park, Abingdon, Oxon OX14 4RN

and by Routledge
605 Third Avenue, New York, NY 10158

*Routledge is an imprint of the Taylor & Francis Group, an informa business*



*British Library Cataloguing-in-Publication Data*
A catalogue record for this book is available from the British Library

*Library of Congress Cataloging-in-Publication Data*
Names: Byrialsen, Mikael Randrup, editor. | Raza, Hamid, editor. | Olesen, Finn, editor.
Title: Macroeconomic modelling, economic policy and methodology : economics at the edge / edited by Mikael Randrup Byrialsen, Hamid Raza and Finn Olesen.
Description: Abingdon, Oxon ; New York, NY : Routledge, 2023. | Series: Routledge frontiers of political economy | Includes bibliographical references and index.
Identifiers: LCCN 2022018139 (print) | LCCN 2022018140 (ebook) | ISBN 9781032182117 (hbk) | ISBN 9781032182131 (pbk) | ISBN 9781003253457 (ebk)
Subjects: LCSH: Macroeconomics—Mathematical models. | Economic policy.
Classification: LCC HB172.5 .M3223 2023 (print) | LCC HB172.5 (ebook) | DDC 339—dc23/eng/20220718
LC record available at https://lccn.loc.gov/2022018139
LC ebook record available at https://lccn.loc.gov/2022018140

ISBN: 978-1-032-18211-7 (hbk)
ISBN: 978-1-032-18213-1 (pbk)
ISBN: 978-1-003-25345-7 (ebk)

DOI: 10.4324/9781003253457

Typeset in Times New Roman
by codeMantra

# Contents

# Figures

# Tables

# Contributors

Mikael Randrup Byrialsen, Associate Professor at Aalborg University Business School

Arne Heise, Professor at Hamburg University

Thibault Laurentjoye, Assistant Professor at Aalborg University Business School

Catherine R Macaulay, GI Think Tank, Melbourne

Mogens Ove Madsen, Associate Professor at Aalborg University Business School

Jacques Mazier, Professor Emeritus at Université Paris-13

Huub Meijers, Associate Professor at Maastricht University

Joan Muysken, Professor Emeritus at Maastricht University

Finn Olesen, Professor at Aalborg University Business School

Christos Pierros, Senior researcher at Labour Institute INE-GSEE

Hamid Raza, Associate Professor at Aalborg University Business School

Luis Reyes, Professor at Kedge Business School

Louis-Philippe Rochon, Professor at Laurentian University

Robert Ayreton Bailey Smith, Assistant Professor at Aalborg University Business School

Sebastian Valdecantos, Assistant Professor at Aalborg University Business School

Guillaume Vallet, Associate Professor at Université Grenoble Alpes

Francesco Zezza, PostDoc at Sapienza Università di Roma

Gennaro Zezza, Associate Professor at Università di Cassino

# 1 Introduction – economics at the edge

*Mikael Randrup Byrialsen, Hamid Raza and Finn Olesen*

## Introduction

Ever since the Great Recession, the modern macroeconomic mainstream has been criticised theoretically as well as methodologically. Did it cope with real-world phenomena in a realistic way? Is a uniform methodological approach of doing macroeconomics with a focus on abstract mathematical reasoning and modelling the only way of addressing important macroeconomics problems? Or should one rather allow for more pluralism presenting not only the theoretical mainstream story but also important alternative heterodox theories and use a variety of methodological approaches?

While neither macroeconomics nor policy recommendation changed significantly following the Great Financial Crisis (GFC) as discussed in Olesen (2016), the reactions to the COVID crisis, however, are more interesting from a heterodox perspective, since Keynesian policy seems to be back in fashion (see, i.e., Byrialsen et al. 2021). The focus on balance on the public budget, which permeated economic policy after GFC, has suddenly been replaced by planned public deficits, just like temporary permission of breaking the 'Budget law' within the EU has been discussed by national institutions (The Danish Economic Council 2021). At the same time, the Rebuilding Macroeconomic Theory Project was launched with the purpose of investigating the need for a change in the benchmark New Keynesian dynamic stochastic general equilibrium (DSGE) model. In Blanchard (2018) it is suggested that the purpose of DSGE benchmark models should be to provide a generally accepted theoretical framework. He states that other types of models should be used as policy models, where the purpose is primarily to fit data and facilitate policy analysis. This statement is an important recognition of the heterodox critique towards the current state of macroeconomic theory; DSGE modelling is not the only approach to macroeconomic modelling. An alternative which has gained much attention especially among Post-Keynesian economists is the approach of Stock-Flow Consistent models following the traditions of Wynne Godley. The work on establishing heterodox empirical macroeconomic models must be seen as an important contribution to create an alternative to the actual focus on replacing the old-fashion structural econometric models with different types of general equilibrium features.

DOI: 10.4324/9781003253457-1

As pointed out by Nikiforos & Zezza (2017), the number of researchers adopting the approach of Stock-Flow Consistent models has been increasing since the publication of Godley & Lavoie (2006) and after the GFC. A growing number of attempts have been initiated to establish a benchmark model, which provides a generally accepted theoretical framework for heterodox economists. While most of the models are theoretical in the sense that they do not aim at reproducing the balance sheet and transactions for any specific economy, the number of models attempting to explain individual economies has also increased over the last decade. A number of empirical SFC models built for specific countries including Argentina (Valdecantos), Denmark (Byrialsen et al.), France (Reyes & Mazier), Italy (Zezza & Zezza) and the Netherlands (Muyskens & Meijers) are collected in this book. This collection of empirical models for different countries enables an important starting point for sharing experiences related to empirical models and comparing different methodologies across the models, which might help modellers in improving their models. These models provide a framework for discussing the interdependencies between the various financial and non-financial flows and stock represented in the economy. From a policy perspective, the formal framework offered by these economic models allows for a discussion on how to design the strategy for conducting economic policy in an effective way as well as discussions regarding the implications of different economic policies.

An important lesson learnt from the years of the Great Recession and the current COVID-19 pandemic is that economic policy should not only focus on designing rules concerning optimal monetary and fiscal policies. Economic policy aspects must be seen in a broader perspective as highlighted by heterodox economists for several decades. The status of Keynesian economics is evaluated in the spring 2020 issue of the *Review of Keynesian Economics*. The perception among the contributors seems to be that Keynesian economics is alive and that Keynesian policy recommendation seems to be an imperative need in times of crisis (see, for instance, (Rowthorn 2020) and (Eichengreen 2020)). As Palley et al. (2020, p. 21) conclude: "We are living in a time which many believe has a distinctly Keynesian character… its legacy remains in place in the sense that discretionary counter-cyclical fiscal policy is back … Likewise, activist monetary policy is back". A Keynesian perspective on economic policy is broader than just arguing for expansionary policies in the short run. A Keynesian policy also focuses on the right policy strategy concerning the longer run. This concerns questions, amongst others, of inequality, environmental sustainability, the design of a well-functioning welfare state and the aim to achieve a satisfactory level of output, close to that of full employment.

To sum up, as the modern macroeconomic mainstream is still challenged by empirical evidence from real life, we think there is an urgent need to present the cutting edge of research within heterodox economic thinking. In doing so, the present book not only aims at addressing problems related to methodological aspects but also tries to highlight the many benefits of using an empirical Stock-Flow Consistent modelling approach. Furthermore, it also attempts to address and discuss important economic policy aspects using a broader perspective than that of the present modern macroeconomic mainstream. The book chapters are divided into three parts.

## Part I: METHODOLOGY

The first part of the book covers various methodological aspects of macroeconomics. It consists of three chapters.

In Chapter 2, Arne Heise discusses how one could try to cope with the problems of ideology and pluralism in economics. He argues that, as a social science, economics studies social interactions. What ostensibly distinguishes it from the other social sciences is, first, its focus on interactions involving the management of scarce resources and the social provisioning process and, second, its conception of itself as generating traceable, verifiable findings that are free of normative judgements but instead yield objective knowledge. Some regard this methodological foundation of positivist fallibilism as the feature that makes economics the queen of the social sciences. However, others are critical of these core assumptions, which they believe have no place in a social science. Interestingly, both critiques and defences of economics often refer to ideology: defenders claim that economics is as free of ideological bias as possible, while critics deny economics' status as a science and instead regard it as an ideology that serves to uphold power relations. The chapter by Arne Heise explores the relationship between ideology and economics with special reference to German academia, asking whether a pluralist approach to economics could help make the discipline less vulnerable to the charge of being ideological.

Chapter 3, written by Finn Olesen, discusses if macroeconomics should deal with ethical considerations. In the years after the Great Recession, modern macroeconomic mainstream has increasingly been criticised for its lack of theoretical relevance. The story the mainstreamers tell is often very far away from the facts of real life. There is hardly any empirical evidence to confirm that agents perform economically perfectly rationally, ensuring intertemporal macroeconomic outputs on the unique intertemporal equilibrium path. However, aside from theoretical and methodological criticisms, as non-mainstreamers have provided for years, the modern macroeconomic mainstream could also be exposed to criticism concerning how it copes with ethical matters. Ought macroeconomics concern itself with ethical considerations and questions of morality? Seen from the perspective of Finn Olesen and others, the answer to this question is of course a yes.

In Chapter 4, Mogens Ove Madsen highlights the importance of coping with the concept of time in economics the right way. As he points out, studies by John Maynard Keynes himself and a number of his professional successors – and not least Victoria Chick – leave no doubt that the concept of time should be of central importance in economic analysis. It is also indisputable that in the sense of one of Keynes' old teachers, the philosopher of time, McTaggart, it is the A-series with past, present and future that should be given important focus rather than focusing only on the B-series with before, now and after. This raises the interesting epistemological problem of being able to distinguish between past, present and future, and how theory formation and methodology should be handled.

## Part II: EMPIRICAL SFC MODELLING

The second part of the book consists of five chapters. It covers modelling aspects of macroeconomics and contains a collection of empirical stock-flow consistent (SFC) models aimed at addressing some general as well as country-specific issues.

In Chapter 5, Mikael Randrup Byrialsen, Hamid Raza and Christos Pierros discuss the link between the house prices, business cycles and credit cycles within the lenses of an empirical SFC model for the Danish economy. In some literature house prices are seen as an important driver behind financial cycles in most countries, since a high correlation between changes in house prices, business cycles and financial cycles can be identified. Focusing on the Danish data since 1950, all financial cycles seem to be led by changes in house prices and business cycles. Contrary to expectations, however, is the current situation in the Danish economy, where house prices (and assets prices in general) have increased significantly, while the demand for credit among the households has stagnated since the crisis. In this chapter Byrialsen, Raza and Pierros build an empirical SFC model for the Danish economy to investigate the different channels through which housing prices affect both business cycles and credit cycles, with specific focus on the period leading up to the latest crisis. Identifying the channels before the latest crisis enables the authors to discuss the effect of a lower accepted debt-to-income ratio introduced by households, banks or the government. While the effects in the short run seem as expected, the medium-run effects provide interesting information.

In Chapter 6, Joan Muysken and Huub Meijers discuss the impact of financialisation and assets price bubbles in the Netherlands. The Dutch economy is an interesting case study, since it experienced an exceptionally strong rise in financialisation during the last decades. The authors present a fully consistent data set of the Dutch economy distinguishing between the following sectors: households, firms, government, pension funds, central bank, banks and the foreign sector. In their simulations, they show that both house prices and asset prices increased in the last years; that forced savings due to the funded pension system exceed total savings in several years, implying negative voluntary savings; that the deposit financing gap of the banking system is still very large; that firms use the majority of their savings to buy financial assets abroad instead of investing them in physical capital;

and that quantitative easing injections by the European Central Bank have mainly resulted in increased foreign asset liabilities by Dutch banks. The latter phenomenon, together with the still high incidence of mortgages and the potential bubble in asset prices, indicates the vulnerability of the Dutch economy in this era of financialisation.

In Chapter 7, Luis Reyes and Jacques Mazier study the implications of two exogenous shocks on the French economy via an empirical macroeconomic SFC for France: housing prices and quantitative easing. They show how an exogenous increase in land prices raises housing investment, which in turn raises housing prices, while at the same time reinforcing land profitability. However, this turns out to be unsustainable given the falling disposable income caused in part by the increase in the interest rate, both of which are determinants of housing investment by households. The financial sector distinguishes Banque de France and other financial institutions. In order to isolate the central bank, and without sacrificing adherence to official data while at the same time keeping the model simple and realistic, Reyes and Mazier split currency and deposits into four sub-items: (1) bills and coins, (2) banks reserves, (3) deposits and (4) refinancing. This allows them to study the impact of an increase in Target 2 (an asset for Banque de France) in the French economy. An exogenous increase in money creation via this variable makes funds available for Banque de France, with which in turn it can refinance other financial institutions. This can have positive effects on the economy if used differently than has been the case in the run-up of the Global Financial Crisis (GFC).

In Chapter 8, Gennaro Zezza and Francesco Zezza present their SFC Quarterly Model of the Italian economy. Macroeconomists and political officers need rigorous, albeit realistic, quantitative models to forecast the future paths and dynamics of some variables of interest while being able to evaluate the effects of alternative scenarios. At the heart of all these models lies a standard macroeconomic module that, depending on the degree of sophistication and the research questions to be answered, represents how the economy works. However, the complete absence of a realistic monetary framework, along with the abstraction of banks and more generally of real—financial interactions—not only in dynamic stochastic general equilibrium (DSGE) models but also in central banks' structural econometric models—made it impossible to detect the rising financial fragility that led to the Great Recession. In this chapter, Zezza and Zezza show how to address the missing links between the real and financial sectors within a Post-Keynesian framework, presenting a quarterly SFC structural model of the Italian economy. They set up the accounting structure of the sectoral transactions starting from the appropriate sectoral data sources. They then "close" all sectoral financial accounts, describe portfolio choices and define the buffer stocks for each class of assets and sector in the model. Furthermore, the authors describe their estimation strategy, present the main stochastic equations and finally discuss the main channels of transmissions in their model.

In Chapter 9, Sebastian Valdecantos discusses the seemingly never-ending balance of payments crisis of Argentina with the use of an empirical SFC model for the Argentinian economy. After the peak registered in 2011 Argentina's per capita GDP has oscillated with a decreasing trend, leaving the economy poorer than it was ten years before. During these ten years different governments with antagonistic macroeconomic programmes were in power, none of them being able to take the economy away from stagflation. In this chapter, Valdecantos tests the hypothesis that the cause of the persistent crisis in the balance of payments lies in the inconsistency of the policy mix adopted by governments, regardless of their ideological orientation. On the premise that external conditions throughout the sample period were favourable for emerging countries (although, for Latin American countries, not as favourable as they were until the GFC), some of the policy variables of each of the regimes implemented are modified to assess whether, given the conditions of the external context, it is possible to find a policy mix that results in a growth rate consistent with the balance of payments equilibrium. The policy tools incorporated into the model comprise many of the dimensions of macroeconomic policy: fiscal, monetary, exchange rate, income and redistribution policies, as well as the capital flow regulation approach. Subsequently, the resilience of the sustainable policy mix found is evaluated using less optimistic scenarios for the external context. The analysis is made through an empirical quarterly SFC model (for the period 2007–2020) to ensure the coherence of the results and to give the outcomes of the simulations a holistic and dynamically consistent interpretation. Finally, the chapter presents a short reflection about the social and political viability of the "optimal" policy mix obtained through the model.

## Part III: Economic policy aspects

The third and final part of the book consists of four chapters. It addresses issues that are important for shaping macroeconomic policies.

In Chapter 10, Louis-Philippe Rochon and Guillaume Vallet discuss the role of central bank policy in the economy and its implications for democracy and social responsibilities. In mainstream macroeconomics, monetary policy is neutral in the long run, but may have some short-term influence on the real economy. While the impact of monetary policy on income distribution has become an important area of research on mainstream theory its impact is considered temporary, shortlived and therefore inconsequential in the setting of monetary policy. The authors argue that Post-Keynesian research shows long-lasting effects of monetary policy on both income and wealth inequality, consistent with the recent work on Post-Keynesian interest rate rules. The authors argue there are important implications for central banks with respect to the social responsibilities of an essentially unelected central banker. Is it time to rethink the relationship between central banks within democratic societies?

In Chapter 11, Thibault Laurentjoye investigates the degrees of freedom of monetary policy in an open economy setup, using as a starting point the monetary policy trilemma, or impossible trinity, which famously states that economic authorities cannot lead autonomous monetary policy – in the form of interest rate targeting – while maintaining their currency exchange rate fixed and allowing capitals to move freely. The author surveys various strains of the existing literature, which include the dilemma vs trilemma debate, the empirical literature on the growing strategic use of foreign exchange reserves and the less well-known quadrilemma theory. He then uses a simple stock-flow model to recreate the experimental conditions posited by the trilemma to analyse the effect of autonomous changes in monetary policy on the central bank balance sheets. The simulations show that short-term and long-term effects differ and therefore need to be distinguished. On the one hand, an autonomous interest rate increase will boost foreign exchange reserves in the short run but will prove unsustainable in the long run. On the other hand, if the negative short-run effects of an autonomous interest decrease can be absorbed through pre-existing foreign exchange reserves, it will be viable in the long run. The author concludes that under certain conditions the usual trilemma can be bypassed and suggests replacing it with a quadrilemma which would include the existence of foreign exchange reserve constraints as a fourth corner.

In chapter 12 Byrialsen, Smith and Olesen provide an introduction to the early contributors to the System of National Accounts for each of Denmark, Finland, Norway and Sweden. Using the data available in the sectoral national accounts for the four Nordic countries we investigate the statistical properties of the net lending of the different sectors of the four Nordic economies. The calculated correlation between net lending of the different sectors of the economy, together with the correlation between the net lending of the sectors and the different phases of the business cycle, confirm the results to be found in the scarce literature analysing the sectoral balances. We use rolling correlations to establish a number of correlations instead of focusing on just one point estimate for the sample as a whole. This raises some concerns about the validity of point estimates over longer periods of time, just like it enables us to identify and discuss radical shifts the correlation between net lending of a certain sector and, for example, the output gap, which might be explained by a change in the behaviour of economic agents, where a change in the behaviour of any broad group of economic agents might modify the effect of any economic policy.

In Chapter 13, Catherine Macaulay questions the conventional approach of economics towards financial markets while focusing on its implication for financial instability. Conventional approaches to economic dynamics generally presume capitalism's hallmark share trading markets are both a 'given' and an inspired innovation. A critical view presents a different picture. History explains why 'the share' remains an enigmatic instrument and why volatile and manipulable share prices cannot be relied upon as realistic measures of value. Conflating primary and secondary markets as 'markets' in economic theory has assisted the rise of unproductive financial market trading within capitalism. The author argues that unwinding this conflation would facilitate development of theories that are more realistic. Despite the 1929 Great Crash and 1970s downturns, economists assisted the share markets' return to prominence in the 1980s, introducing conundrums for monetary policy and economic theory. Changing monetary policy goals from 'price stability' to 'financial stability' has left central banks implicitly responsible for stable share markets, something never proven possible. The author argues that building productive economies by supporting small business' preference for internal or bank finance, directing pension savings towards investment in productive activity and confirming the original monetary policy goal of 'price stability' would help strengthen productive enterprise capitalism. A new direction for economic policy would require a new theoretical approach.

## References

Byrialsen, Mikael R., Olesen, Finn, & Madsen, Mogens O. (2021). The macroeconomic effects of covid-19: The imperative need for a Keynesian solution. *Revue de la Régulation. Capitalisme, Institutions, Pouvoirs*, 29, pp. 1–19.

Danish Economic Council (2021). *Danish Economy Spring 2021.* Danish Economic Council.

Eichengreen, Barry (2020). Keynesian economics: Can it return if it never died? *Review of Keynesian Economics*, 8(1), pp. 23–35.

Godley, Wynne, & Lavoie, Marc (2006). *Monetary Economics: An Integrated Approach to Credit, Money, Income, Production and Wealth.* Springer Verlag.

Nikiforos, Michalis, & Zezza, Gennaro (2017). Stock-flow consistent macroeconomic models: A survey. *Journal of Economic Surveys*, 31(5), pp. 1204–1239.

Olesen, Finn (2016). The making of a revolution: How important are economic crises? In *Macroeconomics After the Financial Crisis*, Madsen, Mogens Ove & Olesen, Finn (eds.), pp. 86–97, Routledge.

Palley, Thomas et al. (2020). Do current times vindicate Keynes and is New Keynesian macroeconomics Keynesian? *Review of Keynesian Economics*, 8(1), pp. 21–22.

Rowthorn, Robert (2020). The Godley-Tobin lecture: Keynesian economics – back from the dead? *Review of Keynesian Economics*, 8(1), pp. 1–20.

# Part I

# Methodology

# 2 Ideology, *Werturteilsfreiheit* and pluralism in economics*

*Arne Heise*

## Introduction

Economics is a social science, which means that it studies social interactions, just like disciplines such as sociology and political science. What distinguishes it from these other disciplines is, first, its focus on interactions involving the management of scarce resources and, second, the fact that the overwhelming majority of academic economists understand themselves to be generating traceable, verifiable findings that are free of normative judgements and individual or group/class-specific perspectives but instead yield 'objective knowledge', whereby only propositions that are deduced in a logically correct manner and cannot be empirically falsified are accepted (see e.g. Drakopoulos 1997). Some regard this methodological foundation of positivist fallibilism as the feature that makes economics the 'queen of the social sciences' (see e.g. Badinger et al. 2017) because it appears to guarantee an objectivity and value freedom analogous to the natural sciences. Others (such as Beschorner 2017) are critical of core assumptions that they believe have no place in a social science, such as the oft-criticised notion of the *homo economicus*.

Interestingly, both critiques and defences of economics often make reference to ideology: defenders claim that economics is as free of ideological bias as it is possible to be, while critics deny economics' status as a science and instead regard it as an 'ideology that serves to uphold power relations' (Girscher 2012:1, author's translation). How did these apparently contradictory positions come about? Is it due to the ambivalent use of the term 'ideology' or, as Joan Robinson believes, the fact that:

> economics has always been partly a vehicle for the ruling ideology of each period as well as partly a method of scientific investigation.
> (Robinson 1962:1)

This chapter will explore the relationship between ideology and economics, in line with the task formulated by Robinson:

> To sort out as best we may this mixture of ideology and science.
> (Robinson 1962: 25)

DOI: 10.4324/9781003253457-3

Special reference is given to German academic economics that is sometimes portrayed as particularly stiff-necked in its alliance with market apologetics (see e.g. Bachmann 2015). Moreover, one particular focus will be to consider whether a pluralist approach to economics, something for which there are growing calls (see e.g. Dobusch & Kapeller 2012; Heise 2017a, 2018; Beckenbach 2019), could help to make the discipline less vulnerable to the charge of being ideological.

## DSGE as standard economics

Like all sciences, economics has a long history of theoretical and methodological development. The discipline's theoretical development is documented in numerous works on the history of economic thought, while its methodological development includes the two *Methodenstreite* ('method disputes') of the 19th and early 20th centuries. These disputes concerned economics' conception of itself as a scientific discipline, something that is important for the internal consolidation of an epistemic community so that it does not have to constantly debate what can and cannot be accepted as a scientifically validated result. In Lakatosian terms, what was at stake in these disputes was economics' methodological dimension as a quality control criterion. Positivist fallibilism prevailed over historico-empirical and normative-evaluative methodologies inasmuch as proponents of the latter approaches left (or were forced to leave) economics as a discipline and instead flocked to the sociological institutions that were also expanding at that time.[1] Inspired by the natural sciences (especially physics), there was a clear ambition to create a science capable of producing generally accepted findings (i.e. 'objective knowledge') on the basis of 'methodological monism'.[2] In line with the Kuhnian theory of science, it is considered a sign of a science's maturity when, after a period of competition between different theoretical approaches, it arrives at a monistic paradigm that can lay sole claim to being the 'objective truth' and ward off any relativism that would undermine this claim.

With the dynamic stochastic general equilibrium (DSGE) model, a paradigm (in Kuhnian terminology), scientific research programme (in Lakatosian terminology) or *Denkstil* ('thought style', in Fleckian terminology) was established that can indisputably be considered 'market-oriented' and 'market-friendly'. It is 'market-oriented' because it takes exchange processes that typically occur in markets as its ontological basis. Decision and action situations under conditions of scarcity are modelled in terms of intertemporal exchange relations. This is done on the basis of certain core epistemological assumptions ('axioms') such as the rationality, substitution and ergodic axioms, which – supplemented by a 'protective belt' of microeconomic assumptions including rational expectation formation, infinitesimal rates of price and quantity adjustment, conditions of perfect competition and the absence of transaction costs (the essential features of 'perfect markets') and the macroeconomic condition of Walras' law – describe a state of general equilibrium. As used here in the sense of 'market clearing' and 'balance of supply and demand', equilibrium can, to be sure, be understood as having positive connotations, since it describes a state in which market actors do not want anything to change. Precisely where the equilibrium state is situated will depend on many subjective factors (preferences, inclinations, utility calculations, etc.), and although attempts to strip away this subjective element to yield a purely objective analysis have been unsuccessful (see Drakopoulos 1997:293ff.), the subjectivity is confined to the model's 'data' and does not extend to the methodology of the inquiry itself.

All other paradigms, scientific research programmes or *Denkstile*, such as Marxian theories, the various post-Keynesianisms, behavioural economics, complexity economics, evolutionary economics, feminist economics and the Austrian School, have been either increasingly marginalised or they form a tolerated 'cutting edge', which according to some commentators is where the truly interesting work within the dominant DSGE paradigm is being done (cf. Colander, Holt & Rosser 2004:486ff.). The status of a paradigm – tolerated or marginalised – depends crucially on whether it shares the ontological, market-oriented and market-friendly core of the DSGE paradigm as a heuristic or at least does not aggressively challenge it ('dissenters' are tolerated) or openly reject it ('heterodox' approaches are marginalised).[3]

## On the concept of ideology

Before turning to the question of the extent to which economics, in the form of the dominant research programme with its aspiration to the status of a science, is or is not ideological, the concept of 'ideology' must be briefly clarified. The sociologist Karl Mannheim (1954) distinguishes between a value-free and an evaluative concept of ideology. The value-free conception understands ideology as a vision of a desired (i.e. positively construed) state. It is thus value-free not in the sense that it does not involve subjective assessments, but in that it is a neutral descriptor of a 'worldview' that serves as a necessary guide to social action. The evaluative concept of ideology, by contrast, refers to an interpretation of reality that, in the service of particular interests, consciously or unconsciously conceals certain facts or makes untrue/unverifiable claims.

In this chapter, I shall be using this negatively connoted concept of ideology. Accordingly, to call economics ideological is to imply that it, consciously or unconsciously, 'sells' untruths as truths so as to promote individual or group/class-specific interests.

But why should economics accept this charge of ideological distortion, if its methodological apparatus is geared precisely towards producing maximally objective 'truths' (i.e. traceable, verifiable findings)? One common argument points to the supposed autism of the theoretical framework, which does not allow any meaningful reference to reality. This criticism thus takes aim at the lack of social context in the often highly formal economic models, and questions the realism of the core axioms, especially the rationality assumption. Critics also argue that the underlying conception of *homo economicus* reduces human beings to 'calculating machines' and represses social ties and motivations in favour of a fully economically rational way of acting, thereby covertly smuggling in normative aspects. Finally, the way that the state of general equilibrium is treated as an 'ideal' or 'model' solution is criticised for constructing a 'Nirvana model', from which (predominantly 'laissez-faire') economic policy conclusions are derived that are adopted uncritically and in extreme form into general conceptions ('supply-side policies' with a primary focus on allocation). According to the critics,[4] the ideological nature of economics thus construed consists in its giving a description of reality that, in virtue of its abstractness and tendency to prefer a particular market solution (equilibrium), must be considered 'untrue' and ultimately only serves the interests of those who profit from uncorrected market outcomes.

## DSGE and ideology

When assessing these interpretations of economics in its current form (i.e. the DSGE paradigm as 'normal science' that claims monistic authority) as an ideological product, we should distinguish between criticism of the paradigm itself and criticism of the way economists operate with it. In response to criticisms of the paradigm, it can always be conceded that of course each individual assumption, whether in the core or the protective belt, can and, in the spirit of critical scrutiny, indeed must be questioned. This happens constantly in scientific practice, and is the source of the myriad variations within the DSGE paradigm, which have given rise not just to the two fundamental strands of standard and new Keynesianism on the one hand and new classical macroeconomics on the other, which differ primarily in the assumptions in the protective belt, but also to extensions of the *Denkstil* such as experimental, behavioural and complexity economics, which take a critical view even of the core axioms, though without questioning the DSGE heuristic. These extensions diverge sufficiently that it is possible to derive alternative economic policy conceptions from them, such as supply- or demand-side policies. We do not have to agree with Hans-Werner Sinn (2014; own translation), who claims that 'economists (like tracking dogs) scour the economy looking for flaws and consider how to rectify them by means of smart state interventions', to concede that this is possible within the framework of the DSGE paradigm, and indeed is often done in practice. Thus, the market fundamentalism often disparaged as 'ideological' is not a feature of the DSGE paradigm per se, but can at most be imputed to certain variants and to those proponents who, at least in the policies they derive from the theory, tend to attribute considerable real-world efficacy to the self-regulatory mechanism of 'perfect markets'.

Another possible criticism is that the entire approach of economics is misguided because human behaviour simply cannot be represented in the deterministic terms of the natural sciences and any attempt to do so will necessarily result in flawed judgements and ideological assertions rather than objective knowledge. However, frequent discussions of this topic have yielded little in the way of results (in the sense of objective knowledge as opposed to ideological distortion; see Adorno 1962; Popper 1962; Keuth 1989). By contrast with economic sociology, economics aspires to produce generally valid 'explanations', not merely to offer contextualised 'understanding'. Whether it is actually possible to satisfy this ambition within the framework of 'positivist fallibilism' depends on conditions that we shall turn to shortly. In any case, the fact that economics relies on model-theoretic abstractions that necessarily make little reference to reality is by itself not enough to ground a charge of ideology.

What really matters is how economists operate with DSGE models. We shall consider, first, the history of DSGE's rise to the status of dominant paradigm, and, second, the prevalence of DSGE modelling in actual educational and political practice.

## From interwar pluralism to DSGE monism

In most highly developed economies, including Germany, economics was not always dominated by the DSGE model. In line with Kuhnian theory, during the interwar period, and also later on in the 1960s and 1970s, there was a wide array of different, competing theories, which were represented at universities by the holders of professorial posts. Until the end of World War II, many of the economics professors at German universities were proponents of the 'historical school', but there were also some Marxist professors (at least until the 1930s). Only in the course of the 'self-Americanisation' of German academic economics post-1945 (cf. Hesse 2010:320ff.; Hesse 2012) did economics professors come to be increasingly recruited from proponents of DSGE modelling, in the form of the then-dominant standard Keynesianism; as with the later restructuring of economics in accordance with 'international standards', this was an expression of a desire to satisfy externally defined 'quality criteria'. This narrowing of the paradigmatic composition of the community of academic economists that had grown so dramatically over the years was interrupted by a brief phase of repluralisation in the 1960s and 1970s, when, in the wake of the student protests and widespread social reforms, more heterodox staff were appointed, especially at the newly founded universities, with the explicit aim of providing an alternative to the standard economics that was only just beginning to consolidate. However, this pluralisation was very limited in quantitative terms and confined to only certain institutions, and gained no purchase in the wider economics community, as evidenced in the dearth of appointments of heterodox economists working in the post-Keynesian or Marxian traditions at the older, traditional universities (see Heise, Sander & Thieme 2017).

The marginalisation of heterodox economics that could be observed in the subsequent three decades and the simultaneous paradigmatic narrowing at German universities[5] conflicts with the myth of the perfect 'market of economic ideas' in which the 'best ideas' (i.e. those with the greatest empirically supported explanatory power) win out, and instead suggests a flawed, unregulated scientific market. The 'market of economic ideas' has a number of notable features: the commodity of 'scientific knowledge' is an (international) public good whose value depends on trust and confidence. What matters on this market is not price-based supply and demand structures, but the reputation of providers. To ensure quality control, the market generally has excess supply (to ensure a 'selection of the best'). High levels of investment in extremely specific human capital and the associated sunk cost give rise to a demand for standardisation in order to reduce systemic risks. Thanks to path dependencies, lock-in effects or what Ludwik Fleck termed *stilgemäße Denkzwänge* ('thought style compulsion'), this standardisation demand is met by a standardisation supply in the form of various paradigms, economic research programmes or *Denkstile*. Which of them is ultimately able to win out and thus transmute the ontological pluralism (i.e. the variety of 'pre-analytic visions' concerning the essence of the object of investigation) into a monism depends on the providers' economic, social and cultural capital.[6] It is highly plausible that the reason why it was a handful of private elite universities belonging to the USA's scientific hegemony that were able to elevate their *Denkstil* to universally valid status, and one of the reasons why its positing of social exchange as the basic ontological constituent of economic interactions is not seriously questioned, is that a more market-critical ontology would not have been able to flourish in the market-oriented US culture, and, just as importantly, that markets and exchange are always presupposed as the basic forms of economic interaction: a 'state of nature' or Kantian a priori analytic judgement (see Aspers 2011:69ff.).

The practice of economics on the basis of methodological and ontological monism is, thus, not the result of fair competition over the best process of inquiry, but rather of a process of standardisation that, like all such processes, can stand in the way of better outcomes (see for instance Arthur 1989). In the case of economics, a better outcome would not be, say, establishing another paradigm as a monistic standard, but rather accepting the pluralist imperative that applies to the social sciences (see Heise 2017a). Positing a pre-analytic vision becomes ideological if alternative ontologies, such as a Marxian power-based or post-Keynesian obligation-based ontology, are discriminated against; and this is true regardless of whether this discrimination is deliberate or a result of ignorance.

## Textbook DSGE and ideology

The practice of a science also includes, of course, passing on knowledge to the next generation of scholars. A value-free, unideological approach here would require teaching future economists about the theoretical foundations of their discipline at the earliest possible stage in their education. Furthermore, true to the didactic principle that students should not be indoctrinated, it should be an explicit aim of educational practice to either teach about the plurality of existing paradigms or make clear the one-sidedness of the approach that is being used. Thus, a class on 'neoclassical economics'[7] or a textbook on post-Keynesianism would definitely be permissible, but a course on the foundations of economics based solely on a textbook that describes just one paradigmatic approach would have to be rejected as value-laden and hence ideological. An increasing number of studies[8] on the content of curricula and choice/content of textbooks suggests that this is the case for the vast majority of economics teaching at German universities: although there exist plenty of textbooks with a pluralist approach,[9] almost all institutions exclusively use the US textbooks that dominate the market (or their German translations), all of which not only relay a decidedly neoclassical approach but also fail to situate this approach within the landscape of different theories, and refer only to developments or refinements within the same paradigm or *Denkstil*; they do not cite any heterodox literature. The approach taken by Blanchard & Illing (2015), the most-used textbook in German university seminars, can serve as an example. Macroeconomic disputes are explained in terms of Keynesian and classical variants of the DSGE paradigm, or by reference to the distinction between the short run (involving temporary disequilibriums and states of market failure, where state interventions would make sense) and the middle/long run (where the 'natural' equilibrium states are reached, and state interventions would be ineffective/unnecessary). Moreover, the distinction between short- and medium-/long-run economics, which differ in terms of their economic policy focus but share the common assumption that the 'market economy' will regulate itself over the long term, was until the fourth edition explicitly described as representing 'common beliefs' about which 'most macroeconomists are in agreement' (Blanchard & Illing 2006:796) and 'propositions accepted by virtually all macroeconomists' (Blanchard & Illing 2006:796). No more is said about the other macroeconomists who disagree, nor is there any critical theoretical reflection on the monism manifested in these statements. Interestingly, in the fifth edition (published after the financial crisis) this section of the textbook was rewritten and replaced by 'First lessons from the financial crisis', though the conclusions it drew from it are conservative in scope: the 'common beliefs' are fundamentally sound, but are only applicable to normal economic situations. Exceptional situations, like the recent global economic crisis, cast the fundamental self-regulation postulate in a more critical light: more research is needed, the authors suggest, though presumably not a scientific revolution (Blanchard & Illing 2015:731). The possibly unconscious, ideological bias in this view is evident from the fact that the instability of the 'market economy' is attributed to the 'exceptional nature' of the situation; whatever does not fit within the explanatory framework of the paradigm is explained away as an 'exception'.

Thus, any attempt to claim economics education in Germany is value-free must itself be regarded as an ideological distortion by groups or individuals misinterpreting reality to suit their own interests.

## Policy consulting and ideology

One especially difficult question concerns the relationship between academia and politics. Politics involves setting and pursuing social goals, guided by values; it is thus pure ideology, at least in the positively connoted sense of the term. But the use of false interpretations of reality to serve one's agenda is also part of the day-to-day business of politics, with policy consultants being brought on board to help provide legitimacy. How can economists working in this field defend their claim to objectivity, or does science always become ideological when put to the service of politics?

To answer this question, it is again necessary to draw a distinction between, on the one hand, the relationship between academia and politics and, on the other, the way in which the policy consulting is practised. A scientific paradigm cannot help being appropriated by political ideologies, just as Marxian economics, the neoclassical Austrian School and standard Keynesianism were respectively used to legitimise communism (see e.g. Ollman 1977), neoliberalism (see e.g. Ötsch 2009) and classical post-war social democracy (see e.g. Przeworski 1985). And of course proposals at the policy/polity level can be derived from scientific paradigms in order to achieve predefined goals (such as the 'magic square of economic policy' or distribution/efficiency targets) or to identify and resolve conflicts between goals. Economic policy is, thus, just like every other area of politics, ideological, whereas economic policy action programmes and their scientific foundations are administrative. Matters become ideological if the competition between action programmes based on the imperative of pluralist economics is suppressed by means of the There Is No Alternative prerogative – but it is *politicians*, not *academics*, who are guilty of this ideological distortion.

Kirchgässner (2013:202) breaks down the actual process of policy consulting (in Germany) into five different categories, the two which most concern us here being proposals addressed to the general public and reports commissioned by political actors or interest groups. If an economist pursues their discipline not just as a purely intellectual challenge or in the spirit of 'l'art pour l'art', they will eventually take some sort of stance on economic policy questions. Their choice of epistemological and ontological frame of reference will be guided either by what they expect will attract the greatest acceptance among colleagues or from the commissioner of their reports or by what they believe will most likely yield the best explanation of, and possibly solution to, the problems or phenomena under investigation (the Lakatosian progressiveness criterion). Paid reports are, without a doubt, the most likely to be ideological, since the rationality of obtaining commissions is at odds with the principle of scientific objectivity. However, not every paid report will necessarily be biased, if the report writer's allegiance to a certain paradigm is known at the time of the commission. In that case, the consultant can abide by the usual scientific criteria enshrined in codes of ethics[10] while simultaneously meeting the commissioner's expectations; however, this presupposes the plurality of economics, a norm that is upheld in reality to only a very limited extent.

If the choice of paradigm is based on the criterion of achieving maximum acceptance in the scientific community or on the progressiveness criterion, this does not necessarily prevent flawed advice, but it does counter the charge of ideology, at least if a paradigm pluralism allows competing advice to be given and it is an explicit condition of the commission that the paradigmatic basis of this advice be made transparent.[11] The (almost)[12] inevitable relativism may be unamenable to politicians in an ideal world in which politics is solely committed to upholding the common good. In the more realistic conception of a world of plural interests, however, pluralist policy consulting allows even non-dominant interests to receive scientific support.[13] This runs counter to the suggestion (cf. Kooths 2018) that science must unify around a consensus in the event of competing advice rather than leaving it to politicians to select whichever advice they deem 'suitable': for if consensus is supposed to mean 'compromise', this would always (assuming one of the initial proposals is correct) result in incorrect policy advice, whereas if it means settling on the smallest common denominator, there would not be much 'policy advice' left over in most cases. Moreover, the reality of policy consulting shows that in many cases, such as the introduction of a minimum wage or the 'debt brake' in Germany or assessments of eurozone austerity, 'consensus' means the majority position of the mainstream, which is 'constantly bandied about with great fanfare' so as to prevent the 'crazy nonsense' of alternative positions from 'becoming respectable' (Potrafke 2017:20; authors translation). Dullien & Horn (2019:930) refute the notion that the correctness or quality of scientific findings and the advice derived from them is a matter of majorities within the scholarly profession. However, it is perhaps more significant that precisely this 'arrogance of the majority' can (and generally does) result in ideological distortion if recommendations are made despite there being empirical evidence that flatly contradicts them. As for instance the statement that rejecting the minimum wage on the basis that it would cause mass job losses despite a demonstrable lack of empirical support for this view; see (Heise 2019a). Or, just to mention another example, the widespread scientific dissent and uncertain empirical evidence as in the case of the 'debt brake' and the effects of austerity, without explicit attention being drawn to the controversial nature and restricted theoretical foundations of these recommendations (e.g. the fact that both examples are based on a 'neoclassical model').

Policy consulting is thus not necessarily at risk of being ideological, at least not if a plurality of advice is ensured by means of pluralist scientific principles and this plurality is actively promoted through transparency about the paradigmatic allegiances of the consultants.[14] The inability of policy consulting to meet these exacting demands is without a doubt the fault of the state that sets the framework and the individual scholars that promulgate ideologies, but only of the discipline of economics as a whole (i.e. the scientific community) insofar as it is unable to ensure the necessary paradigm pluralism.

## Conclusion

This chapter has discussed the relationship between economics and ideology: is economics an ideology-free method of scientific analysis for obtaining objective knowledge, or is it a vehicle of the dominant ideology, or, as Joan Robinson suggested, both at once? The latter option would only be possible if science is attributed a socially formative power and 'ideology' is meant in the positively connoted sense of a social vision.[15] But if 'ideology' means a distortion of reality in the service of certain interests, it is hard to see how economics could be both at once.

However, we have shown that a social science such as economics, particularly if it chooses to understand itself as a positivist science, must necessarily be practised pluralistically, in the sense that multiple paradigms can compete with another over the best interpretation of reality provided that they meet certain methodological standards. This implies that even 'less good' or false interpretations of reality (i.e. interpretations based on false pre-analytic visions) can satisfy the aspiration of scientific analysis if or insofar as they are not clearly falsified by empirical evidence or logical fallacies. However, in order for the relativity of the acquired knowledge not to become ideological distortion, it is necessary that the pluralist imperative be recognised and that there is transparency about the paradigmatic basis of the findings. And it is precisely here that the difference between the fundamental principles of economics and the actual practice of a science by the corresponding scientific community can be seen: if a single monistic paradigm marginalises other competing paradigms and its scientific views and the economic policy recommendations derived from them are 'constantly banded about with great fanfare' (Potrafke 2017:20; authors translation), alternative ideas are rejected as 'crazy nonsense' and the theoretical principles underlying this paradigm are not taught in universities, this must be considered ideological distortion.

The accusation of ideology is sometimes levelled at economics a little overhastily, when its findings do not agree with the views (or prejudices) of the accuser or a cui bono investigation reveals that people who are materially better off will benefit from the economic policy recommendations derived from it.[16] Formal, axiomatic modelling may also be unsuited to understanding social processes – though economists at least (across all paradigmatic divisions), with their positivist self-conception, take a different view (cf. Badinger et al. 2017) – and necessarily requires ungrounded 'value judgements' to be made when selecting the core assumptions (axioms in which the posited ontology is contained). However, this only represents an ideological distortion in the negative sense if a specific model (in this case, the dynamic stochastic equilibrium model that constitutes the contemporary mainstream) claims general validity and rejects all alternative paradigms as 'nonsense' or, under the sway of a 'thought style compulsion', simply ignores realities that contradict theoretical conclusions.[17]

There is little doubt that the current state of economics, and not just in Germany, must be described precisely in these terms: research, teaching and policy consulting are, by and large, based monistically on the DSGE paradigm, even if variations within this paradigm (extensions of the *Denkstil*) are tolerated, especially in research, while alternative paradigms are systematically marginalised.[18] A science whose community[19] is unable to ensure that its discipline is practised in a proper (i.e. pluralist) manner must accept the charge of ideology.

## Notes

* This is a shortened and revised version of an article that has been published in the International Journal of Pluralism and Economics Education

1 Of course, sociology differs from economics not just methodologically, but also in terms of its subject matter (economics: human–object relations, sociology: human–human relations) and epistemological basis (economics: logical explanation of logical action, sociology: logical explanation of non-logical action); cf. Mikl-Horke 2008:25).

2 This refers to uniformity of methodology (not of methods!) within economics and across its various epistemological approaches, and between the natural and social sciences.

3 Keynesianism, which in the form of neo-Keynesianism belongs to the DSGE paradigm and in the form of post-Keynesianism is heterodox, is one example of a paradigm with both heterodox and orthodox variants; others include complexity economics, which can likewise be divided into tolerated orthodox and marginalised heterodox research programmes (see Heise 2017b).

4 See, for example, Wilber and Wisman (1975:672), who speak of an ideal type that 'is treated as if it were a highly confirmed theory of "what is"'.

5 Grimm et al. (2017) estimate that at present over 90% of professors at German-speaking universities use mainstream research approaches.

6 Institutional incentives such as rankings or third-party funding potential can be used as supposedly objective quality criteria in order to consolidate a paradigmatic standard; see, for example, Lee (2007); Lee, Pham and Gu (2013).

7 For instance, the University of Notre Dame's Department of Economics, following an organisational split that saw its heterodox economists hived off into a separate Department of Economics and Policy Studies after decades of coexistence, for a while explicitly referred to itself as 'neoclassical'.

8 See, for example, Beckenbach et al. (2016); Hedtke (2016); Graupe (2017); Peukert (2018a; 2018b).

9 A few examples of such textbooks: for general economics, Heine & Herr (2012); for economic policy, Heise (2010); for microeconomics, Biesecker & Kesting (2003) or Elsner, Heinrich & Schwardt (2015); for growth theory, Hein (2004); and for monetary theory, Ehnts (2017).

10 The German Economic Association's code of ethics, for instance, can be found at www.socialpolitik.de/DE/ethikkodex.
11 Article 2 of the German Act on the Appointment of a Council of Experts on Economic Development can be interpreted in precisely this sense.
12 Different interpretations of reality need not necessarily result in different economic intervention proposals; for instance, it is often hard to distinguish the economic policy approaches of standard, new and post-Keynesian paradigms.
13 This equation of dominant social interests and the dominance of economic paradigms ('the mainstream') that serve these interests is at the core of the socioeconomics of economics (cf. Heise 2016; Heise & Thieme 2016; Heise 2019b).
14 The aforementioned requirement in Article 2 of the German Act on the Appointment of a Council of Experts on Economic Development can be understood in this sense. The same principle was also behind the German Minimum Wage Commission's decision to commission separate reports on the macroeconomic consequences of the minimum wage from Keynesian and neoclassical perspectives; cf. Braun et al. (2017); Herr et al. (2017).
15 It must be noted here that Joan Robinson did not clearly distinguish between positive and negative concepts of ideology, and so her claim that economics is both a vehicle of ideology and a scientific method may be attributable to an insistence on the rationality of visions.
16 Schulmeister (2018:86) appears to be insinuating this when he writes that mainstream economic theories 'are guided by common ideological principles. This is readily evident from the "fruits" of these theories, that is, their recommendations and the consequences of these recommendations, but not so readily from their theoretical constructs. The simplest test is, as ever: whom do the theories benefit?'
17 It follows from the logic of the argument presented here that the accusation of ideology thus formulated does not necessarily mean that the incriminated paradigm must in fact be postulating untruths in favour of specific interests. Only a paradigm that lays claim to sole and objective truth is ideological in this sense.
18 'Systematically' means that it is not simply that more successful scientific networks prevail (e.g. as a result of appointment cartels and close-knit networks between research institutions and funding bodies) but that institutional incentive structures are created (for instance, by introducing appointment criteria and 'performance-based' funding that is awarded according to seemingly objective criteria such as impact-based hierarchies of publications) that privilege the mainstream.
19 With regard to the fundamental right of academic freedom, the state's role as regulator must also be mentioned here. 'Academic freedom' is typically understood as a negative norm that prevents unjustified interventions (especially by the state) in the practice of academic activities. But it can also be understood as a positive, constitutive norm that requires the state to ensure or facilitate proper conduct of academic inquiry.

## Bibliography

Adorno, T. W. (1962) 'Zur Logik der Sozialwissenschaften', *Kölner Zeitschrift für Soziologie und Sozialpsychologie*, 14, pp. 249–263.

Aspers, P. (2011) *Markets*, Cambridge.

Arthur, W. B. (1989) 'Competing technologies, increasing returns, and lock-in by historical events', *The Economic Journal*, 99(394), pp. 116–131.

Bachmann, R. (2015) 'Erkennen, was Quatsch ist'; in: *brand eins*, 17(11), pp. 86–89.

Badinger, H. et al. (2017) 'Pseudowissenschaft in der Volkswirtschaftslehre: "Mainstream" gegen "alternative Zugänge": Über die angebliche Krise der Wirtschaftswissenschaften' in *Der Standard*, 14 July 2017 (https://www.derstandard.at/story/2000061320999/pseudowissenschaft-in-der-volkswirtschaftslehre?ref=article, last accessed 23 August 2019).

Beckenbach, F. (2019) 'Paradigmendominanz in der Ökonomik und die Notwendigkeit eines kompetitiven Pluralismus; in Petersen, D. J. et al., *Perspektiven einer pluralen Ökonomik*, Wiesbaden, pp. 3–24.

Beckenbach, F. et al. (2016) *Zur Pluralität der volkswirtschaftlichen Lehre in Deutschland*, Marburg.

Beschorner, T. (2017) 'Wirtschaft ist Kultur', *ZeitOnline*, 22 August 2017 (https://www.zeit.de/wirtschaft/2017-08/wirtschaftswissenschaften-universitaet-ausbildung-erneuerung/komplettansicht#comments, last accessed 23 August 2019).

Biesecker, A., & Kesting, S. (2003) *Mikroökonomik*, Munich.

Blanchard, O., & Illing, G. (2006) *Makroökonomie*, 3rd expanded edition, Hallbergmoos.

Blanchard, O., & Illing, G. (2015) *Makroökonomie*, 5th expanded edition, Hallbergmoos.

Braun, H. et al. (2017) *Makroökonomische Folgen eines gesetzlichen Mindestlohnes aus neoklassischer Perspektive*, RWI study on behalf of the Minimum Wage Commission, Essen.

Colander, D., Holt, R., & Rosser, B. Jr (2004) 'The changing face of mainstream economics', *Review of Political Economy*, 16(4), pp. 485–499.

Dobusch, L., & Kapeller, J. (2012) 'Heterodox united vs. mainstream city? Sketching a framework for interested pluralism in economics', *Journal of Economic Issues*, 46(4), pp. 1035–1058.

Drakopoulos, S. A. (1997) 'Origins and development of the trend towards value-free economics', *Journal of the History of Economic Thought*, 19(2), pp. 286–300.

Dullien, S., & Horn, G. (2019) 'Replik zum Kommentar von Stefan Kooths', *List Forum für Wirtschafts- und Sozailpolitik*, 44(4), pp. 927–932.

Ehnts, D. H. (2017) *Modern Monetary Theory and European Macroeconomics*, Abingdon.

Elsner, W., Heinrich, T., & Schwardt, H. (2015) *The Microeconomics of Complex Economies: Evolutionary, Institutional, Neoclassical and Complexity Perspectives*, Oxford.

Girscher, C. (2012) 'Wirtschaftswissenschaft als herrschaftssichernde Ideologie. Thesen zum Verhältnis von Herrschaft und Ökonomie', *trend onlinezeitung*, 3, pp. 1–7.

Graupe, S. (2017) *Beeinflussung und Manipulation in der ökonomischen Bildung*, FGW-Studie Neues ökonomisches Denken no. 5, Düsseldorf.

Grimm, C., Kapeller, J., & Pühringer, S. (2017) 'Zum Profil der deutschsprachigen Volkswirtschaftslehre: Paradigmatische Ausrichtung und politische Orientierung deutschsprachiger Ökonom_innen', ICAE Working Paper Series, Johannes Kepler University Linz.

Hedtke, R. (2016) *Paradigmatische Parteilichkeit, lückenhafte Lehrpläne und tendenziöses Unterrichtsmaterial*, FGW-Studie Neues ökonomisches Denken no. 1, Düsseldorf.

Hein, E. (2004) *Verteilung und Wachstum: Eine paradigmenorientierte Einführung unter besonderer Berücksichtigung der post-keynesianischen Theorie*, Marburg.

Heine, M., & Herr, H. (2012) *Volkswirtschaftslehre*, Munich.

Heise, A. (2010) *Einführung in die Wirtschaftspolitik: Grundlagen, Institutionen, Paradigmen*, Münster.

Heise, A. (2016) '"Why has economics turned out this way?" A socio-economic note on the explanation of monism in economics', *The Journal of Philosophical Economics*, 10(1), pp. 81–101.

Heise, A. (2017a) 'Defining economic pluralism: Ethical norm or scientific imperative?', *International Journal of Pluralism and Economics Education*, 8(1), pp. 18–41.

Heise, A. (2017b) 'Whither economic complexity. A new heterodox economic paradigm or just another variation within the mainstream?', *International Journal of Pluralism and Economics Education*, 8(2), pp. 115–129.

Heise, A. (2018) 'Re-claiming the university: Transforming economics as a discipline', *The Journal of Philosophical Economics*, 11(2), pp. 37–66.

Heise, A. (2019a) 'Ludwik Fleck's philosophy and sociology of science and the resilience of modern neoclassical economics – a case study', *The Journal of Philosophical Economics*, 13(1), pp. 1–18.

Heise, A. (2019b) *Socioeconomics of Economics: Essays on the Construction of the Economic Discipline and Its Critique*, Münster.

Heise, A., Sander, H., & Thieme, S. (2017) *Das Ende der Heterodoxie? Die Entwicklung der Wirtschaftswissenschaften in Deutschland*, Wiesbaden.

Heise, A., & Thieme, S. (2016) 'The short rise and long fall of heterodox economics in Germany after the 1970s: Explorations in a scientific field of power and struggle', *Journal of Economic Issues*, 50(4), pp. 1105–1130.

Herr, H. et al. (2017) *Makroökonomische Folgen eines gesetzlichen Mindestlohnes aus keynesianisch geprägter Perspektive*, IMK study on behalf of the Minimum Wage Commission, Düsseldorf.

Hesse, J. -O. (2010) *Wirtschaft als Wissenschaft: Die Volkswirtschaftslehre in der frühen Bundesrepublik*, Frankfurt.

Hesse, J. -O. (2012) 'The, Americanisation' of West German economics after the second world war: Success, failure, or something completely different?', *European Journal of the History of Economic Thought*, 19(1), pp. 67–98.

Keuth, H. (1989) *Wissenschaft und Werturteil: Zu Werturteilsdiskussion und Positivismusstreit*, Tübingen.

Kirchgässner, G. (2013) 'Zur Politischen Ökonomie der wirtschaftspolitischen Beratung', *Wirtschaftsdienst*, 3, pp. 198–203.

Kooths, S. (2018) 'Kommentierung zum Beitrag von Sebastian Dullien und Gustav Horn', *List Forum für Wirtschafts- und Sozailpolitik*, 44(4), pp. 919–926.

Lee, F. S. (2007) 'The research assessment exercise, the state and the dominance of mainstream economics in British universities', *Cambridge Journal of Economics*, 31, pp. 309–331.

Lee, F. S., Pham, X., & Gu, G. (2013): 'The UK research assessment exercise and the narrowing of UK economics', *Cambridge Journal of Economics*, 37(4), 693–717.

Mannheim, K. (1954) *Ideology and Utopia. An Introduction to the Sociology of Knowledge*, New York.

Mikl-Horke, G. (2008) 'Klassische Positionen der Ökonomie und Soziologie und ihre Bedeutung für die Wirtschaftssoziologie' in Maurer, A. (ed.) *Handbuch der Wirtschaftssoziologie*, Wiesbaden, pp. 19–44.

Ollman, B. (1977) 'Marx's Vision of Communism', *Critique*, 8(1), pp. 4–44.

Ötsch, W. O. (2009) *Mythos Markt.* Marktradikale Propaganda und ökonomische Theorie, Marburg.
Peukert, H. (2018a) *Makroökonomische Lehrbücher: Wissenschaft oder Ideologie?*, Marburg.
Peukert, H. (2018b) *Mikroökonomische Lehrbücher: Wissenschaft oder Ideologie?*, Marburg.
Popper, K. R. (1962) 'Die Logik der Sozialwissenschaften', *Kölner Zeitschrift für Soziologie und Sozialpsychologie*, 14, pp. 233–248.
Potrafke, N. (2017) 'Der Letzte der Weisen' in *Frankfurter Allgemeine Sonntagszeitung*, 27 August 2017, p. 20.
Przeworski, A. (1985) *Capitalism and Social Democracy*, Cambridge.
Robinson, J. (1962) *Economic Philosophy*, London.
Schulmeister, S. (2018) *Der Weg zur Prosperität*, Salzburg and Munich.
Sinn, H. -W. (2014) 'Ignorante Kritik an Ökonomen: Sie sind wie Spürhunde' in *Süddeutsche Zeitung*, 1 November 2014 (https://www.sueddeutsche.de/wirtschaft/kritik-an-oekonomen-der-grosse-irrtum-1.2198333, last accessed: 28 June 2019).
Wilber, C. K., & Wisman, J. D. (1975) 'The Chicago school: Positivism or ideal type', *Journal of Economic Issues*, 9(4), pp. 665–679.

# 3 Does macroeconomics have to deal with ethical considerations?

*Finn Olesen*

## Introduction

As we all know, in the aftermath of the years of the global financial crisis and the Great Recession, the modern macroeconomic mainstream – the New Neoclassical Synthesis (NNS) – was criticised by, not surprisingly, most heterodox economists for its lack of theoretical relevance as the mainstream was seen as out of sync with empirical evidence. Real life did not seem to match the description given in mainstream macroeconomic textbooks very well. However, this time, even some members of the macroeconomic establishment raised critical voices against the mainstream story – they also found the theory of harmoniously functioning modern global interrelated economies that was put on the unique equilibrium path by necessary changes in relative price relationships to be too far from what was experienced in real life.

Furthermore, the mainstream understanding was and still is also open for methodological criticisms. The macroeconomic system cannot be characterised as a closed system as mainstreamers usually do. This system is not to a huge degree deterministic when it unfolds its processes of adjustment. Rather, it is a unique open, changeable, socially determined and path-dependent system; see Chick & Dow (2005). Or put differently, as Davidson (2016) explains, modern financially global integrated economies are functioning in a non-ergodic manner.

However, in addition to criticising the mainstream theoretically and methodology as mentioned above, which non-mainstreamers have done for years, the modern macroeconomic mainstream can also be exposed to criticism concerning how it copes with ethical matters.

Ought macroeconomics to concern itself with ethical considerations and questions of morality?

The answer to this question is a 'yes, of course' as argued in the following sections of the present chapter.

## Ancient times and what follow

In ancient times – somewhat around 400 B.C. to 400 – Greek, Roman and early Christian philosophers addressed questions of the quality and justice of life. Not surprisingly, later at the very beginning of economic thinking

DOI: 10.4324/9781003253457-4

scholars were inspired by these moral considerations. It became essential that prices at the marketplace had to be seen as just and fair. Therefore, the focus went beyond the problems of having a willing buyer meeting a willing seller and making free choices. Actions of trade also had to include doing good applying the ethics of love (Wittmer 2017). The understanding of economic behaviour in early economic thought was thereby anchored by ethical frames (Stapleford 2000).

However, a thorough focus on market economy processes was first given by Adam Smith in his *Wealth of Nations* in 1776. And Smith, hardly surprising as he started out his academic career by writing *The Theory of Moral Sentiments* in 1759, also put his economic understanding into a framework of morality as he thought it necessary to have an ethical foundation for economics and society. As Keynes later did, so did Adam Smith early on define economics as a moral science (Malek et al. 2016). In the old days, as well as now in modern times, every society is inhabited by human beings who at least sometimes take moral and ethical concerns into consideration when they act as economic units (and, of course, also when they act otherwise). That we know with certainty.

And when the era of classical economics evolved after Adam Smith the moral dimension was kept on board. There are traces of moral statements and ethical concerns in much of classical and early neoclassical theory, e.g., in the writings of Thomas Malthus, John Stuart Mill and Alfred Marshall. However, neoclassical theory soon developed into a purer science leaving aside questions of morality and ethics, thereby regrettably narrowing the scope of economics. Strangely enough, the efforts made to put economic understanding on this kind of track is a normative choice (although not that many modern economists may accept this as a fact). Therefore, of course, neoclassical theory – in its old as well as in its more modern version of the present dominant macroeconomic mainstream – is built on its own normative values that is given by a basic neoliberal ideology. That is, it is not value-free despite its declared objective of only doing positive economics.

## Micro versus macro

As discussed in Best & Widmaier (2006), one should probably separate the ontology of microeconomics from that of macroeconomics as they describe fundamentally different economic universes.[1] Basically, microeconomics uses an atomistic ontology whereas macroeconomics – that is the Keynesian type – uses a broader ontology as it includes social entities and forces combined with some kind of microeconomic universe. To a true Keynesian, macroeconomics is more than just the sum of individual actions. Microeconomic optimality does not necessarily lead to optimal macroeconomic outcomes.[2]

Therefore, the two do not apply to the same kind of ethical orientation. At least they did so in the old days where macroeconomic theory was more Keynesian dominated than today's modern mainstream understanding.

Nowadays, the mainstreamers try to apply a microeconomic approach to macroeconomics which is in good accordance with the strategy implemented a long time ago by Robert Lucas when he sounded the trumpets of the rational expectations revolution and the need of giving macroeconomic theory an explicit traditional microeconomic foundation (Lucas 1976; Lucas & Sargent 1979). If his efforts were crowned by success, one needed no more to distinguish between macro- and microeconomics, he claimed. The two would coincide with the term *economics*.

And success was indeed achieved. We have been introduced to the representative agent heavily reliant on supply-side matters only and witnessed how a behaviour of perfect maximation ensured that the economy was put smoothly on the unique intertemporal path of optimality completely ignoring the severe problems of uncertainty, especially concerning the crucial aspects of focusing on ontological uncertainty. Mainstreamers might somehow try to cope with the epistemological kind of uncertainty – the one that can be modelled when the economic system is working like a closed deterministic system. But they do not address ontological uncertainty at all, not surprisingly, as this requires the economy to be an open and changeable system that develops over time at least to some degree to be unpredictable.

Furthermore, economic policy has, until recently at least, been governed by rigid rules aiming it to become optimal. Monetary policy should focus on achieving low and stable inflation rates. Fiscal policy, almost completely deprived of its potential regulatory role, should only focus on balanced budgets and tax cuts primarily aiming at high-income groups.

In short, victory was achieved. The Keynesians, that is, the real ones, were defeated.[3]

## The modern macroeconomic mainstream

As argued in Olesen (2021), the modern macroeconomic mainstream with its built-in neoliberal ideology relies essentially on the existence of a perfect working market mechanism – in the short run, economies might be out of a general equilibrium due to various imperfections and rigidities, however, in the longer run, with certainty, they are brought back on the unique intertemporal optimal equilibrium path. The strength of the market mechanism ensures that the right changes in relative price relationships are brought about eventually. That is, the outcome of an economy's economic processes is stated always to be effective and successful. But, of course, as we know from history this harmonious picture of how modern economies are supposed to function is far from correct. In real life, there are many limits to the way markets work.[4] Nevertheless, mainstreamers go on pursuing their vision – ideology – of efficient markets ensuring a macroeconomic outcome of optimality in the longer run. Likewise, the approach you must use if you want to do macroeconomics the right way is to rely on mathematical formalism making analysis using supply-side dominated DSGE (dynamic stochastic general equilibrium) models.

Therefore, at its core, the macroeconomic mainstream of today echoes the fundamentals of two earlier paradigms: the old neoclassical paradigm and the neoclassical synthesis that for years became the dominant mainstream interpretation of Keynes' *General Theory*. As such, the modern understanding includes the same normative values as the two previous mentioned paradigms. And, of course, to accept such an ideology has consequences. Of crucial importance is especially not only consequences concerning the design of economic policy but also how mainstreamers view institutional changes in society as potential game changers (Ramazzotti 2019). Accepting this as a fact, the previous strategy of austerity within the EU as *the* economic policy response to the global financial crises and what later became known as the Great Recession from 2008 and onwards comes as no surprise.[5]

Although the macroeconomic mainstream might be coloured by what Lee & Schug (2011) terms a kind of mundane morality,[6] mainstreamers hardly ever include ethical considerations in their analysis. Following a tradition from Friedman (1953) and onwards the focus has in general been one on doing positive economics.[7] However, ethical considerations are of course important. We know that as a fact from real life. To pursue one's self-interest and relying on the strength of the market mechanism cannot in itself ensure an outcome of harmonious equilibriums all over in the economy. There is more to economics than just that. Norms and values are determinants of human behaviour. Moreover, human behaviour is purposeful. Just to give an example, you can hardly talk about the problems of environmental sustainability seriously without including ethical aspects. For instance, which weight should you put on the happiness and prosperous life of future generations? And trying to achieve the best outcome for the next generations also includes aspects concerning distributional matters – how could we act today with a perspective on the future without considering certain principles of equality?

Furthermore, mainstreamers do not focus that much on institutions and institutional changes. That task is normally left to heterodox economists to pursue. Post-Keynesians have for decades argued about the importance of including these matters in macroeconomics. Essentially economics is a story about continuous change. From the very beginning, societies have changed over time affecting the rules of the game of how the economic system works. Therefore, it is important to have a constant focus on the ongoing processes of transition in the economy. Economies change in a path-dependent way. And as they change so does the institutional framework – sometimes only marginally but at times much more dramatically. And society changes because it is inhabited by human beings that have their own free will to act and not by robots that react as iron particles drawn to magnet.[8] That is, societal changes, as of course also macroeconomic changes, are often, at least to some degree, difficult to predict correctly.

In general, mainstream textbooks present an economic worldview on modern economies that is too perfect, too harmonious and too much out of sync with empirical evidence to its readers. As Juselius (2009; 2011) so convincingly points out, in general, what the mainstream theory predicts about the outcome of economic processes of intertemporal optimalisation is not found empirically. Given the evidence from the latest global financial crisis and the Great Recession this should not come as a surprise. Rather, the degree of lack of realism of mainstream macroeconomic theory should be conspicuously obvious to all.[9] No wonder that students in economics have reacted and are demanding changes in their economic curriculum, e.g., the 'Rethinking Economics' movement.

Furthermore, it must be remembered that there are more stories to tell than just the one on mainstream macroeconomics. So why not try to follow a teaching strategy of pluralism[10] which unfolds the mainstream understanding as well as selected alternatives as advocated by Olesen & Madsen (2017)? Apart from this, such an approach also helps students to develop their capabilities to become more critical minded and more reflective. However, changes in mainstream textbooks have been slow and minor recently despite what happened from 2008 and onwards. As indicated by Juniper et al. (2021) this may have something to do with the fact that economists experience increasing career pressure at mainstream economics departments combined with the need to publish in leading mainstream journals.[11] And this, of course, is of relevance when economists are seen as scientists working in academia.

However, as discussed by Su & Colander (2021), there are many sides to being an economist. The job of an economist might be humbler, but nevertheless as important or even at times much more important than working as a scientist employed at an economics department. Often the job of the economist has to do with practical problem-solving activities. Therefore, as argued by Galbraith (2021, p. 67), probably many economists see economics as "a policy discipline" where they are engaged in finding the best solution to a variety of problems. As such, acting like this, the role of the economist has been described as a dentist, an engineer, a surgeon or a plumber. Engaging in these roles, some of the above discussed aspects might be of a minor importance.[12]

## Economics is a moral science

As Adam Smith did, so did Keynes: they both considered economics to be a moral science. That is, economic reasoning should contain ethical consideration.[13] Such a view on economics comes as no surprise for Post-Keynesians as they are quite familiar with the following citation from a correspondence that Keynes had in 1938 with Roy Harrod:

> Economics is a science of thinking in terms of models joined to the art of choosing models which are relevant to the contemporary world ... **Progress** in economics consists almost entirely in a progressive improvement

> in the choice of models ... I also want to emphasize strongly the point about economics being a moral science. I mentioned before that it deals with introspection and with values. I might have added that it deals with motives, expectations, psychological uncertainties.
>
> (CW XIV, pp. 296 & 300)

In Keynes' perspective, perhaps sadly, there is no *one* unique model that can analyse all relevant economic problems. The quest for finding such a model is futile. Contrary to what many mainstreamers believe, the DSGE models are not the right models for analysing all macroeconomic problems.[14] Therefore, to Keynes and Post-Keynesians, economics is 'the art of choosing' the right model for the problem at hand to be analysed. Furthermore, such a view on economics was old news to Keynes in 1938 as he as early as in 1922 wrote the following statement in his Introduction to *Cambridge Economic Handbooks*:

> The theory of economics does not furnish a body of settled conclusions immediately applicable to policy. It is a method rather than a doctrine, an apparatus of the mind, a technique of thinking, which helps its possessor to draw correct conclusions.
>
> (CW XII, p. 856)[15]

Therefore, to Keynes, it can be difficult to be an economist. Up front it might be very troublesome to get your hands on the right model to be able to carry out the economic analysis in the most appropriate way, maybe you must struggle to succeed; however, that is not a motive for not trying. Eventually, you might just do the right thing.

Or as Keynes stated in his famous essay on Alfred Marshal, a master economist must cover many areas of competence:

> He must be mathematician, historian, statesman, philosopher – in some degree. He must understand symbols and speak in words. He must contemplate the particular in terms of the general, and touch abstract and concrete in the same flight of thought. He must study the present in the light of the past for the purposes of the future. No part of man's nature or his institutions must lie entirely outside his regard.
>
> (Keynes 1924, p. 322)[16]

## A concluding remark

As argued in the above sections, economics is and has always been a moral science. That is, it includes ethical considerations at least to some degree. Therefore, the quest for only doing positive economics is in vain. The normative dimension in economics will always somehow be present.

Society is inhabited by real human beings not by textbook monsters or robots that act predictably and deterministically in a perfect manner. In real life people are bound to make economic mistakes as the future in some dimensions is truly unknown. Furthermore, the macroeconomic universe is in general not one of perfection and harmony. Likewise, economic activity is more than just market-related activity. Suffice it to mention the important part played by public sector activities in every modern economy.

As such, even modern global integrated, financially, and otherwise, economies can be hit hard by various demand and supply shocks. That we know as a fact. Therefore, individuals are not themselves fully responsible for their own economic welfare as the traditional ontological individualism of microeconomics and as many modern macroeconomic mainstreamers might argue. Not surprisingly, the ontology of the old neoclassical paradigm and that of the modern macroeconomic mainstream – the NNS – coincide in its core elements.

Being a moral science, macroeconomics must deal with ethics and morality. And there exists an alternative to the modern macroeconomic understanding, which does exactly that. There is a Keynesian alternative. Once again, you can learn from reading Keynes. As Best & Widmaier (2006, p. 622) remind us:

> Starting from a social economic ontology, Keynes's economic proposals clearly articulated a socially-attuned ethical vision. In this moral and economic universe, responsibility for economic success or failure was not borne alone by individuals but was instead shared by the social collective. This collective – and the state as its practical policy-making expression – had, in turn, the moral agency to resolve economic dilemmas and thus to achieve economic ends.

But, of course, both Western societies and the macroeconomic landscape of these countries have changed significantly since the days of Keynes. Some of the old problems have been solved while others have not and new problems have arisen. Today, the green dimension is high on the public agenda as there is an imperative need of taking climate changes seriously. Environmental sustainability must be achieved otherwise everything breaks down. If the ecological system is gone, so is society. And, of course, the care for the planet and future generations' welfare by the present generation has do with various aspects of a political, an economic and a technical kind. But it also has to do with ethics and morality. Economics is indeed a moral science. Therefore, macroeconomics must deal with ethical considerations. These are just as important considerations in our present time as they were in the old days.

## Notes

1 'The very distinction between micro and macro theory is both ontological and ethical: micro and macro theories not only describe but also seek to create fundamentally different economic worlds ... micro- and macroperspectives embody

both different ontological assumptions regarding agents and structures and different methodological assumptions regarding the proper means of economic analysis … a predictable microclassical universe made up of rational isolated individuals and a much more uncertain macro-Keynesian world of both individuals and social forces' Best & Widmaier (2006, pp. 611, 615 & 618).

2 Just to mention one example, as stated by Keynes in his Chapter 3 in *The General Theory* – The principle of effective demand – firms could be in a position where they maximize their expected profits (an equilibrium outcome) without that ensuring an equilibrium at the macroeconomic level with full employment as the level of effective demand in the economy might be too low.

3 Or as Best & Widmaier (2006, pp. 610–611) point out: 'the methodological emphasis on establishing microfundations has hardened into a liberal-individualist normative bias … while the microclassical ontology produces a very individualist morality, the macro-Keynesian approach implies a far more public ethics'.

4 As pointed out by Stahel (2021, p. 13) these might be political, administrative or even moral limits.

5 But perhaps, as a response to the Covid-19 pandemic, the strategy for conducting economic policy – monetary as well as fiscal policy – is becoming more Keynesian-like. This time, the combined supply and demand shock was immediately counteracted by huge expansive policy initiatives all around including the EU (Byrialsen et al. 2021).

6 Such a kind of morality is described by Lee & Schug (2011, p. 75) "as obeying the generally accepted rules and norms of engaging in impersonal exchange, such as being honest, keeping our promises and contractual obligations, respecting the property rights of others, and not intentionally harming others".

7 But to some not successfully as "In spite of the rhetorical effort to separate positive from normative economics, ethics continue to intrude in economic analysis" (Best & Widmaier 2006, p. 614).

8 As Slade-Caffarel (2019, p. 532) concludes:

> social reality is … brought into existence by, and depends on, human beings. It emerges from, and is reproduced and transformed by, our interactions. Social structures are the … results of socio-historically specific social relations … these structures have a power of conditioning over the actions of human beings who, in turn, transform and reproduce them. It is a never-ending dynamic back and forth.

9 Or as Norgaard (2021, p. 56) harshly states:

> Economists have become unhinged from reality. Economists' own limited understanding and false portrayal of their discipline corresponds with their efforts to reduce reason to mathematical models, market data, and econometrics. When that is not possible, they pretty much ignore any discrepancies from reality and morality.

10 Accoording to Negru & Negru (2017, p. 195), pluralism can be defined as

> ways of recognising and accepting the variety of economic ideas and schools of thought in economics and in economic curriculum. Pluralism represents an attitude of openness towards theories and models that are not necessarily heterodox. Pedagogically, pluralism envisages the willingness to produce a diverse curriculum and the introduction of various modes to represent and interpret the economic world different than one's own … Pluralism encompasses the constant movement of change in ideas and theories when considering different approaches in order to understand the real world.

11 Or as Colander (2015, p. 232) somewhat similarly explains:

> The economics profession, like the economy, is best thought of as an evolving complex system. By that I mean that it is composed of hundreds of thousands of economists each trying to survive and get ahead in the existing institutional structure.

12 According to Su & Colander (2021, pp. 298, 304 & 309):

> economics is not a single entity and each entity is better done with different methodologies and mindsets ... unlike economic science ... applied policy economics adopts much wider ranges of methods ... in real life economists fulfil many different roles ... That's what makes economics so difficult.

13 As pointed out by Makashova (1993, pp. 34–35):

> Keynes struck the palpable blow against the objectivist tendency. He spoke out against the ethical neutrality of economic theory, against the dominance of methodological individualism, and for the normative orientation of economic science.

Or as O'Donnell (1989, p. 165) points out, in a letter to the Archbishop of York from 1941, Keynes confirmed the ethical anchoring of economics. Keynes wrote:

> economics more properly called political economy is a side of ethics. Marshall always used to insist that it was through ethics he arrived at political economy and I would claim myself in this, as in other respects, to be a pupil of his.

14 However, there are, of course, exceptions among mainstreamers to this view as expressed by, for instance, Blanchard (2018). Perhaps, DSGE models are the most important macroeconomic models at present but there are other models as well that can be used to address macroeconomic problems, as he points out.

15 Furthermore, Keynes goes on characterising economics:

> It is not difficult in the sense in which mathematical and scientific techniques are difficult; but the fact that its modes of expression are much less precise than these, renders decidedly difficult the task of conveying it correctly to the minds of learners
>
> (CW XII, p. 856)

16 In line with this view advocating a strategy of pluralism, Su & Colander (2021, p. 311) concludes: 'If an economist's training could be structured to let students know that a master economist is an all-rounder, needing many different skills, that would be wonderful'.

## References

Best, Jacqueline & Widmaier, Wesley (2006). Micro- or macro-moralities? Economic discourses and policy possibilities, *Review of International Political Economy*, 13(4), pp. 609–631.

Blanchard, Oliver (2018). On the future of macroeconomic models, *Oxford Review of Economic Policy*, 34(1–2), pp. 43–54.

Byrialsen, Mikael R. et al. (2021). The macroeconomic effects of covid-19: The imperative need for a Keynesian solution, *Revue de la regulation – Capitalisme, institutions, pouviors*, 2021, No. 29, May 2021, 17 pages, https://journals.openedition.org/regulation/18405.

Chick, Victoria & Dow, Sheila (2005). The meaning of open systems, *Journal of Economic Methodology*, 12(3), pp. 363–381.

Colander, David (2015). Why economics textbooks should, but don't, and won't, change, *European Journal of Economics and Economic Policies: Intervention*, 12(2), pp. 229–235.

CW (XII) (1983). *The Collected Writings of John Maynard Keynes, Vol. XII, Economic Articles and Correspondence – Investment and Editorial.* Macmillan Cambridge University Press.

CW (XIV) (1973). *The Collected Writings of John Maynard Keynes, Vol. XIV, The General Theory and After, Part II: Defence and Development.* Macmillan Cambridge University Press.

Davidson, Paul (2016). Rejoinder to Rosser, O'Donnell, and Carrión Álvarez and Ehnts on their criticisms of my ergodic/nonergodic formulation of Keynes's concept of an actuarial certain future vs. an uncertain future, *Journal of Post Keynesian Economics*, 39(3), pp. 308–333.

Friedman, Milton (1953). The methodology of positive economics, in Friedman, M. (Ed.), *Essays in Positive Economics*, The University of Chicago Press, Chicago, pp. 3–43.

Galbraith, James (2021). What is economics? A policy discipline for the real world, *real-world economics review*, issue no. 96, pp. 67–81.

Juselius, K. (2009) The long swings puzzle: what the data tell when allowed to speak freely, in Patterson, K. and Mills, T.C. (Eds.), *Palgrave Handbook of Econometrics*, Vol. 2: Applied Econometrics, Palgrave Macmillan, New York, pp. 349–384.

Juselius, K. (2011) On the role of theory and evidence in macroeconomics, in Hands, W. and Davis, J. (Eds.), *The Elgar Companion to Recent Economic Methodology*, Edward Elgar, Cheltenham, UK, pp. 404–26.

Juniper, James et al. (2021). Orthodox macroeconomic textbooks: A critical evaluation using institutional practice as a benchmark, *International Review of Economics Education*, 37(June number), pp. 1–11.

Keynes, John Maynard (1924). Alfred Marshall, 1842–1924), *The Economic Journal*, 34(135), pp. 311–372.

Lee, Dwight & Schug, Mark (2011). The political economy of economic education: The moral dimensions, *Journal of Markets & Morality*, 14(1), pp. 71–84.

Lucas, Robert E. (1976). Econometric policy evaluation: A critique, in Karl Brunner and Allan H. Meltzer (eds.) *The Phillips Curve and Labor Markets*, Carnegie-Rochester Conference Series on Public Policy, Volume 1, North-Holland Publishing Company, pp. 19–46.

Lucas, Robert E. & Sargent, Thomas J. (1979). After Keynesian macroeconomics, *Federal Reserve Bank of Minneapolis Quarterly Review*, Spring 1979, pp. 1–16.

Malek, Ninos et al. (2016). The relationship between economics and ethics and the effectiveness of normative economics on students' attitudes and learning, *Journal of Economics and Economic Education Research*, 17(1), pp. 16–24.

Makashova, Natalia (1993). Ethics and economic theory, *Problems of Economic Transition*, 35(10), pp. 25–44.

Negru, Ioana & Negru, Anca (2017). Modes of pluralism: Critical commentary on roundtable dialogue on pluralism, *International Journal of Pluralism and Economics Education*, 8(2), pp. 193–209.

Norgaard, Richard B. (2021). Post-economics: Reconnecting reality and morality to escape the Econocene. *real-world economics review*, issue no. 96, pp. 49–66.

O'Donnell, Rod M. (1989). *Keynes: Philosophy, Economics and Politics – The Philosophical Foundations of Keynes's Thought and their Influence on his Economics and Politics*, MacMillan.

Olesen, Finn (2021). Macroeconomics must have an ethical foundation, *International Journal of Pluralism and Economics Education*, 12(2), pp. 138–151.

Olesen, Finn & Madsen, Mogens Ove (2017). Problem-based learning: A non-mainstream way to teach economics, *International Journal of Pluralism and Economics Education*, 8(3), pp. 300–311.

Ramazzotti, Paolo (2019). Homo oeconomicus returns: Neoliberalism, socio-political uncertainty and economic policy, *Journal of Economic Issues*, 53(2), pp. 456–462.

Slade-Caffarel, Yannick (2019). The nature of heterodox economics revisited, *Cambridge Journal of Economics*, 43(3), pp. 527–540.

Stahel, Andri (2021). Has economics become a new theology? Some comments about the practice of modern economists and medieval theologians, *real-world economics review*, issue no. 97, pp. 2–19.

Stapleford, John (2000). Christian ethics and the teaching of introductory economics, *Journal of Markets & Morality*, 3(1), pp. 67–87.

Su, Huei-Chun & Colander, David (2021). The economist as scientist, engineer, or plumber?, *Journal of the History of Economic Thought*, 43(2), pp. 297–312.

Wittmer, Michael (2017). Is a just price enough?, *Journal of Markets & Morality*, 20(2), pp. 263–278.

# 4 Understanding the temporal in Keynesian economics

*Mogens Ove Madsen*

## Introduction

In John Maynard Keynes' own work with time, there are contributions to be found from his time as a student, both in lecture notes and in his unpublished lecture manuscript "Time" from 1903. Keynes has been so close to the time philosopher J.M.E. McTaggart that his concept of time has become part of his understanding, both in terms of time, as something that has to do with change, and at the same time the need to distinguish between past, present and future.

How Keynes later handles this is made very clear in a letter to Harrod in which he states that economics is a science where one must think in models and where the art consists in choosing models that are relevant to the contemporary world (Keynes, 1938). This is necessary because the material available in economics – unlike the natural sciences – is not homogeneous over time. The purpose of a model is to distinguish the semi-permanent or relatively constant factors from those that are transient or oscillating, allowing to develop a logical way of thinking and understanding the time sequences that they may give rise to. Keynesian theory – which will be shown here – is thus characterized by adding a new aspect of economic thinking around time, which is done – is my claim – through the explicit inclusion of an approach very close to the A-series in McTaggart (1908).

McTaggart's division of life's temporal relation has since manifested itself in two schools – the dynamic conception of time based on the A-series and its tensed theory of time and the static conception of time based on the B-series and a tenseless theory of time.

The B-series is to be seen to define the time of the physicist's spacetime continuum whereas the A-series is to be seen as the time of the psychologist's introspective subject (Chung, 1999, p. 304). It matches the ancient Greeks' definition of time: Chronos is closely related to the B-series while Kairos is related to the A-series. Jaques (1982) thus suggested that the two dimensions of time be Succession and Intention.

If the language one uses allows for changes in tenses, it is the same as positions in McTaggart's A-series. And theories described, using such language,

DOI: 10.4324/9781003253457-5

should be an explicit part of post-Keynesian theory. B-series give a different analysis without tensed facts, and this is the kind of analysis which is normally presented in mainstream economics. An economic theory that does not make use of the A-series cannot explore an economy in motion. Focus on B-series alone ends up as a static description.

It may seem paradoxical that relatively little has been said about general requirements for explicit management of time in economics. And, thus, what it means if McTaggart's A-series of past, present and future is to be integrated into economic theory. There is no doubt that it is more complicated than if one only understands time as simple B-series with before and after and where only a mechanical model is involved. This is known from, for example, the IS-LM or multiplier-accelerator models. These are analyses that often try to predict causes based on actions that have already taken place, which is why the researcher cannot manipulate or change the actions or behaviors that have already occurred.

Fortunately, there are attempts to think economics including time in the McTaggart's sense. In what follows the focus is especially on some attempts that are made to introduce McTaggart's A-series into economic theory.

## Some frontrunners

An interesting interpretation of Keynes' method is Shackle (1974) on Keynesian Kaleidics. This stems from Shackle's three main interests, namely, time, expectations and uncertainty, which should be seen in relation to Chapter 12 of Keynes' *General Theory*. He introduces the present as a moment-in-being and following Keynes' letter to Harrod about the art of choosing a model – one could say that Shackle is also approaching a form of analysis in which one not only can view the world as a panorama but must be present in the present. Therefore, he believes that a panorama outside view should be contrasted with an inside view. The latter situation is one in which an economist, on the basis of his knowledge, thoughts and ideas, decides in Keynes' sense which model to use.

Keynesian Kaleidics is a difficult methodology, but it illustrates quite well how changes in a single relationship in an economy can lead to a dramatic change in the overall picture of an economy. The kaleidic factor is uncertainty, which excludes symmetry between explanation and prediction. Thus, it is not possible to make deterministic predictions. In turn, there is room for imagination to play a role in setting up scenarios.

Hicks (1976), like Shackle, has had a lifelong job of bringing economic theory closer to reality – they have both been preoccupied with Keynes' concept of expectations in *The General Theory* since the beginning of their careers. The path for Hicks is quite interesting because it is not so direct, and it takes time before he seriously recognizes the limitations of general equilibrium theory and in his own IS-LM diagram (Madsen, 2018). Hicks gradually becomes quite explicit about the concept of time and notes that unlike the natural sciences, as Robinson (1953) did, time in the social sciences must be perceived as irreversible and like Keynes he states that the facts one works with in economics are not permanent. This leads him to the work of three types of causalities, where he prefers sequential causality (Hicks, 1980).

Thus, Hicks approaches the possibility of studying dynamic processes by wanting to study not only a period, but the connection between several periods. This is the theme of Continuation Theory, which allows the study of effects on economic processes of changing expectations.

Sometimes post-Keynesians provide a quite uncritical reference to Path Dependence in dealing with time and the past. Admittedly, Path Dependence can be taken as an expression of hysteresis, cumulative causality and/or technological lock-ins, but it also illustrates a problem, namely, how far can one go in letting past events determine conditions that will happen in the future? The simple and traditional version in the form of Qwerty-nomics holds no viable path for economics. The approach is retrospective and again too much space is given to the past and too little space to the future and uncertainty. On the other hand, the learning from other social sciences' use of Path Dependence could make the concept more relevant to economics (Madsen, 2016).

The concept of Path Dependence is weak because it is neither a clear theory nor an explicit method; neither has it been conclusively proven empirically. And the question is, in which degree any paths can be identified as generalizable when history actually never repeats itself? A move away from Querty-nomics toward a new and reformulated Path Dependence provides an opportunity to leave functional explanations of historical development to take intentional explanations into use (Madsen, 2016).

This calls for studies of social mechanisms in the form of institutional changes. This may involve a showdown with, for example, traditional regression analysis. Instead, there is a need for studies of causal complexities such as tipping points, higher-order interaction effects, strategic interaction, two-way causality or feedback loops that require new forms of process detection and systematic case studies to address Path Dependence issues (Bennett & Elman, 2006). There needs to be more room for case-study methods that shed light on how causal mechanisms work in a context, but also detection of rare events and "omitted variables".

The explicit insights of Keynes, Shackle, Hicks have some implications for how time is to be handled in economics. This will be summarized in the coming sections.

## Victoria Chick

Victoria Chick[1] has an explicit and interesting approach to the concept of time. She has explicitly formulated herself about time in many of her contributions and not least based on her book *Macroeconomics after Keynes from* 1983. Time is the key to understanding Keynes, she argues. As such, Chick sees his General Theory as a static model for a dynamic process.

Why then is time so important?

Primarily it is easy to see that it's just one of the crucial areas where post-Keynesian theory stands out in direct continuation of Keynes and demonstrates that the relationship between economics and reality should be taken seriously.

And, second, there is another good reason. As stated by Currie & Steedman (1990, p. 241) in their book on wrestling with time: "It is extremely healthy that more and more economists seem to be acknowledging that substantive progress in economic analysis can only come from confronting the formidable difficulties associated with time".

It is important to note that a basic trend of modern philosophy is the desire to unite the various branches of science's understanding of time. The idea of this unification tendency is to unite our daily experience of self and the world with our academic theories of nature and man. In the second half of this century a more general concept of time has been developed and implemented at the interface between physics, chemistry and biology within the framework of the so-called theories of 'self-organization'. According to the proponents of the new view, this allows it to overcome the old duality between natural and historical time; see Prigogine & Stengers (1985).

Chick says in her 1995 article "Order out of Chaos in Economics" that the contribution of Prigogine and Stengers is of vital interest to economists because of the connection between chaos and time.

Chick's notion of Prigogine and Stenger's self-organizing system is a concept for economists as an evolutionary system with a strong instinct for self-sufficiency. And the rediscovery of time that is happening in the natural sciences is a support to economists who believe that the history of economics and the history of thought about economics have something important to tell.

For the same reason, Chick is amazed at the powerful position that closed, deterministic models occupy in economics where physics moved away from deterministic systems many years ago.

In particular, the point of irreversibility that Chick raises is a milestone in the effort to advance economic science with the obvious assistance of science as a significant contribution to taking the concept of time seriously.

The recent financial and economic crisis should be an eminent example to demonstrate the need for time consciousness and especially the relationship between money and time, that is, the increasing importance of the financial sector.

As Chick & Dow (2013) portrayed it in an article on the present crisis the financial system was in

> Keynes's times, tightly controlled and quite well behaved. But today the practice of executive remuneration in the form of stock options has

> increased the focus on the stock price for investment decisions beyond anything Keynes had portrayed in chapter 12 of the GT. The picture is darker for us now than it was for Keynes.
>
> (Chick & Dow, 2013, p. 23)

They subsequently pointed out

> the complete disconnection of finance from the real economy and of big business from national and local economies. Predatory capitalism has become the norm, with "bubbles" being created in order to allow those involved in them to gain at the expense of consumers, shareholders and other industries. And some would argue that the financial system has been starving the real economy of funds.
>
> (Chick & Dow, 2013, p. 18)

The development of financialization may lead to another conception of temporality. Money is not created on the stock market by realizing a possibility, but simply by selling an idea as an option. An investment loses all its direction and purpose toward accomplishment and financialized money is bound to a virtual reality. Projects that begin with a tangible vision corrode more and more into pieces of artificial game. It is a shift from a world with realizable dreams to a virtual world, constantly chasing its own tail. Time spent on productive work requires linear time: Time is linear because of the different and cumulative ways we can record and measure it, but the financial sector makes money in terms of timing.

Here, a concept like perishability offers a good way to understand the economic changes that take place up to a financial and economic crisis. This is true when the relationship between work and money burns out completely. This is where an economic bubble bursts.

In other words, the financial economy is on the verge of losing its connection to the rest of the economy.[2] Speculation has now proven to be such a potent force in the currency and equity markets that we would be fools if we ignore this important part of Keynes' analysis. And *The General Theory* still pertains to an advanced capitalist system.

In the way described Victoria Chick (1983, 1995, 1985[2009]) has been of great importance and is highlighted because she has continuously helped to clarify the explicit use of temporality in the Keynesian economy.

## Keynesian economics in real time

For economic science as treated by the introduced Keynesian pioneers, therefore, it is about how to find a useful path for economics that moves in and through real time.

This brings us back to McTaggart's A- and B-series, which is a similar way of approaching the issue of what brings an economy through real time.

In fact, both types of time concepts are needed for this to succeed, as Subert (2001, p. 212) states:

> In order to investigate the human world, however, it is necessary to use both types, as human awareness of time contains both the experience of real successions, and the ability to remember, reflect and expect. Series B (before/after) creates a time structure that refers to relationships and events that are identical for all observers. Conversely, in series A (past, present, future) the definition of today, tomorrow and yesterday change in connection with the observer and the observer's awareness.

Historical development can be considered as continuous development of ideas, actions and events. Or with a slightly different approach, it can be said that economic activities consist of continuous processes. Both a choice and an action require a course over time and involve both mental and physical experiences that are felt over time. The process of making a choice and implementing a decision is quite complex. It involves subjective as well as objective assessments. It is at this level that the psychic aspects associated with the conceptualization of time in the A-series become relevant.

However, one must be aware that the human consciousness varies from individual to individual in terms of perception and assessment of reality as well as its influence on behavior.

Although McTaggart (1908) ends up giving the A-series primacy in understanding time, the question still remains as to how the B-series can be maintained. It is clearly an interesting approach that Turk (2010, 2015) and Subert (2001) take on a dualistic approach to time, where both the A- and B-series are included. This is also stated in Jaques (1982, p. 24):

> Mink (1960) has realized that the true resolution of the McTaggart paradox is to recognize that it is necessary to keep hold of both the A-series and the B-series. He saw clearly that the two series reflect two different ways of looking at the world: what he calls the discursive aspect, which throws up our tendency to fix on points, to perceive things in succession, as earlier and later, and hence to construct B-series; and what he calls the transient aspect, in which we have a sense of a moving series of A-series (which he constructs as a series of vertical past-present-future lines), this series of transient and changing A-series being identifiable as earlier and later than each other, and hence giving the sense of succession that goes with the B-series.

And how do we handle that? There are two possibilities for connecting the two angles: a strategy can be to internalize the external or alternatively to externalize the internal as inspired from science (Atmanspacher & Dalenort, 1994, p. 9):

> ... the first of these possibilities might be found in realizing that a vivid and active relationship of man to his "internal world" is required for a humane, future-oriented science. This implies that the way science is practiced on a day-to-day basis has to change accordingly, if our civilization is to keep pace with its enormous amount of theoretical knowledge about the external world. In a broad sense, this is the way of introspection. An option for the second possibility might be the study of toy models, of a virtual reality, transforming Rösslers endo- and exolevels into an empirically domain. The exo-observer is brought down from a superobserver existing in the hidden world of a human observer. The price to be paid is that the endo-world he observes is not real nature but an artificial cyberspace – and the observer's role switches between superobserver and participator.

Rössler's (1992) division into endo- and exo-levels must be understood as an attempt to do away with centuries of Western European thinking, where a distinction is made between inside and outside. But if we take Rössler's distinction we have either an endosystem without an external observer or an exosystem with an external observer.

This means that in order to move through time, we must choose introspection over toy models.

What implications does this particular approach have for modeling an economy that moves through real time?

Here one has – perhaps as expected – again to look back to Keynes himself. And here it is quite surprising that very little development work has actually taken place, despite the fact that Keynes states a methodology for dealing with both a successive and an intentional concept of time at the same time.[3] Even despite the fact that in some economic thinking there is a recognition that uncertainty and expectations play a crucial role in understanding economics, it still fails to include these conditions explicitly in analyses. That is probably related to the stationary interpretations of Keynes – for example, 45-degree or IS-LM interpretations, etc., – that have been allowed to dominate in both teaching and research for far too long without the distinction that Keynes actually very explicitly emphasized that he operated with a different methodology.

In a study, Madsen (2017), of the anatomy of time in Keynes, different assumptions about expectations in the short and long term must be established and when this is done, a multiplier process can be allowed to unfold and determine the total income. However, it is important to draw attention to Chapter 19 of *The General Theory*. This chapter is about how to analyze the consequences of changes in the money-wages (Madsen (1986), which can be quite a complicated affair, as it is closely related to the methodology used.

The analysis of a money-wage reduction in Keynes' system is considerably more complex than the neoclassical (Pigou) analysis – it has no method of analysis wherewith to tackle the problem, as Keynes said, and:

> … the precise question at issue is whether the reduction in money-wages will or will not be accompanied by the same aggregate effective demand as before measured in money, or, at any rate, be an aggregate effective demand which is not reduced in full proportion to the reduction in money wages.
>
> (Keynes, 1936, pp. 259–260)

Keynes presented after this definition an otherwise incomplete catalog with examples of the most obvious reactions to such a change in money-wages. Some of the most important repercussions are that a reduction of money-wages can reduce prices or can result in better money-wages than abroad, or can worsen the terms of trade, or will increase the marginal efficiency of capital, or diminish the need for cash, or weakening effective demand. In Keynes' view it is very complex to analyze in the same way as with monetary policy.[4]

This is a result of his method being quite different from what classical theory supposes:

> Thus the reduction in money-wages will have no lasting tendency to increase employment except by virtue of its repercussion either on the propensity to consume for the community as a whole, or on the schedule of marginal efficiencies of capital, or on the rate of interest. There is no method of analysing the effect of a reduction in money-wages, except by following up its possible effects on these three factors.
>
> (Keynes, 1936, p. 262)

Also, Chapter 21 of *The General Theory*, which deals with price theory, contains considerations regarding the use of a different method:

> … we might make our line of division between the theory of stationary equilibrium and the theory of shifting equilibrium – meaning by the latter the theory of a system in which changing views about the future are capable of influencing the present situation. *The importance of money essentially flows from it being a link between the present and the future.*
>
> (Keynes, 1936, p. 293)

This quotation is very explicit as Keynes points out that one thing is to take as a starting point what can be called heroic assumptions that expectations and motives are fixed, which makes it relatively easy to do equilibrium analyses, but it is a completely different thing to study the real world where expectations under uncertainty can be disappointed and how it can just have a contemporary effect.

The research perspective with a background in Keynesian time perspectives is based on a fusion of the intentional and the successive concept of time. Keynes' theory of shifting (as distinct from stationary) equilibrium can as stated by Carabelli and Cedrini (2016) to provide a new starting point where history so to speak is brought back into economic analysis.

## Conclusion

J.M.E. McTaggart's dual theory of time contributes to a breakthrough in the method of economic analysis. Keynes is fully aware of the content of this approach and uses it in his analyses. This has a number of implications for the way analyses should be performed.

A number of post-Keynesian writers have explicitly worked on this. Shackle has developed the Keynesian Kaleidics method. Hicks has developed Continuation Theory. Supporters of Path Dependence have elaborated on Qwerty-nomics. And Victoria Chick has prepared Keynes' method as a static model for a dynamic process.

To study the human world, it is necessary for Keynesian theory to use both the A- and the B-series, as human time consciousness contains both the experience of real successions and the ability to remember, reflect and expect. This is illustrated by Keynes himself with his analysis in General Theory of the consequences of a money-wage reduction and his price theory, respectively.

## Notes

1 This chapter is inspired by a speech I gave to Victoria Chick on her 80th birthday at University College London, Gustave Tuck Lecture Theatre, July 11, 2016.

2 It may seem superfluous, yet also appropriate referring to Keynes (1936, p. 142):

> Speculators may do no harm as bubbles on a steady stream of enterprise. But the position is serious when enterprise becomes the bubble on a whirlpool of speculation. When the capital development of a country becomes a by-product of the activities of a casino, the job is likely to be ill-done.

3 There are, of course, exceptions and one of the good ones is Kregel (1976).

4 "There is, therefore, no ground for the belief that a flexible wage policy is capable of maintaining a state of continuous full employment; any more than for the belief that an open-market monetary policy is capable, unaided, of achieving this result" (Keynes 1936, p. 267).

## References

Atmanspacher, H. & Dalenort, G.J. (eds.) (1994). Introduction, from *Inside Versus Outside, Endo- and Exo-Conepts of Observation and Knowledge in Physics, Philosophy and Cognitive Science*. Springer-Verlag, Berlin, pp. 1–15.

Bennett, A. & Elman, C. (2006). Complex Causal Relations and Case Study Methods: The Example of Path Dependence, *Political Analysis*, 14(3), Special Issue on Causal Complexity and Qualitative Methods (Summer 2006), pp. 250–267.

Carabelli, A.M. & Cedrini, M.A. (2016). This Time Is... Complex. Keynes on Time. Paper presented at the ESHET XX Annual Conference, Paris, May 2016. Post-keynesian.net

Chick, Victoria (1983). *Macroeconomics After Keynes*, Phillip Allan; First Edition.

Chick, Victoria (1995). Order Out of Chaos in Economics? Some Lessons from the Philosophy of Science, from Dow, S.C. & Hillard, J. (eds.), *Keynes, Knowledge and Uncertainty*. Edward Elgar, Cheltenham, pp. 25–42.

Chick, Victoria (1985[2009]). Time and the Wage-Unit in the Method of the General Theory: History and Equilibrium, from Lawson, T. & Pesaran, H. (eds.), *Keynesian' Economics*. Routledge, London, pp. 195–208.

Chick, V. & Dow, S. (2013). Keynes, the Long Run, and the Present Crisis, *International Journal of Political Economy*, 42(1), pp. 13–25.

Chung, Chen H. (1999). Balancing the Two Dimensions Of Time For Time-Based Competition, *Journal of Managerial Issue*, 11(3), pp. 299–314.

Currie, M. & Steedman, I. (1990). *Wrestling with Time: Problems in Economic Theory*. Manchester University Press.

Hicks, John Richard (1976). Some Question of Time in Economics, from Tang, Anthony M. et al., (eds.), *Evolution, Welfare and Time in Economics*. Lexingtom Books, pp. 135–151.

Hicks, John Richard (1980). *Causality in Economics*. Basill Blackwell, Oxford.

Jaques, Elliott (1982). *The Form of Time*. Crane, Russak, New York.

Keynes, J.M. (1903). Essay on Time. Kings College Archive, Cambridge, UK: JMK/UA/17.

Keynes, J.M. (1936). *The General Theory of Employment, Interest and Money*. MacMillan, London, 1973.

Keynes, J.M. (1938). Letter to Harrod, 4 July. *The Collected Writings of John Maynard Keynes XIV, The General Theory and After: Part II, Defence and Development*, pp. 295–297.

Kregel, J. (1976). Economic Methodology in the Face of Uncertainty: The Modelling Methods of Keynes and the Post-Keynesians. *The Economic Journal*, 86(June), pp. 209–225.

Madsen, Mogens Ove (1986). Lønpolitik – "The Missing Link"? (Wagepolicy – The Missing Link?) *Samfundsøkonomen*, 4(7), pp. 17–21.

Madsen, Mogens Ove (2016). Two Generations of Path Dependence in Economics? from Madsen, M.O. & Olesen, F. (eds.), *Macroeconomics After the Financial Crisis: A Post-Keynesian Perspective*. Routledge, London, pp. 171–191.

Madsen, Mogens Ove (2017). An Anatomy of the Concept of Time in Maynard Keynes, *Economics World*, 5(2), pp. 146–153.

Madsen, Mogens Ove (2018). Hicks's Progress from Statics to Historical Time, from Dow, S., Jespersen, J. & Tily, G. (eds.), *Money, Method and Contemporary Post-Keynesian Economics*. New Directions in Modern Economics series. Edward Elgar, pp. 120–133.

McTaggart, J.M.E. (1908). The Unreality of Time. *Mind*, 17, pp. 457–473.

Mink, Louis O. (1960). Time, McTaggart and Pickwickian Language, *The Philosophical Quarterly*, 10(40), pp. 252–263.

Prigogine, Y. & Stengers, I. (1985). *Order Out of Chaos: Man's New Dialogue with Nature*. Flamingo Fontana, London.

Robinson, Joan (1953). A Lecture Delivered at Oxford by a Cambridge Economist, from *On Rereading Marx, 10–18*. Cambridge Students' Bookshops Ltd. Reprinted in *Collected Economic Papers, Vol. 4*, 1973, Basil Blackwell, Oxford, pp. 254–263.

Rössler, O.E. (1992). *Endophysics. Die Welt des Inneren Beobachters*. Merwe Verlag, Berlin.

Shackle, G.L.S. (1974). *Keynesian Kaleidics: The Evolution of a General Political Economy*. Edinburgh University Press.

Subert, J. (2001). The Problem of Time from the Perspective of the Social Sciences, *Chech Sociological Review*, 9(2), pp. 211–224.

Turk, M.H. (2010). The Arrow of Time in Economics: From Robinson's Critique to the New Historical Economics, *History of Economics Thought*, 17(3), pp. 471–492.

Turk, M.H. (2015). *The Idea of History in Constructing Economics*. Routledge, London.

# Part II

# Empirical SFC Modelling

# 5 House prices, financial cycles and business cycles

## An empirical stock-flow consistent (SFC) model for the Danish economy

*Mikael Randrup Byrialsen, Hamid Raza and Christos Pierros*

### 1 Introduction

The build-up of the Global Financial Crisis (GFC) and its consequences are well documented in the literature. Financial cycles – usually driven by credit accumulation – have received a lot of attention in macroeconomic debates as reported by Grinderslev et al. (2017) and Borio (2014). The aggressive build-up of the financial cycles was believed to have set a perfect stage for a serious crisis. The financial cycles of several advanced countries peaked shortly before the crisis in 2007–2008 as shown in Stremmel (2015) and Borio (2014). In countries where the peak of the financial cycle was high, the resultant crisis was also more severe. There seems to be consensus emerging on the argument that credit creation is important for the economy but too much credit can also damage the economy through various feedback channels, which can sometimes turn into a full-blown crisis. Credit growth is one of the central variables when discussing the dynamics of a financial cycle.

From a long-term perspective, it has been argued that aggressive credit accumulation has made growth rates more fragile. That is, aggressive credit accumulation was the driver of high and persistent growth rates in the pre-crisis period, but this made the whole economic and financial system more vulnerable to a serious crisis. Due to the importance of financial cycles in understanding financial crises and monitoring financial risks, it is imperative to examine how these cycles evolve over time and how they affect the entire economic system. Despite the strong empirical evidence regarding the relationship between business and financial cycles, the theoretical foundation for understanding the build-up of a financial cycle and its subsequent impact on the real economy is weak. This is primarily due to the complex and innovative nature of the financial markets, which makes its relationship with the real side of the economy very complex. At a broader theoretical level, the work of Hyman Minsky is considered to be the most appropriate in addressing the build-up of a financial cycle and identifying its impacts on the economy.

DOI: 10.4324/9781003253457-7

This chapter is an attempt to identify the drivers of a financial cycle and understand the interdependence between financial and real variables in an explicit and rigorous manner. Doing so, however, requires understanding the dynamics of a financial cycle as well as the transmission mechanism through which financial cycles can create booms and busts. We use Denmark as a case study, representing a small open economy with a modern financial system, to explore these linkages. First, we investigate the dynamics of the Danish business and financial cycles using historical data since 1950. We then adopt an SFC approach to model the Danish financial cycle and carefully capture its interlinkages with the real side of the economy. We then look at the pre-crisis scenario and perform counterfactual analysis to address the following question: What would be the potential status of an economy, if it accumulated lower credit and built up a less extreme financial cycle prior to the crisis. That is, we attempt to create and discuss an alternative path of the economy and explore its dynamics. We do so by creating a scenario where the pre-crisis financial cycle, due to strict constraints on credit, has a lower peak than the actual financial cycle and study its implications on macroeconomic outcomes. Our findings suggest that a financial cycle of lower peak leads to a boom and bust of lower amplitude, which is not surprising. However, the most interesting result is related to the post-crisis phase where we find that the post-crisis output is higher when the pre-crisis financial cycle was less extreme. We explain the underlying reason for this result and also discuss the policy implications of our findings.

The structure of the chapter is as follows. In Section 2, we provide a preliminary statistical description of the dynamics of business and financial cycle for the Danish economy. In Section 3 we discuss the relevant literature. In Section 4, we present the data and explain the structure of the empirical macroeconomic model for Denmark, containing various features inspired by the work of Hyman Minsky. In Section 5, we discuss the results of our model and discuss the policy implications of our empirical finding. The final section concludes this chapter.

## 2 House prices, financial cycles and business cycles in Denmark

While there seems to be consensus regarding the choice of keys variables for identifying business cycles (GDP), several variables have been suggested as indicators of financial cycles. Following the tradition of Stremmel (2015), Borio (2014) and Grinderslev et al. (2017), financial cycles are expressed as credit cycles in our plots.

The development in all three time series from 1950 to 2017 is presented in real terms in Figure 5.1:[1]

While the development in real GDP seems to follow a long-term linear trend, the development in real house prices and real credit is far less linear. The accumulation of credit seems to be almost exponential with a few exceptions. Especially, between 2000 and 2009 the increase had been steep, presumably due to the introduction of a new type of mortgage loans – delayed

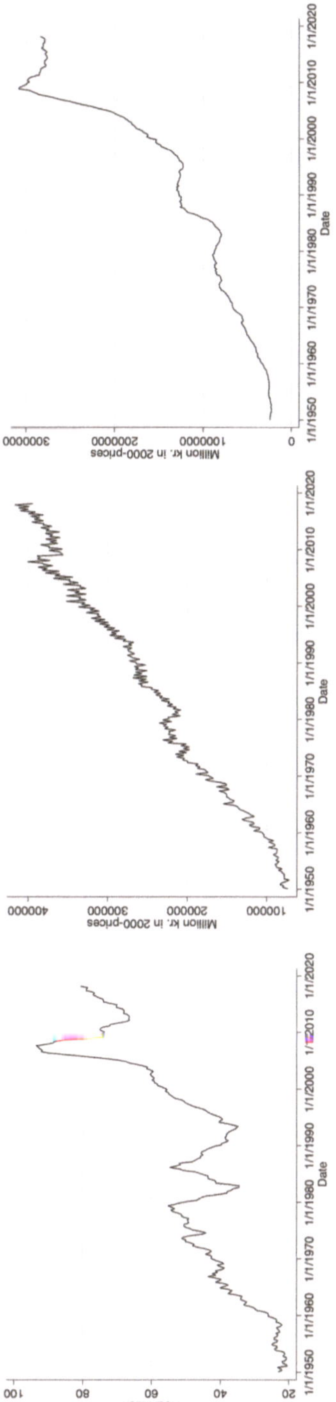


*Figure 5.1* Real house prices (left), real GDP (center) and real stock of credit (right).

amortization[2] – in 2003. Apart from the 1950s, the house prices showed a positive trend over the years, but three major falls can be identified in the figure: around 1980, from 1986 to 1993 and around the GFC. Since the crisis, the real house prices have increased considerably and are about to approach the pre-crisis level.

In times of growth, the correlation between all three variables seems to be high. However, when, focusing on the three aforementioned episodes their relationship is not that straightforward. In the beginning of the 1980s, following the bust in the housing market and the economic crisis, the real stock of credit fell, pointing to a close connection between the variables under consideration. The crash in the housing market in the first half of the 1990s did not result in a recession even though the stock of credit stagnated. This indicates a very close connection between house prices and credit, but not with real GDP. In the aftermath of the GFC, all the three variables (house prices, GDP and the stock of credit) fell. In the post-crisis period, house prices resurged whereas GDP has been growing following its long-term trend. The stock of credit, however, has remained stagnant. The current situation clearly constitutes a break from the long-term pattern.

Other interesting insights can be drawn by focusing on the cyclical deviations from the trend. If we estimate the cycles of the time series using an HP filter for real GDP, real house prices and real credit provide interesting insights. Cycles in house prices and credit have larger amplitudes, while cycles of GDP seem to be comparatively shorter (Figure 5.2). This result is also suggested when looking at the autocorrelations, which are higher for house prices and credit rather than GDP.

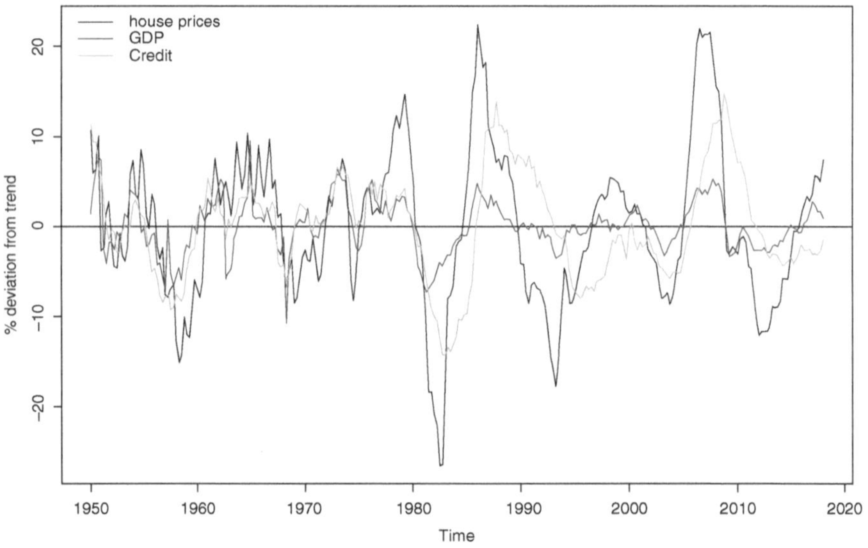


*Figure 5.2* House price cycles, GDP cycles and credit cycles.

Unsurprisingly, all three cycles co-move and are positively correlated. The figure shows that credit cycles lag the cycles of the two other components in most cases. This is confirmed by looking at the cross correlation among the three time series, which indicates that house prices and GDP are drivers of credit cycles.

As stated above, both the amplitude and the length of the GDP cycles are much smaller than the amplitude of the other cycles, especially in the period after 1980 (see Figure 5.4). Before 1980, the cycles of GDP and credit were quite similar in magnitude. The house prices on the other hand deviated much more from their long-run trend. Concerning the trough of the cycle, the house prices in the last half of the 1950s were around 15% lower than their long-run trend, while the deviation of GDP was around 5% and the deviation of credit about 10%. Looking at a peak instead, the house prices in the last half of the 1970s were much higher than their trend value, while the levels of both credit and GDP were much closer to their trend values. Since the 1980s, the amplitude of credit increased both absolutely and relatively to the amplitude of the GDP cycle. Two peaks of a credit cycle can be identified since 1980: (i) in the end of 1980s and (ii) around the GFC. At the end of 1980s, the upswing of the credit cycle lagged behind the upswing of house prices and GDP. The house prices fluctuated quite a lot. Their rapid fall in the early 1980s was the result of low growth rates and the ensuing crisis in the Danish economy, which was aggravated by the second oil crisis in the late 1970s. In the middle of the 1980s, house prices resurged, simultaneously with a rapid increase in domestic demand. Excessive demand resulted in a record high deficit on the current account and increased public and foreign debt, which in turn signified the change in the government's policy toward fiscal consolidation including tax reforms (e.g. the Potato diet), so as to cope with private consumption. On the positive side, the current account went into surplus, while both public and foreign debt were reduced. On the negative side, the demand dropped considerably, the level of unemployment increased rapidly and house prices started to fall up until 1993. Since 1993, a new era of tranquility can be identified in the Danish economy, with rapid fall in the level of unemployment, moderate growth rates in real GDP and increases in house prices and the demand for credit. In 2003, this phase of tranquility was ensued by a boom in both business and financial cycles, until they burst in 2007–2008. Since then, the Danish economy has been relatively stagnant. At the same time house prices have increased significantly and seem to be either at or above their long-run trend.[3] The credit, however, has not increased since 2009, indicating a clear break in the long-run relationship between house prices, business and financial cycles.

All in all, there seems to be a high correlation between the three time series, with the cycles of house prices seemingly leading the cycles of real GDP and the real stock of household credit. To analyze the effect of a shock to one of these components, their link must be well integrated into a formal macroeconomic model. But before doing so we first briefly review the relevant literature.

## 3 Literature review

Our empirical results above are in line with several important findings of the literature: (i) high correlation between house prices, GDP and credit, (ii) house prices and GDP are leading credit cycles and (iii) business cycles are shorter and smaller in amplitude as compared to cycles in house prices and financial cycles (see i.e. Borio, 2014; Grinderslev et al., 2017; Stremmel, 2015). A common feature for the aforementioned literature is the lack of theoretical foundations for the findings. Stockhammer and Wolf (2019) point out that despite the role played by real estate prices in booms and busts housing is an underestimated topic in macroeconomics and the political economy. In their review they conclude:

> What emerges from this brief survey of mainstream economics is a tension between a theoretical framework that, with its rationality and market clearing assumptions, is ill-suited to explain recent dynamics and crises emanating from the real estate sector and, at the same time, a dynamic empirical research program that bypasses the rigidities of the theoretical framework.
>
> (Stockhammer and Wolf, 2019, p. 48)

Outside the general equilibrium methodology, Minsky has been recognized as one of the economists providing a theoretical framework for understanding cycles generated by the connection between financial markets and the real economy. In Minsky et al. (1995) authors argue that 'over a run of good times the liability structures of households and firms change so that ever larger proportions of their gross cash-flows (incomes) are prior committed to the fulfillment of obligations as specified in their liabilities'. In case of a drop in cash flow, households will try to compensate by selling assets, which might lead to a 'serious decline' in the market price of both financial and capital assets. The fall in asset prices affects the net worth of households, which might adversely affect the demand for consumption and investment. This decline in demand can result in a collapse of income, employment and asset prices. According to Minsky et al. (1995) the relative size of government demand vis-à-vis private demand is an important factor for the sensitivity of profits to investment.

Minsky et al. (1995) present a theoretical model in which financial instability is endogenous. The business cycle follows four phases: (i) a recovery in which profits are increasing even as indebtedness falls, (ii) a robust expansion during which profits increase as debts increase, (iii) a boom in which indebtedness increases even as profits begin to fall and (iv) a deflation phase in which both debts and profits fall. In Zezza (2008) the housing market is taken explicitly into account. In this model an increase in the expected house prices will generate a price bubble since the supply of house is inelastic. These capital gains boost the overall economic activity, through higher consumption and investment in housing (and thereby a fall in rate of saving). Rosser et al. (2012) employ a Minsky-Kindleberger perspective to discuss the nature of different bubbles from a historical perspective. According to their study, three types of bubbles can be identified. The authors claim Minsky to be the one who identified and labeled the third type,[4] which according to Kindleberger is the most frequent one. It is characterized by a rise in prices up to a peak after which the prices fall, panic arises and the economy crashes. In Nikolaidi (2015) house prices are integrated into the analysis, pointing out that their growth increases the net wealth of households, which results in higher credit and demand and house price inflation. From a Minskyan perspective this might result in a Ponzi scheme, where a continuous increase in house prices is critical in rolling over debt. Dafermos (2017) integrates endogenous stock-flow norms into a Godley-Minsky-inspired SFC framework. In his model, the propensity to consume or invest in the private sector increases (decreases) when the target debt-to-income ratio increases (decreases), which generates fluctuations in the system. These endogenous norms vary with economic activity and financial innovation. In periods with booms both the economic activity and the level of financial innovations is high, which has a positive effect on the targeted debt-to-income ratio and the consumption as well as investment.

In Nikolaidi and Stockhammer (2017) a survey of Minskian models is carried out. The authors define a Minskyan model as a macroeconomic model with a focus on analyzing the interdependence between financial and real variables through channels identified by Minsky. They divide Minskyan models into two different types, with the first one characterized by a focus on debt and/or interest dynamics, while the focus in the second type is on asset price dynamics. Asset prices are typically being split into equity prices and real estate prices. As pointed out by Nikolaidi and Stockhammer (2017) real estate prices have only very recently been incorporated into the Minskyan framework. In these models, house prices are expected to play a central role in both cycles and instability (see i.e. Ryoo, 2016).

The following model contributes precisely in this part of the literature. In particular, the underlying mechanism highlights the dual role of housing prices as drivers of demand and credit growth. For instance, a higher expected rate of return on houses boosts the demand for houses. In turn, it increases their price and, thus reinforces the expectations regarding a higher rate of return. The aggregate demand is positively affected by both higher investment in the housing market and the wealth effect on consumption. At some point expectations are lowered due to the excessive increase of the stock-flow norm, wealth over consumption. This feeds back negatively to the demand for and the prices of housing. The housing wealth to capital ratio moves procyclically. Once the ratio is low, households are again willing to take up investment in housing. At the same time, housing wealth also functions as a collateral in a procyclical manner. A higher housing wealth renders the credit constraints less binding. Credit growth boosts demand and price of houses. Gradually, the interest payments to the bank, or the leverage ratio, become too large. Households have difficulties in meeting their debt payment commitments. This affects the housing market negatively as the respective demand and prices drop. In this sense, a financial cycle is generated.

## 4 The model

To explore the link between asset prices, business cycles and financial cycles, we adopt a Minskian SFC approach to modeling. The model is a modified version of the benchmark model presented in Byrialsen and Raza (2020). We use annual sectoral national account data from Eurostat covering a period from 1995 to 2016. The balance sheet and transaction matrices can be found in the Appendix along with the structure of the model. To confine the length of the chapter, the presentation of the model focuses on some important characteristics that extend the work of Byrialsen and Raza (2021) and Byrialsen and Raza (2022).

### Model structure

Following the identification of Nikolaidi and Stockhammer (2017), we analyze the interdependence between financial and real variables through channels identified by Minsky. In a sense, the model presented here can be seen as a hybrid model of several of the existing theoretical Minskyan models, as its focus is on both the debt and interest dynamics, as well as on asset price dynamics. The dynamics are identified within the model through different channels:

1. Debt and interest dynamics work through both the interest flows between sectors and the stock of debt, which affects both consumption and investment. The effect on consumption is formalized under the standard Keynesian consumption function. In terms of investment, a rule of thumb is applied, according to which households and banks evaluate the actual stock of debt compared to an 'targeted stock of loan'. This 'targeted stock of loan' is determined as a proportion of the disposable income and can be interpreted as both households' willingness to borrow and banks' willingness to lend.
2. The actual stock of debt also affects the households' demand for credit, in the respective credit demand function.
3. Changes in house prices affect the aggregate demand through investment, since the ratio between the value of housing and the cost of

producing houses provides financial incentives for building new houses. In addition, there is a wealth effect on consumption in the structure of the model.

4 Housing price inflation increases the value of the collaterals and thus the demand for credit.
5 Changes in equity prices affect both the portfolio decision and the financial wealth of households, which in turn have a wealth effect on aggregate demand.

These channels enable us to investigate the linkages between asset pricing, business cycles and financial cycles, identified with changes in prices of houses, economic activity and credit flows as well as the feedback mechanism in the model.

Since the model refers to Denmark, we assume away any impact of the domestic economic activity on international trade and capital flows, while the central bank is assumed to take any action necessary to maintain a fixed exchange rate. All domestic production takes place in non-financial corporations (NFCs). Changes in aggregate demand, and thereby in economic activity, reflect the business cycles. Total demand is given by the standard accounting identity:

$$Y = C + I + G + X - M \qquad \text{(Eq. 5.1)}$$

$Y$ represents total demand,[5] $C$ private consumption, $I$ investment, $X$ exports and $M$ imports. Government consumption ($G$) is exogenous in this model. Exports are modeled as a function of relative prices and the weighted import of the trading partners, while imports are a function of relative prices and domestic private demand.

Following standard Keynesian theory, private consumption is a function of disposable income, one period lagged net wealth, while inertia is reflected in the lagged term of consumption.

$$\Delta ln(c_t) = \beta_i \Delta ln(yd_t) + \beta_i \Delta ln\left(nw_{t-1}^{H}\right) + \beta_i \Delta ln(c_{t-1}) \qquad \text{(Eq. 5.2)}$$

Two components of investment are endogenous: investment of NFCs and households' residental investment. NFCs' investment is a function of the capacity utilization and the rate of capital accumulation in the last period.

$$\frac{i_t^N}{k_{t-1}^N} = \beta_i + \beta_i \frac{i_{t-1}^N}{k_{t-2}^N} + \beta_i \frac{y_t}{k_{t-1}^N} \qquad \text{(Eq. 5.3)}$$

The level of housing investment is determined by the incentive to invest in new housing, real disposable income, the accumulation of housing in the last period and the difference between the current debt-to-income ratio and the 'targeted debt-to-income ratio' or leverage. The incentive to invest in new housing – known as Tobin's q for housing – is usually defined as the ratio of house prices to construction cost ($P^i$). The expectation is that an increase in the house prices relative to construction costs would induce investments in housing (Kohlscheen et al. 2020).

Real investment $\left(i_t^H\right)$ in fixed assets (housing) is as follows:

$$\left(\frac{i_t^H}{k_{t-1}^H}\right)=\beta_i\left(\frac{i_{t-1}^H}{k_{t-2}^H}\right)+\beta_i\left(\frac{P_t^H}{P_t^i}\right)+\beta_i\left(\frac{yd_t^H}{k_{t-1}^H}\right)+\beta_i\left(\frac{IBL_{t-1}^H}{k_{t-2}^H}\right)-\phi\beta_i\left(lev_{t-1}^h-lev_{t-1}^{tar}\right)$$

(Eq. 5.4)

The inclusion of real disposable income[6] makes demand for investment procyclical as it reflects an accelerator mechanism. The procyclicality of investment is further reflected in lenders' and borrowers' risk which in practice is the deviation of actual debt-to-income ratio from the targeted debt-to-income ratio.[7] Increases in disposable income result in a higher accepted stock of debt that the households are willing to hold. In this sense, the paradox of tranquility is integrated in the model. A phase of tranquility therefore increases the accepted stock of debt of both households and banks. An increase in the house prices $\left(P^H\right)$ motivates the households to invest more in construction, while an increase in the construction costs $\left(P^i\right)$ would lower housing investment. The house price index is modeled as a function of the real stock of houses to real investment in housing ratio, which can be interpreted as an inverse rate of accumulation of houses, the economic activity and the lagged house price index.

$$P_t^H=\beta_i+\beta_i ln\left(P_{t-1}^H\right)+\beta_i ln\left(\frac{k_{t-i}^H}{i_{t-i}^H}\right)+\beta_i ln\left(y_t\right) \qquad \text{(Eq. 5.5)}$$

As described above, housing prices affect the demand for houses. At the same time, the economic activity (including investment in housing) affects housing prices. Thus, there is a simultaneous feedback effect between the two variables as indicated in the literature. The stock of debt might affect both the demand for consumption and investment, but the decision to consume and invest also affects the demand for credit. On the financial side of the economy, the households take on loans to finance mainly investment in housing and allocate their wealth in pension, equities or interest-bearing assets following a modified Tobin portfolio allocation. The relative return of the different assets determines the allocation. The current debt-to-income ratio is modeled as a function of investment to disposable income ratio, the interest rate (representing the cost of borrowing) and the previous period debt-to-income ratio.

$$lev_t^h = \beta_i \left( \frac{IBL_{t-1}^H}{YD_{t-1}^H} \right) + \beta_i \left( \frac{I_t^H}{YD_t^H} \right) - \beta_i r_{L,t-1}^H \qquad \text{(Eq. 5.6)}$$

Following Minsky et al. (1995) investment is financed by internal funds as well as loans. An increase in the investment-to-income ratio is therefore expected to increase the demand for credit. As the interest rate represents the cost of borrowing, an increase in the interest rate would affect the demand for credit negatively.

## Estimation and simulation

Our model has several structural parameters which are estimated using annual Danish data from 1995 to 2016.[8] While our model selection for each equation is purely econometric in nature aiming to obtain statistically valid estimators, our choice of variables in every equation is purely theoretical as discussed earlier.

After estimating the structural parameters, we numerically solve the model to establish a baseline scenario. To evaluate the overall performance of our model, we compare the baseline scenario with actual data for the period 1995–2016. The overall performance of the model is satisfactory, as it is able to explain the macroeconomic dynamics of the Danish economy to a reasonable extent.[9]

## 5 Results and discussion

An important aspect of this simulation exercise is to investigate the linkage between house prices, business cycles and financial cycles within the model. The simulation of the model clearly reproduces this interdependence between these variables.

Focusing on the period before the crisis, there was a bubble in housing prices, ensued by high growth rates in GDP and high household credit demand. From a Minskyan point of view, the period preceding the crisis can be seen as clear evidence of a tranquil state of growth, in which both banks and households were willing to increase the stock of credit. Its increase buoyed up demand for investment in housing and increased the associated prices. This bore a significant wealth effect on consumption and investment and the demand for credit. Housing prices were inflated through higher aggregate demand. This positive correlation between housing prices, business cycles and financial cycles reinforces itself. In order to investigate these feedback mechanisms, the first scenario examines the evolution of business and financial cycles following a drop of the housing prices.

In the second scenario, we analyze the macroeconomic effect of a reduction in the accepted debt-to-disposable income ratio. The banks grant less loans and simultaneously households demand less credit. The implications of this change affect, directly or indirectly, households, banks but also the government. From the perspective of households, the fall in the accepted debt-to-income ratio reflects a drop in optimism or willingness to get further into debt. From the perspective of banks, the drop in the accepted debt-to-income ratio illustrates a lower willingness to lend money and thereby reduce the risk for the banks (this can also be interpreted as applying credit constraints). Finally, the reduction in the debt ratio can be initiated by new regulations made by the government aiming to stabilize the financial markets.

## Shock 1: A drop in house prices

As presented in the literature, changes in house prices are expected to play an important role in explaining changes in the stock of household debt and the economic activity. To investigate the propagation of this mechanism, we introduce a negative shock in the house price index of five units during the booming period 2003–2007. The shocks are considered as what-if scenarios, which take place as a counterfactual analysis.[10]

In Figure 5.3 we illustrate the development in housing prices, household debt and real GDP compared to the baseline scenario.

The drop in housing prices affects aggregate demand through investment and consumption to a smaller extent. The negative effect on consumption comes as a result of a drop in the net wealth of the households, while the negative effect on investment is due to the drop of Tobin's q. The fall of both investment and consumption reduces total demand, which necessarily implies a lower demand for imports. The drop in the overall economic activity feeds back into investment and consumption, which aggravate the initial effects (see Figure 5.3). The lower demand for housing and lower economic activity exacerbate the initial shock to house prices, as illustrated in Figure 5.3. Finally, the lower demand for housing leads to a lower demand for loans, which reduces the stock of household debt (see Figure 5.3).

In the period after 2009, during which the Danish economy was trapped in stagnation, the economy seems to perform better in case of Shock 1; between 2009 and 2012 the GDP is at a higher level as compared to the baseline. Similarly, housing prices are lower than the baseline scenario prior to 2009, but higher between 2009 and 2013. The drop in investment in this scenario is much more modest as compared to the actual fall. The relatively higher level of investment boosts the demand for credit, while since 2010 the stock of household debt in scenario 1 exceeds that of debt of the baseline scenario.

Following Minskyan theory, large capital gains on housing before the crisis led to a high level of demand partly financed by new household credit, which further boosted housing prices, and the process reinforced itself. By reducing the level of housing prices before the crisis, both economic activity and credit was reduced, which confirms the Minskyan idea. The lower level of debt before the crisis resulted in a quicker recovery in the years after the

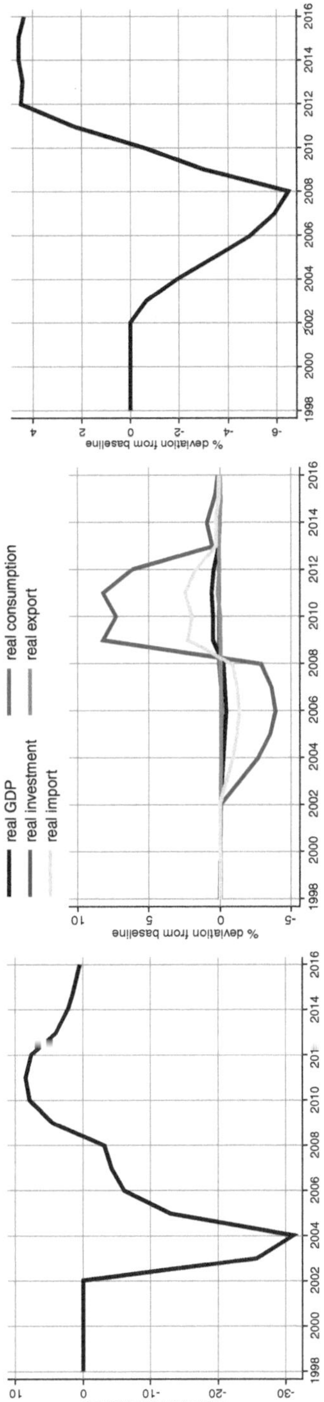


*Figure 5.3* The effect on house prices (left), demand (center) and credit (right).

crisis, both for investment and for imports. Furthermore, housing prices increased faster in this scenario. However, the real stock of credit is higher in Shock 1 as compared to the baseline scenario.

The above insights imply that the stability of the macrofinancial system is critically dependent on the regulation of the credit and housing market. The financial and the business cycles are strongly interconnected with the fluctuations being triggered by capital gains in the housing market. The speculative behavior emanating from the financial gains out of the housing market generates booms and busts and debt dynamics. Policy makers need to reduce the sensitivity of the economy to the housing price fluctuations, so as to ensure the stability of the macrofinancial system.

## Shock 2: A fall in the accepted debt-to-disposable income ratio

As seen in our baseline scenario and in scenario 1, a sudden drop in housing prices affects both the household credit demand and the economic activity. As reported in Figure 5.4, there is a notable exception in this pattern from 2015 onward. This exception might be explained by a change in the behavior of the economic agents, or a structural break. For this reason, we investigate the macroeconomic consequences of a reduction in the accepted debt-to-disposable income ratio. Note that, as mentioned above, this drop might be initiated by the households, the banks or the government. To perform this shock, we fix the accepted debt-to-disposable income ratio to the same ratio as in 2003 for the period from 2003 to 2007.

In the short run, the lower accepted debt-to-income ratio reduces the demand for investment in houses. The fall of the residential investment reduces both the economic activity and the housing prices as seen in Figure 5.4.

In the short run, a lower accepted debt-to-income ratio therefore has a braking effect on the economy as expected. Similar to the result from scenario 1, the medium-term impact seems surprising at first glance, though the underlying mechanism can be well explained within the model. The fall in residential investment lowers both aggregate demand and the demand for credit. At the same time, the effect on other financial assets in households' balance sheet is indirect. There is a reallocation of wealth to other assets leading to an increase in the income of the households from capital gains (increase in the stock of financial assets and fall in the stock of debt). The rise in disposable income results in higher consumption and aggregate demand. The positive effect in the medium term can also be reflected in the asset prices, where housing prices are higher than in the baseline.

From a Minskyan perspective, these results can be explained by a change in the risk behavior between the lender and the borrower. If the households and/or the banks were less willing to increase the level of credit in the system, the housing bubble and economic boom before the

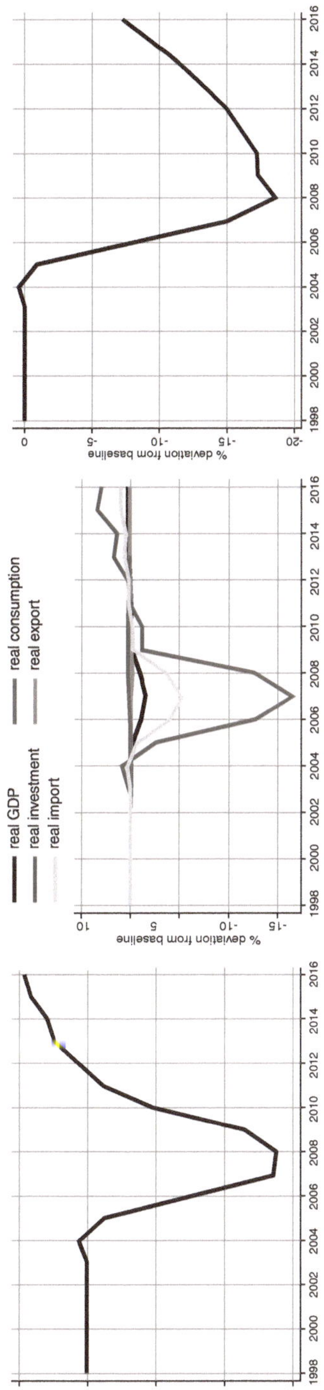


*Figure 5.4* The effect on house prices (left), demand (center) and credit (right).

crisis would have been smaller, just like the recovery from the crisis would have been faster in an economy with less debt. This finding conforms with the one from Shock 1. Riskier behaviors tend to generate financial cycles and amplify their impact on the business cycles. Therefore, regulating the housing market and especially its financial aspects reduces the instability of the system and allows the economy to recover faster in the presence of negative shocks.

## 6 Conclusion

Since the GFC politicians and economists have focused on creating financial stability by focusing on medium-term target for specific ratios. From the perspective of this chapter, the focus on specific stock-flow norms becomes relevant. The interplay between housing prices, stock of credit and real GDP is key to understanding the linkages between financial and business cycles. For this reason, we have developed an empirical SFC model, applied to the economy of Denmark, in order to investigate cycles that were triggered by capital gains in the housing market. In this respect, the model introduced important Minskian aspects that were considered important for carrying our task.

Our empirical findings indicate not only that changes in the housing prices explain financial and business cycles but that the reduction of their impact on economic activity, via regulation of the housing market, renders the economy more prone to recover in the presence of a negative shock. Regulation can further stabilize the macrofinancial system by making households less risky in taking up more debt, or banks less willing to lend. In this respect, under a stricter macroprudential policy the Danish economy would be less susceptible to housing bubbles. Furthermore, our findings reflect to some extent the international experience. Despite the rather significant particularities and specificities of each economy, the burst of the housing bubble in the US, Greece, Spain and Ireland had similar effects to those provided by our analysis. The recent situation, however, is in contrast to the expectations where the house prices (and assets prices in general) have increased significantly, while the demand for credit among the households has stagnated since the crisis.

## References

Borio, Claudio. 2014. "The Financial Cycle and Macroeconomics: What Have We Learnt?" *Journal of Banking & Finance* 45: 182–198.

Byrialsen, Mikael Randrup, and Hamid Raza. 2020. "An Empirical Stock-Flow Consistent Macroeconomic Model for Denmark." Working Paper No. 942. *Levy Economics Institute.*

Byrialsen, Mikael Randrup, and Hamid Raza. 2021. "Assessing the Macroeconomic Effects of COVID-19 in an Empirical SFC Model for Denmark." *International Journal of Political Economy* 50 (4): 318–350.

Byrialsen, Mikael Randrup, and Hamid Raza. 2022. "Household Debt and Macroeconomic Stability: An Empirical Stock-Flow Consistent Model for the Danish economy." *Metroeconomica* 73 (1): 144–197.

Grinderslev, Oliver Juhler, Paul Lassenius Kramp, Anders Farver Kronborg, and Jesper Pedersen. 2017. "Financial Cycles: What Are They and What Do They Look Like in Denmark?" Danmarks Nationalbank Working Papers.

Kohlscheen, Emanuel, Aaron N Mehrotra, and Dubravko Mihaljek. 2020. "Residential Investment and Economic Activity: Evidence from the Past Five Decades." *International Journal of Central Banking* 16 (2020): 6

Minsky, Hyman P et al. 1995. "Sources of Financial Fragility: Financial Factors in the Economics of Capitalism." *Hyman Minsky archive*, Paper No. 69.

Nikolaidi, Maria. 2015. "Securitisation, Wage Stagnation and Financial Fragility: A Stock-Flow Consistent Perspective." *Working paper GPERC27*

Nikolaidi, Maria, and Engelbert Stockhammer. 2017. "Minsky Models: A Structured Survey." *Journal of Economic Surveys* 31 (5): 1304–1331.

Rosser, J Barkley, Marina V Rosser, and Mauro Gallegati. 2012. "A Minsky-Kindleberger Perspective on the Financial Crisis." *Journal of Economic Issues* 46 (2): 449–458.

Ryoo, Soon. "Household debt and housing bubbles: a Minskian approach to boom-bust cycles." *Journal of Evolutionary Economics* 26.5 (2016): 971–1006.

Stockhammer, Engelbert, and Christina Wolf. 2019. "Building Blocks for the Macroeconomics and Political Economy of Housing." *The Japanese Political Economy* 45 (1–2): 43–67.

Stremmel, Hanno. 2015. "Capturing the Financial Cycle in Europe." ECB Working paper, No. 1811.

Zezza, Gennaro. 2008. "US Growth, the Housing Market, and the Distribution of Income." *Journal of Post Keynesian Economics* 30 (3): 375–401.

## Notes

1 In real terms, the house price index is still at a lower level than before the latest crisis. In nominal terms, however, the nominal house price index is at the highest level ever.

2 In 2003 a grace period of maximum ten years was introduced on Danish mortgage loans, which allowed households to postpone installments.

3 The result depends on the choice of the value for $\lambda$ in the HP filter.

4 In the first type, the price rises in an accelerating manner before it crashes sharply. The second type is associated with a rise in price before a parallel decline happens (no need for a crash).

5 Upper case letters represent nominal variables, while lower case letters represent a real variable.

6 This behavior is similar to the model proposed in Zezza (2008) where an increase in expected disposable income positively affects the demand for houses.

7 To integrate a threshold into the model, the shift parameter $\phi$ is used. If the debt-to-income ratio in the last period exceeds the targeted debt-to-income ratio, this parameter is equal to 1.

8 To estimate the equations, in most cases, we start our estimation by including 2 lags due to small sample. We then follow a general to specific methodology and fit a parsimonious model. We also test for unit roots and account for any significant structural breaks in our estimations.

9 For a graphical evidence of this we refer to Byrialsen and Raza (2020).

10 The reader should be aware of the fact that except from the discussed parameters, none of the exogenous variables or parameters are changed in the shocks.

# Appendix

# Balance sheet and transaction flow matrix

*Table A5.1* Balance sheet

| | *NFC* | *FC* | *G* | *H* | | | *W* | $\Sigma$ |
|---|---|---|---|---|---|---|---|---|
| | | *A* | *L* | | *A* | *L* | | |
| Interest bearing (*IB*) | | $IBA^F$ | $IBL^F$ | | $IBA^H$ | $IBL^H$ | | 0 |
| Net interest bearing (*NIB*) | $NIB^N$ | $NIB^F$ | | $NIB^G$ | | | $NIB^W$ | 0 |
| Net equities (*NEQ*) | $NEQ^N$ | $NEQ^F$ | | | $EQA^H$ | | $NEQ^W$ | 0 |
| Pensions (*PEN*) | | | $PEN^F$ | | $PEN^H$ | | $NPEN$ | 0 |
| Financial net wealth (*FNW*) | $FNW^H$ | $FNW^F$ | | $FNW^G$ | $FNW^H$ | | $FNW^W$ | 0 |
| Fixed assets (*K*) | $K^N$ | $K^F$ | | $K^G$ | $K^H$ | | | $K^T$ |

*Table A5.2* Transaction flow matrix

| | *NFC* | *FC* | *G* | *H* | *ROW* | | | | | | |
|---|---|---|---|---|---|---|---|---|---|---|---|
| | *Current* | *Capital* | *Current* | *Capital* | *Current* | *Capital* | *Current* | *Capital* | *Current* | *Capital* | $\Sigma$ |
| Private consumption | $+C$ | | | | | | $-C$ | | | | 0 |
| Government consumption | $+G$ | | | | $-G$ | | | | | | 0 |
| Investment | $+I$ | $-I^{N}$ | | $-I^{F}$ | | $-I^{G}$ | | $-I^{H}$ | | | 0 |
| Exports | $+X$ | | | | | | | | $-X$ | | 0 |
| Imports | $-M$ | | | | | | | | $-M$ | | 0 |
| [GDP] | $[Y]$ | | | | | | | | | | 0 |
| Taxes | $-T^{N}$ | | $-T^{F}$ | | $-T^{G}$ | | $-T^{H}$ | | $-T^{W}$ | | 0 |
| Gross operating surplus | $-B2^{N}$ | | $-B2^{F}$ | | $-B2^{G}$ | | $+B2^{H}$ | | | | 0 |
| Wages | $-W\ B^{N}$ | | | | | | $+W\ B^{H}$ | | | | 0 |
| Capital income | $rK^{N}$ | | $rK^{F}$ | | $rK^{G}$ | | $rK^{H}$ | | $rK^{W}$ | | 0 |
| Transfers | $STR^{N}$ | | $STR^{F}$ | | $STR^{G}$ | | $STR^{H}$ | | $STR^{W}$ | | 0 |
| Pension adjustments | | | $-CPEN^{F}$ | | | | $-CPEN^{H}$ | | | | 0 |
| Savings | $-S^{N}$ | $+S^{N}$ | $-S^{F}$ | $+S^{F}$ | $-S^{G}$ | $+S^{G}$ | $-S^{H}$ | $+S^{H}$ | $-S^{W}$ | $+S^{W}$ | 0 |
| Capital transfers | | $KTR^{N}$ | | $KTR^{F}$ | | $KTR^{G}$ | | $KTR^{H}$ | | $KTR^{W}$ | 0 |
| Acquisitions – disposals of | | $NP^{N}$ | | $NP^{F}$ | | $NP^{G}$ | | $NP^{H}$ | | $NP^{W}$ | 0 |
| Net lending | | $NL^{N}$ | | $NL^{F}$ | | $NL^{G}$ | | $NL^{H}$ | | $NL^{W}$ | 0 |

*Table A5.3* Estimates

| |
|---|
| $\Delta ln(c_t) = 0.37*\Delta ln(yd_t)+0.03*\Delta ln\left(nw_{t-1}^{H}\right)+0.46*\Delta ln(c_{t-1})$ |
| $\frac{i_t^N}{k_{t-1}^N} = -0.18+0.24*\frac{i_{t-1}^N}{k_{t-2}^N}+0.36*\frac{y_t}{k_{t-1}^N}$ |
| $\left(\frac{i_t^H}{k_{t-1}^H}\right) = 0.22*\left(\frac{i_{t-1}^H}{k_{t-2}^H}\right)+2.34*\left(\frac{P_t^H}{P_t^i}\right)+0.09*\left(\frac{yd_t^H}{k_{t-1}^H}\right)-0.01*\left(\frac{IBL_{t-1}^H}{k_{t-2}^H}\right)-\phi*0.003\left(lev_{t-1}^h-lev_{t-1}^{tar}\right)$ |
| $P_t^H = -6.44+0.41*ln(P_{t-1}^H)-0.05*ln\left(\frac{k_{t-i}^H}{i_{t-i}^H}\right)+0.46*ln(y_{t-1})$ |
| $lev_t^h = 0.88*\left(\frac{IBL_{t-1}^H}{YD_{t-1}^H}\right)+3.23*\left(\frac{I_t^H}{YD_t^H}\right)-1.55*r_{L,t-1}^H$ |

# 6 Globalisation and financialisation in the Netherlands, 1995–2020

*Joan Muysken and Huub Meijers*

## Introduction

Total assets of the financial sector in the Netherlands increased over the past 25 years from 600% of GDP in 1995 to over 1400% in 2020. This size is large compared to international standards. Moreover, there are specific features of the Dutch economy that caused the financial sector to continue to grow strongly after the financial crisis. Two outstanding features are the continued growth of net trade surplus and the presence of a funded pension system with defined benefits.

We want to analyse the growth of the financial sector in more detail below using balance sheet data from the national account statistics. The advantage of using national account data is that these are comprehensive and internationally agreed upon. Moreover, they are consistent with the flow data, for instance, income data and GDP, and they can be compared relatively easily across countries. There is a big problem, however, when using this kind of data. While data are available on balance sheet totals and incomes of various sectors and subsectors, the transactions between the sectors are not documented. For instance, the amount of loans that banks, other financial institutions (OFIs) and foreign financial institutions has provided in a certain year is reported, as well as the amount of loans households, firms and foreign received in that year. But which sector issued loans to which sector – f.i. which loans to firms were issued by banks, by OFIs or by foreign – is not reported. This problem complicates the analysis of the data considerably and requires a theoretical background. Such a background is also important to better understand the reasons for the growth of the financial sector.

In our analysis we use the tradition of stock flow consistent modelling as a background. The stock flow consistent approach, summarised in Godley and Lavoie (2007), promises a very interesting way to model the interaction between the monetary and the real sphere in a coherent framework. The explicit role of balance sheets and portfolios of financial assets of the various sectors in the model, together with the detailed impact of wealth effects on expenditure, enables us to identify the impact of financial sector operations in detail. We used this approach in Meijers, Muysken and Sleijpen (2014, 2015 and 2016) to analyse several features of the position of the financial sector in the Dutch

DOI: 10.4324/9781003253457-8

economy, as we elaborate below for the position of the funded pension system, the deposit financing gap of banks and the financialisation of firm savings, respectively. Moreover, in Meijers and Muysken (2016) we used this approach to model the impact of quantitative easing on the Dutch economy. In the present chapter, we employ the insights from our earlier analyses to construct a coherent data set from the national account data and to use these data to analyse the growth of the financial sector in the Netherlands over the past 25 years in a descriptive way. To our best knowledge, this is the first time that such a coherent overview has been presented, consistent with national account data.

The outlay of the chapter is as follows. In Section 2 we identify the open nature of the Dutch economy. This is reflected in the large part foreign trade plays in this economy: exports increased from almost 60% of GDP in the mid-1990s to over 80% of GDP nowadays, and imports followed a similar pattern, albeit at a somewhat lower level. We show how this led to an increase in national wealth, accompanied by expanding foreign assets and liabilities – exacerbated by the nature of the Netherlands being a conduit country. The expansion of financial assets and liabilities is a broader phenomenon as we demonstrate in Section 3, where we also highlight the role of the pension funds. We claim in Section 4 that the monetary policy pursued by central banks all over the world provided an important impetus for the expansion of the financial sector. Concluding remarks are presented in Section 5.

## Net export surplus and accumulating national wealth

Although the importance of foreign trade for the Dutch economy is widely recognised, the consistent and increasing surplus on the balance of trade is not often mentioned as an important issue. Net exports increased from around 6% of GDP in the mid-1990s to around 10% recently.[1] Next to trade, incoming and outgoing primary income flows are also substantial. This is due to the nature of the Netherlands as a conduit country (Suyker and Wagteveld, 2019). For instance, retained earnings of foreign subsidiaries of multinationals are counted as income receipts, even though these earnings are reinvested abroad. Also, the Netherlands hosts a huge amount of Special Purpose Vehicles (SPVs) created for tax reasons, leading to earnings earned abroad which do not remain domestically. Therefore, net income flows are small, but fluctuating.[2]

The current account balance of the Dutch economy is dominated by the trade balance and has been increasing steadily over time, in particular after 2008. This was accompanied by a decrease in net foreign wealth from a foreign debit position of around 100% of GDP in the mid-1990s to a credit position of around 100% nowadays (Figure 6.1). Thus, over the past 25 years, foreign liabilities increased by 200% of GDP relative to foreign assets.

The development of foreign assets and liabilities over time has three interesting features. First, there is a huge expansion of both foreign assets and liabilities over time due to the abovementioned creation of SPVs for tax reasons. As can be observed from Figure 6.2, domestic liabilities of SPVs towards foreign, hence foreign assets, were around 175% of GDP in the mid-1990s and peaked at 600% of GDP in 2017 – they decreased slightly afterwards. The liabilities of foreign sectors that are held by domestic SPVs, hence domestic assets, follow a similar pattern over time, albeit at a somewhat lower level.

The second feature is that the remaining financial foreign assets and liabilities (excluding SPVs) also increased over time, as is illustrated in Figures 6.3 and 6.4, respectively. From Figure 6.3 one observes that foreign direct investments from abroad in domestic firms are relatively stable at around 300% of GDP, with a slight upward movement after 2008. Next to

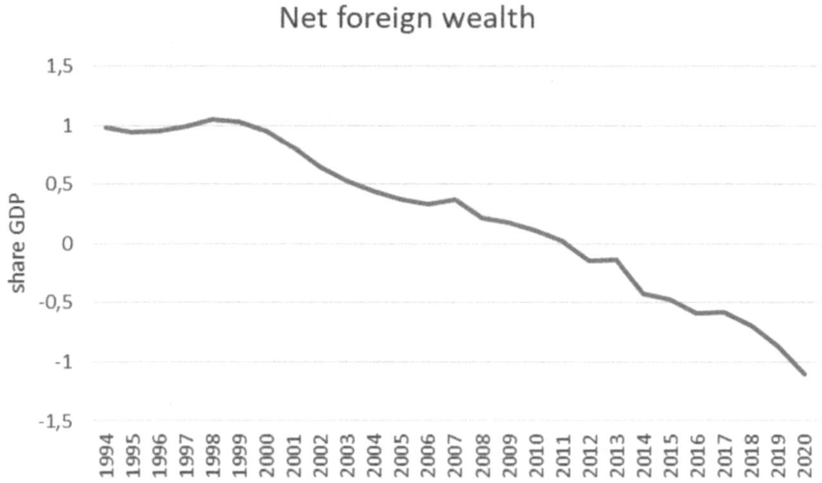


*Figure 6.1* Net foreign wealth.
Source: CBS, national accounts.

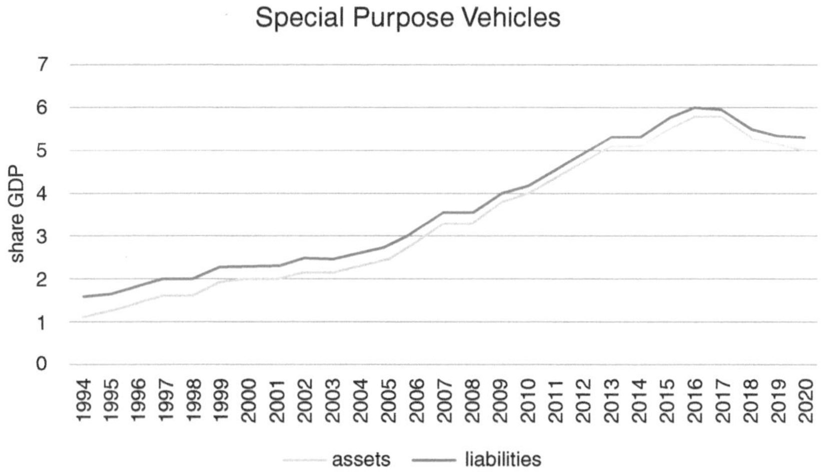


*Figure 6.2* Special Purpose Vehicles.
Source: CBS, national accounts.

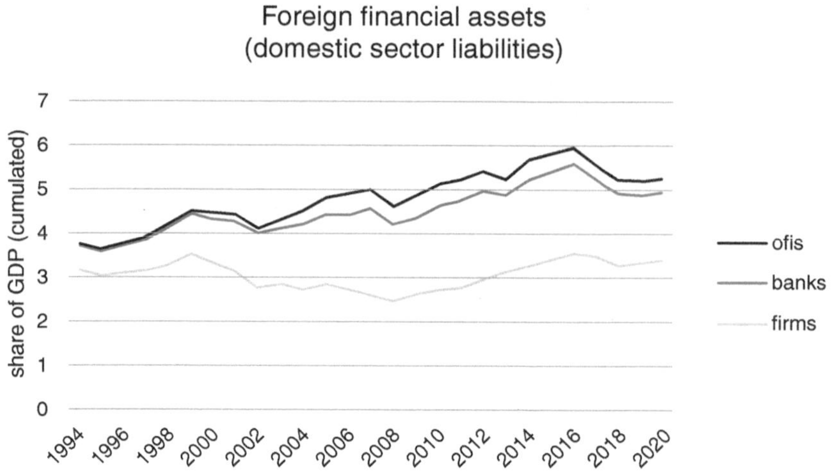


*Figure 6.3* Foreign financial assets (domestic sector liabilities).
Source: CBS, national accounts.

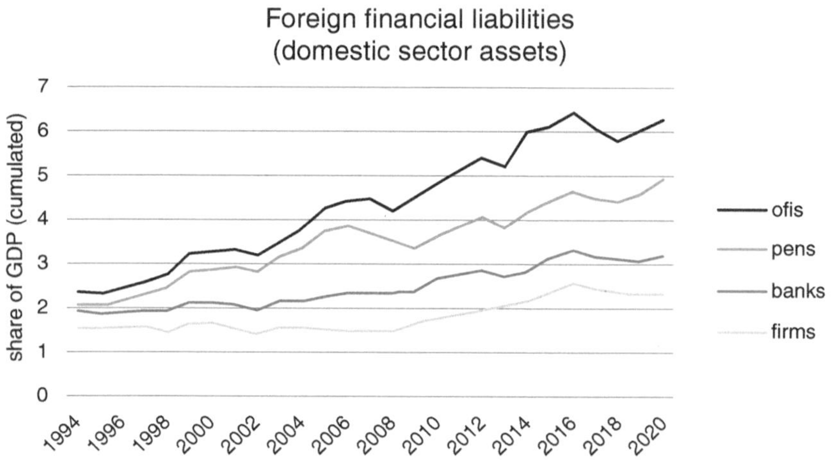


*Figure 6.4* Foreign financial liabilities (domestic sector assets).
Source: CBS, national accounts.

that, banks hold an increasing share of assets borrowed from the foreign sector in their portfolios, amounting from 50% of GDP in the mid-1990s to 150% of GDP in recent years – this leads to the deposit funding gap, as we discuss in the next section. Finally, OFIs play a small role.

In Figure 6.4 we observe that investments of domestic firms abroad are lower than foreign direct investments, albeit still at a level of about 200% of GDP, and have been increasing after 2008. This implies that domestic firms have a large portfolio of both foreign assets and foreign liabilities, with a net borrowing position vis-à-vis the foreign sector.[3] Banks also hold lower foreign liabilities relative to foreign assets, although the foreign liabilities are at a substantial level of around 75% of GDP in recent years. An interesting phenomenon is a strong growth in foreign liabilities held both by pension funds and by OFIs, relative to GDP – this is the main explanation for the growth of foreign liabilities relative to foreign assets. Together these liabilities held by pension funds and OFIs amount to almost 300% of GDP in recent years. Moreover, the pension funds outsourced part of their foreign investments to OFIs since 2008 as we elaborate below – this explains the diverging gap between pension funds and OFIs in Figure 6.4.

Figures 6.3 and 6.4 illustrate on the one hand that the involvement of the financial sector in holding financial assets and liabilities has increased over time. On the other hand, the figures demonstrate that next to banks on the liability side, OFIs and pension funds have become more important over time as participants in the financial sector. We analyse these developments in more detail in the next section.

The third feature regards the development of prices of the foreign financial assets and liabilities in Figures 6.3 and 6.4 (i.e. excluding SPVs).[4] The development of these prices since the mid-1990s is such that in 2008 the value gains of both assets and liabilities fell short of GDP price development and were clearly influenced by the financial crises in 2000 and 2008. However, from 2009 onwards the prices of assets and liabilities increased almost consistently relative to GDP, resulting in value gains of 6 and 13 percentage points, respectively, relative to GDP – cf. Figure 6.5. We will point out a

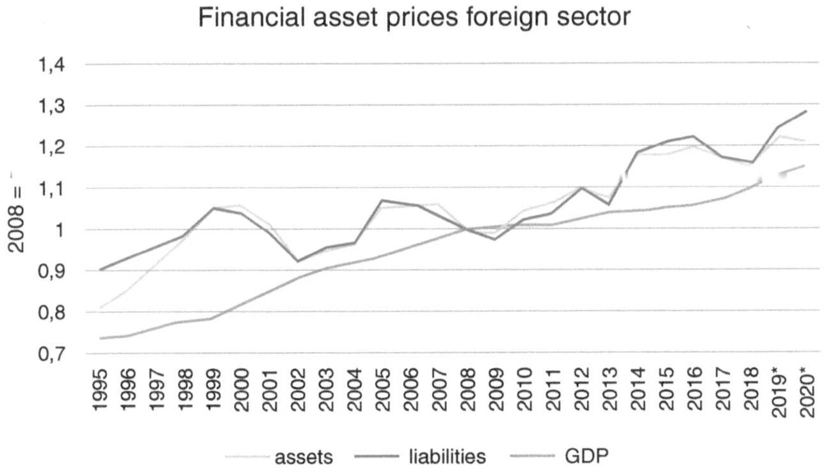


*Figure 6.5* Financial asset prices, foreign sector.
Source: CBS, national accounts.

connection with the quantitative easing policies of central banks world-wide after 2008 in Section 3.

## The expanding financial sector

We mentioned already that, next to banks, the financial sector also consists of OFIs and pension funds. Banks are under the supervision of the central bank and accept deposits. OFIs consist of investment funds, financial intermediaries and special financial institutions.[5] Pension funds are financial institutions that manage the funded pension system – they also include insurance companies, which are dominated by life insurance companies who have the same function as pension funds. In Figure 6.6 we show the development of the assets for each of these sectors over time, relative to GDP. Since liabilities show a similar development, we do not present these.

The growth of the financial sector is also summarised in Table 6.1, to emphasise how each of the three subsectors of the financial sector has developed in a different way over time. The banking sector has grown relative to GDP till 2012, OFIs have mainly grown relative to GDP in the period 2004–2012 and pension fund assets have increased consistently relative to GDP, accelerating after 2007.

With respect to banks, the main growth in assets and liabilities took place in the period prior to the financial crisis in 2008 – cf. Figures 6.7 and 6.8.[6]

On the asset side, the growth of household assets was due to mortgages, which doubled in size relative to GDP and stabilised at a level around 100% of GDP – we elaborate on the impact of quantitative easing on this development below.[7] Next to that loans to firms also increased over time.

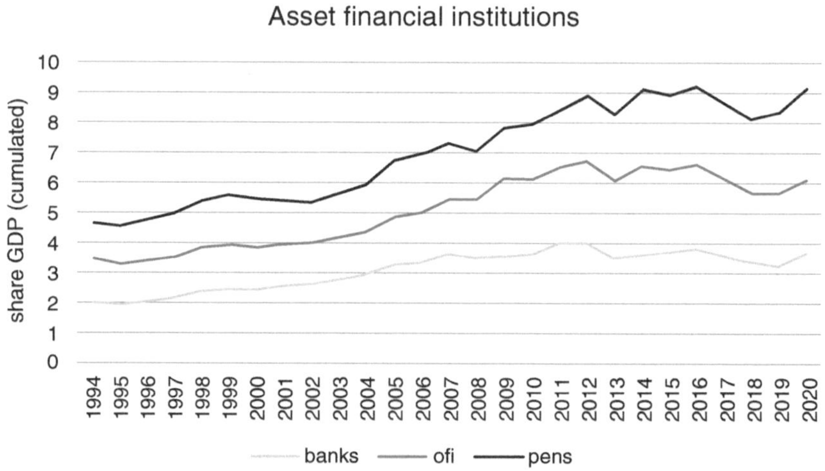


*Figure 6.6* Assets of financial institutions.
Source: CBS, national accounts.

*Table 6.1* Share of total assets in GDP of the financial sector

| | *1995* | *2004* | *2012* | *2019* |
|---|---|---|---|---|
| Banks | 2,00 | 2,97 | 4,02 | 3,26 |
| OFIs | 1,44 | 1,46 | 2,71 | 2,41 |
| Pension funds | 1,25 | 1,55 | 2,18 | 2,73 |
| Total | 4,69 | 5,97 | 8,91 | 8,40 |

Source: CBS, national accounts

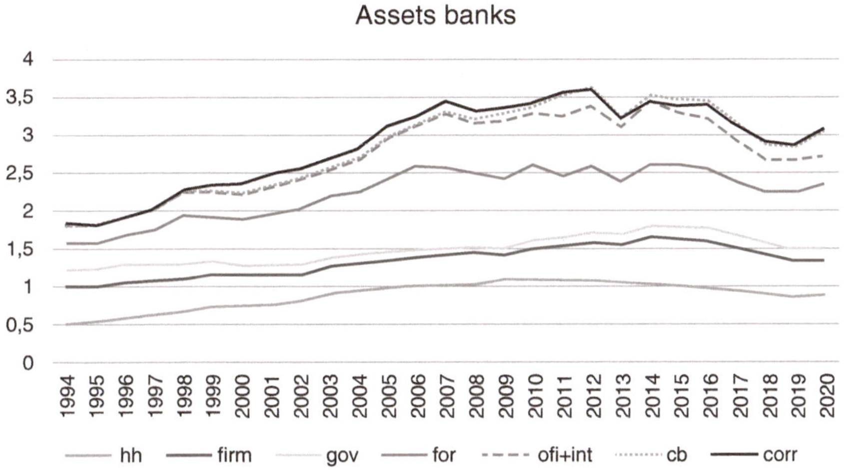


*Figure 6.7* Assets of banks.
Source: CBS, national accounts.

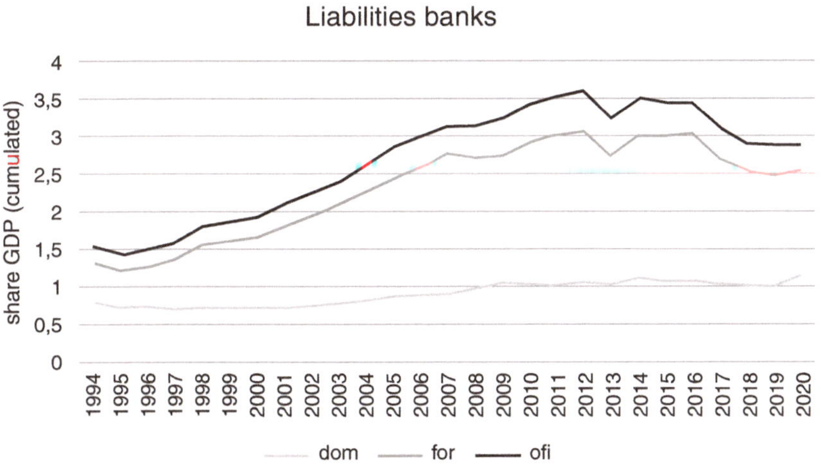


*Figure 6.8* Liabilities of banks.
Source: CBS, national accounts.

Foreign assets increased initially relative to GDP, but are relatively stable after the financial crisis. The substantial share of the OFIs in bank assets reflects mainly financial intermediation. On the liability side, both deposits held by domestic sectors (dom) and OFIs are stable over time. However, foreign liabilities increased strongly relative to GDP till 2011, then they stabilised for a few years, and subsequently decreased from 200% of GDP in 2016 to 150% in 2020.

The composition of assets and liabilities of banks implies that the outstanding mortgages and loans to firms of about 150% of GDP are only covered by domestic deposits around 100% of GDP. The remaining gap is covered by foreign liabilities. This gap is identified in the literature as the 'deposit financing gap' (Meijers, Muysken and Sleijpen, 2015) – it was considered as a dangerous development by the supervising central bank DNB (Jansen et. al., 2013) and the IMF (IMF, 2013). The reason is that foreign liabilities are very volatile, whereas domestic deposits are considered to be stable. Surprisingly, the central bank DNB nowadays is silent about the problem of the deposit financing gap, although the problem persists.

The foreign orientation of banks reflects first of all the open nature of the Dutch economy – the many international contacts are reflected in the financial contacts. This holds for both assets and liabilities. Next, banks want to diversify their portfolios. Since the Dutch economy is a relatively small economy, this implies that banks will look beyond the national borders to find sufficient means, i.e. liabilities, to finance their loans and mortgages. Finally, the increase of financial liabilities was facilitated by new financial instruments, including securitisation of mortgages and other loans. These instruments are mainly traded abroad.

An important reason for the stabilisation of the growth of the banking sector is the bailing out by government after the financial crisis. Out of the four large banks in the Netherlands, three were effectively nationalised after the financial crisis – two are still under the control of the Dutch state.[8] Next to that, the use of financial instruments is restricted due to tightened regulation – for instance, the securitisation of mortgages dropped from almost 45% of GDP in 2009 to below 20% in 2020. Banks nowadays have around 10% securitised mortgages on their balance sheets and increasingly substitute these by covered bonds, which are also 10% of GDP.

While the growth of banks relative to GDP stabilised after 2008, pension fund assets and liabilities continued to grow. It is important to understand that the Netherlands has a funded pension system with defined benefits. This implies that employees are mandatory members of a pension fund and have to pay a mandatory contribution, which is withheld from their wage. In return, they receive a monthly benefit after retirement, which is related to their average lifetime wage. As a consequence, each pension fund has to have enough financial assets to cover future claims. These claims are discounted at a predetermined rate, which implies that a drop in the discount rate leads to an increase in claims. Total claims will also increase when longevity increases. Finally, there is an increasing number of flexible workers – about 28% of the workforce – who have no pension rights, and hence pay no mandatory pension contributions.[9]

The total assets of the pension funds are presented in Figure 6.9 and are more or less equal to the total claims.[10] The growth prior to 2008 is mainly due to ageing – pension claims increased due to an increasing longevity after 1970. However, after 2008 this development was exacerbated due to the fall in the interest rate as the reaction of the central banks to the financial crisis – this led to a lower predetermined discount rate and hence higher claims. In order to cover the growth in liabilities, the assets had to grow proportionally. From Figure 6.9 one observes that while prior to the mid-1990s pension funds had to finance their assets domestically, asset management was liberalised in the late 1990s. As a consequence pension funds started to increasingly invest abroad in order to diversify and to obtain higher returns. In that context one should realise that the sheer magnitude of assets required to match the liabilities can hardly be found in a small economy like the Netherlands; thus expansion abroad is required.

The pension funds also outsourced part of their foreign investments to investment funds (OFIs in Figure 6.9) from 2009 onwards. This outsourcing can also be observed in Figure 6.10, depicting the assets of OFIs – we mentioned earlier that OFIs consist of investment funds, intermediaries and special financial institutions.[11] From Figure 6.10 we observe both a jump in the total assets of OFIs relative to GDP and a relative increase in the importance of investment funds, towards which the pension funds have outsourced their investment.

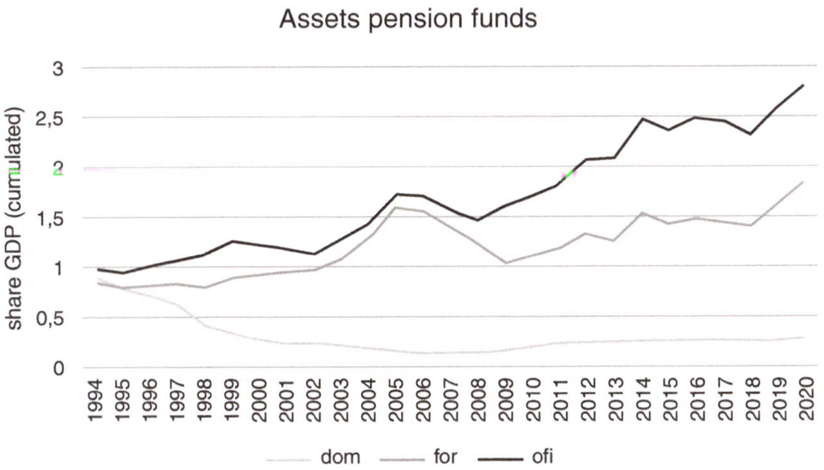


*Figure 6.9* Assets of pension funds.
Source: CBS, national accounts.

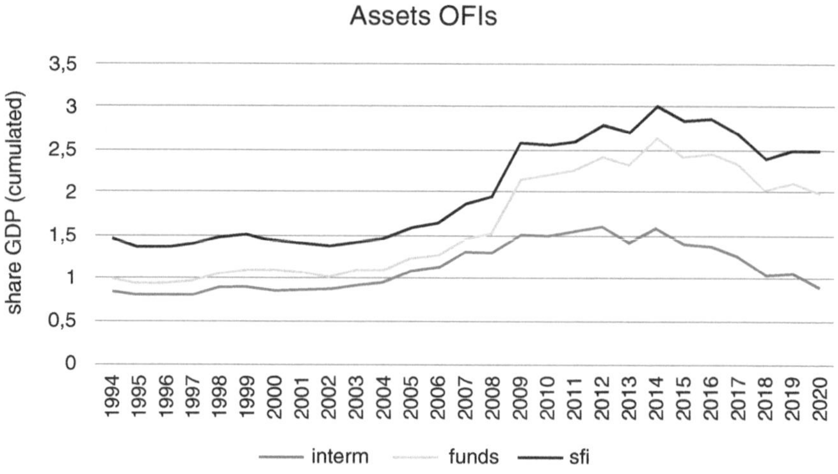


*Figure 6.10* Assets of OFIs.
Source: CBS, national accounts.

The observations above explain why: i) the assets of pension funds continued to grow relative to GDP, while the growth of banks relative to GDP stabilized after 2008. ii) why OFIs assets and liabilities continued to grow relative to GDP till 2014. Since the balance sheets were multiplied by two, this resulted in a strong growth of the total assets and liabilities of the financial sector.

After 2014 the asset growth of pension funds stagnated relative to GDP. Since the predetermined discount rate met a zero lower bound, liabilities no longer increased due to a decrease in the interest rate, which explains the stagnation in assets relative to GDP. The subsequent increase in assets in 2019 and 2020 is mainly due to an increase in asset prices, as can be seen from Figure 6.11.

Even when no transactions take place, but prices of financial assets increase relative to the price of GDP, the share of assets and liabilities will grow relative to GDP. This is illustrated in Figure 6.11 for the prices of the assets of pension funds and investment funds. One observes that in particular after 2008 prices of financial assets of both sectors increased systematically relative to the GDP price. Since 2008 GDP price increased from 1 to 1.15, while the funds' price increased from 1 to almost 2.3. This implies that since 2008 the share of fund assets in GDP increased by 200% points due to price changes only.[12] The development of prices of firm liabilities and houses (Figure 6.12) will be discussed in the next section.

The better performance of fund assets relative to pension fund assets also explains why the pension funds have outsourced their asset investment. However, the outsourcing comes at a high cost (Bezemer, 2022). While the direct returns on pension fund assets increased by about 250% over the

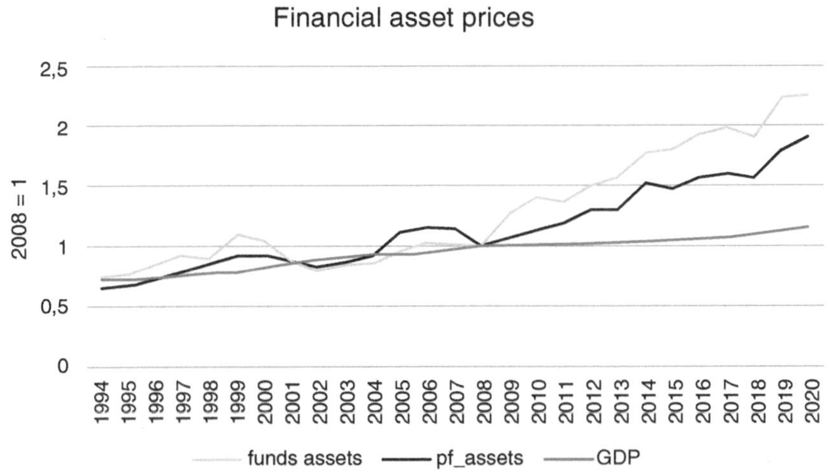


*Figure 6.11* Financial asset prices.
Source: CBS, national accounts.

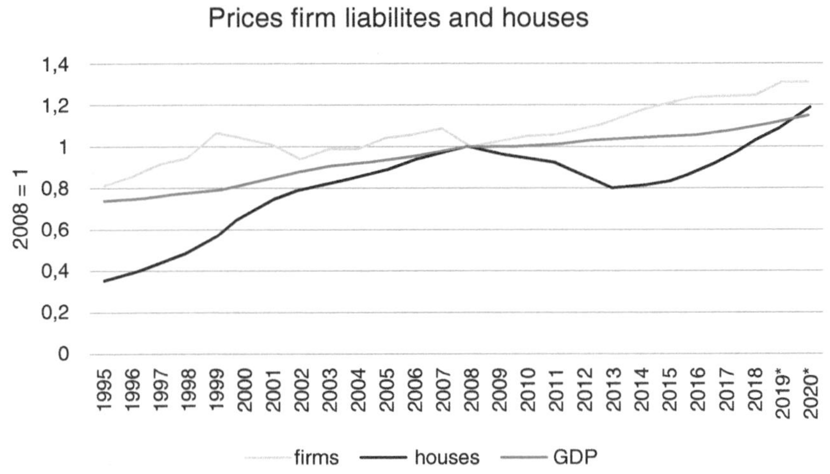


*Figure 6.12* Prices of firm liabilities and houses.
Source: CBS, national accounts.

period 2009–2020, the managing costs increased by more than 1000%.[13] In 2020 almost half of the direct returns were absorbed by managing costs.

## The impact of monetary policy

Till the last decade, monetary policy used its deposit rate to influence the economy, with a special aim to keep inflation under control. In the period 1995–2008 inflation was low and the long-term interest rate was falling.

As can be observed from Figure 6.13, the European Central Bank managed the economy by varying its deposit rate (dep) around 2% and setting the rate on advances (adv) slightly higher. Following the reaction of central banks around the world, the ECB dropped the deposit rate sharply in reaction to the financial crisis in order to stimulate the economy, from 3% in 2008 to almost zero in 2009. The rate remained low till 2014 and even became negative thereafter – with no apparent positive effect on the economy. The negative interest rate induced central banks around the world to resort to unconventional means to stimulate the economy, dubbed as quantitative easing –this involved, amongst other measures, buying government bonds.

When implementing quantitative easing, the ECB delegated the responsibility for buying and holding bonds and other selected financial assets to the national central banks in the Eurozone. Therefore, we consider the amount of bonds held by DNB in Figure 6.14. This increased from around 4% of GDP in 2011, which is already twice the usual amount held relative to GDP prior to the financial crisis, to above 12% in recent years. We analyse the impact below.

The monetary policy, and in particular the low interest rate policy, influenced the Dutch economy in several ways. First, the impact of the policy is an increase in both house prices and prices of financial assets. This is well recognised in the literature – see Mersch (2020) and the references therein. This impact might also explain the relative increase since 2009 of financial asset prices of the foreign sector in Figure 6.5, of pension funds and investment funds in Figure 6.11 and firm's liabilities in Figure 6.12.[14] One also observes in Figure 6.12 that house prices decreased initially after the financial crisis, but that was due to the mortgages crisis (Meijers and Muysken, 2016). The house prices recovered strongly after 2014, increasing by almost 50% in

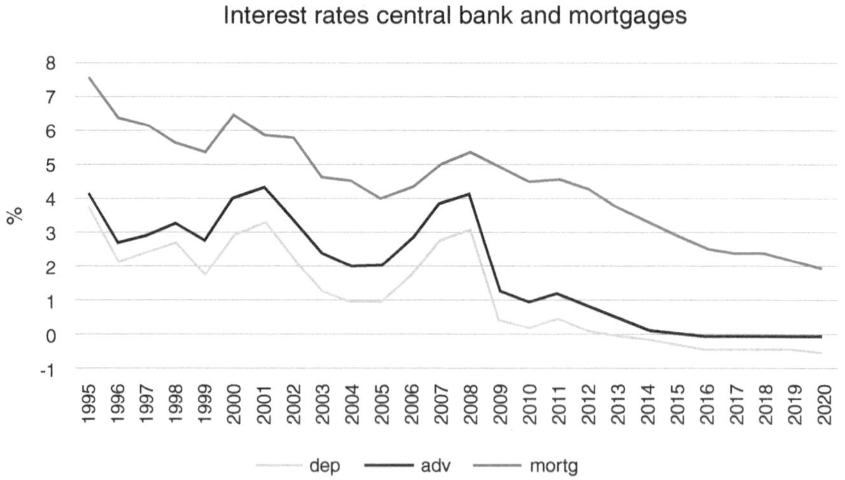


*Figure 6.13* Interest rates of the central bank and mortgages.
Source: CBS, national accounts.

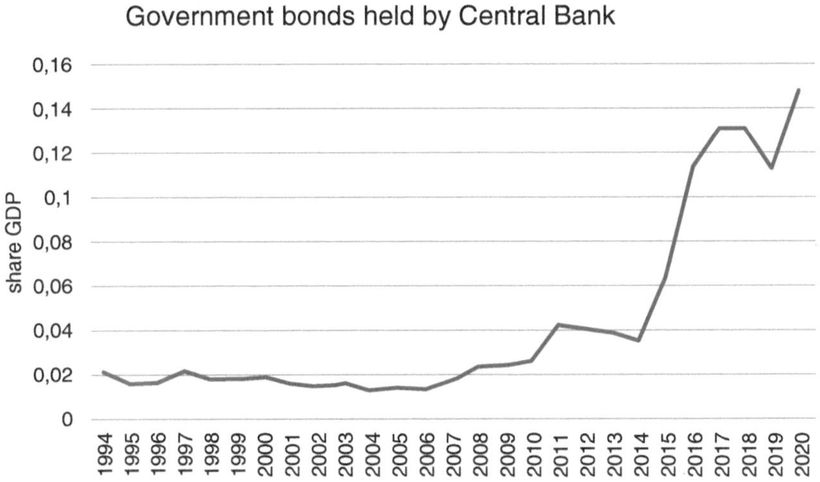


*Figure 6.14* Government bonds held by the central bank.
Source: DNB statistics.

the last five years. What is not well recognised in the literature and the policy debate is that the increase in house prices and asset prices stimulated wealth inequality, since only house owners and owners of financial assets profit from this consequence of monetary policy (Alves and Silva, 2021; House of Lords, 2021, pp. 21–23).[15] Also, there is a danger that the increase in asset prices might induce a bubble with negative consequences (Blot et al., 2020).[16]

An important second consequence of the low interest rate policy is that pension claims increased strongly, as we discussed above. Amongst others, this implies higher mandatory pension contributions for employees, while flexible workers do not have to pay contributions (but also don't receive pensions). This development created social tensions in the pension system which induced reforms for both regular and flexible workers that will be implemented in the coming years.[17]

The third influence of monetary policy on the Dutch economy is more evasive. It is related to the attitude that rules that held prior to the financial crises should no longer be followed too close – some lenience should be allowed to enable individual banks to survive and to enable central banks to influence the economy directly since the low interest rate policy is no longer effective. An example of the former is that Dutch banks have systematically lowered eligibility requirements for mortgages in recent years to compete on the market for mortgages. DNB (2020) identified this development as an important determinant of the increase in house prices. An example of the latter is that central banks, including the ECB, resorted to 'unconventional monetary policies', resulting in quantitative easing. Amongst others, this resulted in the developments presented in Figure 6.14.

To illustrate the pervasive and elusive workings of the financial sector, we look in more detail at the impact of quantitative easing on the Dutch economy. The result of the unconventional monetary policies can be observed from Figure 6.15, which shows how DNB assets more than tripled relative to GDP after the financial crisis. Initially, this was driven by the increase in Target2 balances – the main component of advances to banks issued by DNB (the orange line in the figure). This increase is due to capital flight from Southern Europe – see also DNB (2016).[18] Effectively the foreign sector transferred money to the domestic banks, increasing their positions in those banks, at the expense of increased liabilities towards DNB, which appear as increased advances (Target2) on the asset side of DNB's balance sheet. The domestic banks in turn increased their deposits at DNB (or paid back advances), which appear as liabilities on the balance sheet of DNB – this explains why deposits and advances go hand in hand over the years 2011–2013.

The reason why banks hold deposits at DNB to such a large extent, despite the negative interest rate, can be understood from the analysis of Asriyan et al. (2021) who emphasise the role of money as a store of value. They argue that money provided by central banks provides a viable alternative to assets backed only by their expectations of future value (unbacked assets). This explains why both in the US and in the Euro Area the monetary base grew approximately fivefold in the aftermath of the financial crisis.

After the situation calmed down in 2014, the ECB started its QE operations. DNB began to buy government bonds to stimulate the economy. In Figure 6.15 we observe a new surge in Target2 balances, accompanied by a growing gap with deposits of domestic banks from 2015 onwards – this gap corresponds to the amount of government bonds acquired by the DNB. In

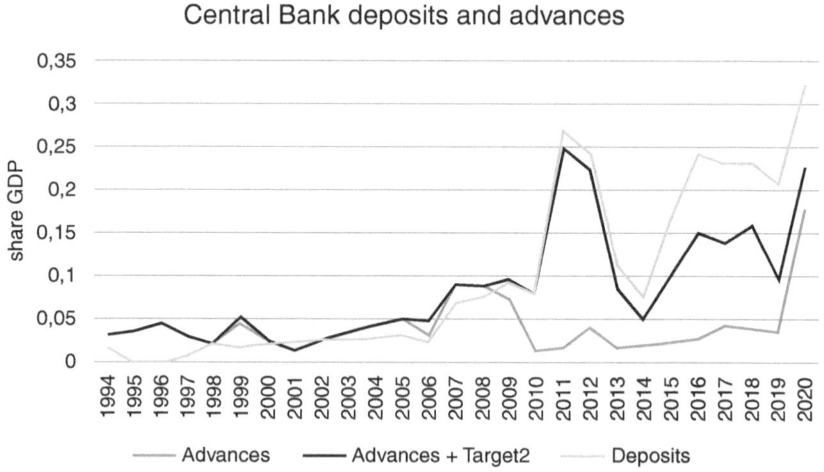


*Figure 6.15* Central bank deposits and advances.
Source: DNB statistics.

Meijers and Muysken (2016) we explain these developments as resulting in a new wave of capital flight from Southern Europe. Pension funds and other asset holders in the South sell their domestic bond holdings to DNB and replace these by positions held at the domestic banks. Moreover, domestic banks again deposit their proceedings at the central bank. That is the reason why we observe in Figure 6.15 that the deposits banks hold at DNB during 2014–2019 equal Target2 balances plus government bonds held by DNB.

The recent surge in assets and liabilities of DNB is of a different nature. Previous expansions of DNB assets were substitutions of ownership of bonds from other bond holders (in particular from Southern Europe) to DNB, while government debt decreased relative to GDP. However, the expansion from 2020 onwards is accompanied by an increase in government debt from 48.5% of GDP end 2019 to 54.3% end 2020 in reaction to the COVID pandemic. As can be seen from Figure 6.14, most of this additional debt has been bought by DNB. And, since this was bought on the secondary market according to ECB rules, bank deposits have increased proportionally. The use of quantitative easing to finance COVID debt is a contentious issue, since it might lead to inflation given the current bottle-necks in production and trade, together with rising energy prices.[19] Moreover, quantitative easing nowadays also leads to many other distortions in the economy as is spelled out in the fascinating report 'Quantitative easing: a dangerous addiction?' (House of the Lords, 2021). Next to the danger of inflation, the report mentions the credibility of monetary policy and the distributional consequences.

## Concluding remarks

We analyse the question why total assets of the financial sector in the Netherlands increased over the past 25 years from 600% of GDP in 1995 to over 1400% in 2020. A first answer is found the nature of the Netherlands as a conduit country. The Netherlands hosts a huge amount of SPVs created for tax reasons, and the assets of SPVs increased from about 150% of GDP in the mid-1990s to over 500% in 2020.

The growth of the remaining part of the financial sector was, prior to the financial crisis, mainly due to the growth in the banking sector relative to GDP. This was primarily driven by mortgages, expanding hand in hand with house prices, and to some extent also by an expansion in loans to firms and to Rest of the World. During this period, foreign liabilities of banks increased strongly relative to GDP, while domestic deposits remained stable. This led to deposit financing gap, which was considered a serious problem a decade ago, but surprisingly is ignored nowadays.

Due to the financial crisis, in which three of the four major banks in the Netherlands were bailed out, the growth of the banking sector stagnated after 2008. However, the assets of pension funds accelerated their growth relative to GDP. As a consequence of the low interest rate policy of the central banks after the financial crisis, pension funds' liabilities increased dramatically, and assets followed. The sheer magnitude of assets required to match the liabilities can hardly be found in a small economy like the Netherlands; thus pension fund assets expanded abroad. Moreover, the pension funds outsourced part of their foreign investments to investment funds from 2009 onwards. This induced further growth in the financial sector.

Monetary policy after the financial crisis facilitated the expansion of the financial sector in three ways. First, the low interest rate policy induced an increase in prices of financial assets and houses. This induced growth in the balance sheets of the pension funds and investment funds directly. Indirectly the house price growth induced growth in mortgages, which further enhanced house price growth – once the mortgage crisis after 2008 was under control. Second, the low interest rate policy led to a strong increase of the liabilities of the pension funds, and assets followed. Third, once central banks all over the world resorted to unconventional monetary policies, the rules on the financial sector started to loosen. This allowed for more risk taking and growth of the financial sector. We point out that these developments led to increasing wealth inequality.

Finally, we use the quantitative easing programme of the ECB to illustrate the pervasive and elusive nature of the financial sector. The large amount of government bonds bought by DNB was mostly provided by the Southern financial sector to smooth the results of current account imbalances between Northern and Southern Europe. There was no discernible impact on the Dutch economy – the resulting balance expansions remained within the financial sector.

Summarising, we observe that the growth of the financial sector in the Netherlands manifested itself foremost in the spectacular rise of SPVs with only foreign assets and liabilities, created for tax reasons. Another reason is the growth of credit provided to households and firms by banks, not based on domestic savings, but borrowed from abroad. Next to that financial intermediation and specialisation contributed to the growth of the financial sector, enlarging the combined balance sheets without an increase in underlying real assets. Even more important is that liabilities of pension funds increased strongly due to the mandatory funded pension system, leading to a surge in assets mostly issued abroad.

Each of these aspects should be scrutinised more closely and how it contributes to well being of society should be evaluated. With our analysis here we hope to have provided a good starting point for such an evaluation. This evaluation might lead to proposals for reform of the financial sector, which we think are necessary, but that lies outside the scope of the present analysis.

## Notes

1 A substantial share of imports is re-exported (excluding transit): this share increased from about 35% of total imports in 1995 to almost 45% in 2020.

2 A considerable part of net primary income is primary income from pension funds and investment funds since most of their assets are invested abroad. This is compensated by 'other income' transfers, for instance, due to foreign aid.

3 On average over the past 25 years, firms used 22% of their net savings (retained earnings) for investment in capital goods. The remaining part was invested in financial assets abroad (or used for share buy-backs).This is further analysed in Meijers, Muysken and Sleijpen (2016).

4 Asset prices are identified in the national accounts by subtracting the transactions made in a certain year from the change in the total amount of assets in that year. The resulting 'other' changes are identified as value changes due to price changes till 2012. From 2012 onwards, these 'other' changes are subdivided in 'value changes due to price changes' and 'changes for other reasons'. Thus, the identification of prices from 2012 onwards is more precise than prior to 2021. However, the 'changes for other reasons' after 2012 are usually very small compared to the 'value changes due to price changes'. For that reason we interpret the 'other changes' prior to 2012 as stemming from price changes.

5 The special financial institutions or 'captive financial institutions and money lenders' subsector consists of all financial corporations and quasi-corporations which are engaged neither in financial intermediation nor in providing financial auxiliary services, and where most of either their assets or their liabilities are not transacted on open markets. We have subtracted from these the SFIs that have exclusively foreign assets and liabilities.

6 In both figures we ignore the small contribution of the central bank and miscellaneous items.

7 In recent years an increasing share of mortgages, 16% in 2020, is being financed by pension funds and insurance companies.

8 Only the largest bank, RABO, survived without bail-out. The third largest bank ING repaid its last debt in 2014, the second largest bank ABN/AMRO is still owned by the Dutch state for 56%, and the fourth largest bank SNS (recently renamed as Volksbank) is now fully owned by the Dutch state. The four banks taken together cover at least 90% of the Dutch market.

9 Some self-employed have life insurances. These are included in the national accounts under pension funds.

10 The mandatory pension contributions are such that when the claims increase relative to the available assets, the contributions increase. Only in very exceptional circumstances do the benefits decrease – albeit that they are regularly not corrected for inflation. The contributions of households, net of benefits, imply forced savings each year amounting to 6.5% of net disposable household income, according to the national accounts.

11 The assets of the special financial institutions are mainly held by households (in special entities) and the assets of financial intermediaries are held partly by banks (Figure 6.0).

12 The price of total assets and liabilities of banks hardly increased over time; hence not all financial asset prices increased.

13 Source: Statistics DNB. Relative to total assets, the costs increased from 0.1% in 2006 to 0.35% in 2020.

14 The price of firm assets did not increase, but the poor relative performance of firms' direct investment abroad relative to foreign direct investment is well recognised in the Dutch literature (Eggelte et al., 2014).

15 It is also emphasised in the Dutch debate that the recent surge in house prices also led to a considerable distortion of the housing market, prohibiting newcomers from entering.

16 Asriyan et al. (2021) provide a more nuanced view, emphasising that bubbles may have a cleansing effect on the economy.

17 In the mandatory pension system, defined benefits have been replaced by qualified defined contributions. Next to that, flexible workers must accept some aspects of a mandatory pension system.

18 The underlying current account imbalances between Northern and Southern Europe are analysed in Holinski et al. (2012).
19 D'Acunto and Weber (2022) provide a balanced survey of the recent literature on the danger of inflation, emphasising the role of expectations.

## References


Alves, J., and Silva, T. (2021). An empirical assessment of monetary policy channels in income and wealth disparities, *Comparative Economic Studies*, 63(3), pp. 432–449.

Asriyan, V. et al. (2021). Monetary policy for a bubbly world, *The Review of Economic Studies*, 88(3), pp. 1418–1456.

Bezemer, D. (2022). Pension fund capitalism and capital market inflation: A case study of the Netherlands, *IMK Working Paper* (forthcoming).

Blot, C. et al. (2020). Monetary policy and asset prices in the Euro Area since the global financial crisis, *Revue d'économie politique*, 130(2), pp. 257–281.

D'Acunto, F., and Weber, M. (2022). Rising inflation is worrisome. But not for the reasons you think, *column VOX Europe*, 04 January 2022.

DNB (2016). Target2 imbalances reflect QE and persistent fragmentation within the euro area, *Themes 16–6–2016*, De Nederlandsche Bank, Amsterdam.

DNB (2020). House prices are more closely related with borrowing capacity than with housing shortage, *Themes 16–7–2020*, De Nederlandsche Bank, Amsterdam.

Godley, W., and Lavoie, M. (2007). *Monetary Economics: An Integrated Approach to Credit, Money, Income, Production and Wealth*. London: Palgrave Macmillan.

Holinski, N. et al. (2012). Persistent macroeconomic imbalances in the Euro area: Causes and consequences, *Federal Reserve Bank of St. Louis Review*, 94(1), pp. 1–20.

House of Lords (2021). Quantitative easing: A dangerous addiction?, *House of Lords Economic Affairs Committee 1st Report of Session 2021–22*, HL Paper 42.

International Monetary Fund (IMF) (2013). The Netherlands- 2013 Article IV consultation: Concluding statement of the IMF Mission, *retrieved from www.imf.org*.

Jansen, J. et al. (2013). Financieringsproblemen in de hypotheekmarkt, *DNB Occasional Studies*, 11(1), pp. 1–28.

Meijers, H., Muysken J., and Sleijpen, O. (2014). The Dutch balance sheet recession: A stock-flow consistent approach, *Paper presented at FMM 2014*, Berlin.

Meijers, H., Muysken J., and Sleijpen, O. (2015). The deposit financing gap: Another Dutch disease, *European Journal of Economics and Economic Policies: Intervention*, 12(1), pp. 32–50.

Meijers, H., Muysken J., and Sleijpen, O. (2016). Firms' excess savings and the Dutch current account surplus: A stock-flow consistent approach, *European Journal of Economics and Economic Policies: Intervention*, 13(3), pp. 339–353.

Meijers, H., and Muysken, J. (2016). The impact of quantitative easing in the Netherlands: A stock-flow consistent approach, *UNU-MERIT Working Paper series 2016–067*.

Mersch, Y. (2020). Asset price inflation and monetary policy, Keynote speech by Yves Mersch, Member of the Executive Board of the ECB and Vice-Chair of the Supervisory Board of the ECB, at the celebration of INVESTAS' 60th anniversary, Luxembourg, 27 January 2020.

Suyker, W., and Wagteveld, S. (2019). A fresh look at the Dutch current account surplus and its driving forces, *CPB Background document*, CPB, The Hague.

# 7 A stock flow consistent model for the French economy

*Jacques Mazier and Luis Reyes*

## Introduction

The first stock flow consistent (SFC) models built by Godley were well-adapted to study financialized economies as well as the international imbalances of the 1990s and 2000s. The application to the American economy was particularly relevant to analyze the 1999 and 2008 crises (Godley, 1999; Godley et al., 2005). The fruitful collaboration with Lavoie turned into a modeling of financial cycles for a domestic economy (Lavoie and Godley, 2001) and into two- to three-country models taking into account imbalances at a European and world scales (Godley and Lavoie, 2003; 2005; 2006). Complementary works dealt with European imbalances and alternative monetary regimes. The book *Monetary Economics* (2007) presented a detailed synthesis of this approach. In each case the same analytical framework was found: a complete balance sheet of the main domestic and foreign agents allowing for an SFC integration of the real and financial sectors, a macroeconomic integration without micro-foundations, demand-led Kaleckian dynamics. Budget constraints and alternative monetary regimes were overwhelmingly better described than in general equilibrium models (Obstfeld and Rogoff, 2005) or portfolio models (Blanchard et al., 2005). In the 2010s better calibrated or econometrically based SFC models became more frequent. The most recent developments are presented in this book. The Levy model of the US (Godley et al., 2005) was a forerunner. The Cambridge Alphametrics Model (CAM), for the world economy with ten regions, also appears as a pioneer (Cripps, 2016). A calibrated and partially econometric detailed SFC modeling of the financial and real sectors provided the Bank of England with useful insights (Burgess et al., 2016). The econometric SFC model of the Italian economy (Zezza and Zezza, 2020) is without a doubt the most complete version. These works took place after the 2008 crisis, in a context of criticism of DSGE (dynamic stochastic general equilibrium) models and rehabilitation of structural econometric models, illustrated by the publication of "Rebuilding macroeconomic theory" by the Oxford Review of Economic Policy (see in particular Blanchard, 2018, and Wren-Lewis, 2018).

DOI: 10.4324/9781003253457-9

In France and elsewhere, since the 1970s macro-econometric models were neo-Keynesian/neo-classical, Keynesian in the short term but dominated by supply-side factors in the medium term, with partial microeconomic foundations and a limited place for finance. The MESANGE model (Allard-Prigent et al., 2002), often updated and used for providing insight on economic policy to the administration (Institut national de la statistique et det études économiques (INSEE), Treasury), is a case in point. Certain more heterodox models had, however, been developed within the administration based on the national accounts and some early elements of the accumulation (or wealth) accounts – the STAR model (Boyer et al., 1974) of the early 1970s and COPAIN (*COmportements PAtrimoniaux et INtégration financière*, Dehove et al., 1981). The latter translates into "wealth behaviors and financial integration", clearly showing the ambition of the project. These models, however, only had a limited impact. The accumulation accounts (*comptes de patrimoine*) from INSEE and the financial accounts by Bank of France nevertheless provide a detailed statistical framework, well-adapted for an econometric SFC model. It is in this perspective that this chapter builds on the work of Reyes (2015). It is organized as follows. A second part presents the overall structure of the model; a third one describes the main equations. A fourth section displays the simulations/projections carried out, the simulations in the past and some basic shocks. This also illustrates how the model allows studying unconventional policies, helicopter money and a partial cancellation of debt held by the central bank. The last part concludes.[1]

## The overall structure of the model

The structure of the model is analogous with that of already existing national-level SFC models. The economy is divided into five domestic agents: firms, households (including non-profit institutions serving households), banks, the central bank, the government, all of which interact with the rest of the world. The monetary and financial operations from the European central bank are included with the rest of the world (which is in a way quite symbolic) in the statistical conventions adopted. The model is aggregate with a single product. Production (in volume, at constant prices) is determined by domestic demand (investment and change in inventories by firms, consumption and investment from households, the government and banks) and foreign demand (exports net of imports). A supply constraint is introduced and results, at this stage of the model, in a simple production function that determines potential output and allows for computation of an output gap. The general price level depends on a mark-up pricing rule, and is a function of unit labor costs with an effect from demand pressures. Value added is calculated from GDP in value after deduction of the VAT and import duties and taxes. This value added is split among the different agents depending on simple structural parameters. Its distribution between wages, profits, social contributions, taxes and other redistribution operations is described in order to arrive at the balance of the agents' accounts, taking into account their expenditure: disposable income, savings and financing capacity/need. Exports and imports are analyzed at the level of all goods and services according to demand (foreign and domestic, respectively) and relative prices (Tables 7.1 and 7.2).

Financing methods via bank credit, bond and equity issuing, as well as financial investment behavior are then described for each agent. An adjustment item is the statistical discrepancy between the real sector accounts from INSEE and the financial accounts by the Bank of France. Changes in assets and liabilities, as well as investments and changes in inventories, combined with the revaluation accounts for capital gains or losses, allow for the transition of the accumulation accounts from one year to the next in an SFC manner.[2] Table 7.1 provides the balance sheet structure of the domestic and foreign sectors. With respect to non-financial assets, a distinction is made between produced capital (productive capital and housing), outstanding stocks and non-produced capital (land), the sharp rise in price of which is one of the characteristics of financialized capitalism and has had a significant macroeconomic impact. Among the financial assets, two deserve particular attention. On the one hand, the government's account at the central bank is isolated in order to study the effects of helicopter money. On the other hand, TARGET2 corresponds to the balance of the real and financial exchanges between France and the rest of the Eurozone. They are, respectively, on the asset side of the Bank of France and on the liability side for the ECB, thus appearing in the column rest of the world in the convention that has been adopted, and are considered exogenous because their determinants lie largely outside of the model. Bonds are domestic, public as well as foreign. Equities are also split between domestic and foreign.

The main closures are the following. Firms balance their accounts by issuing the necessary shares, households by issuing debt. Bank reserves balance the banks' accounts. The equilibrium of the central bank corresponds to the missing equation of the model deducted from the writing of the other balances. Public debt, in the form of bank debt and bonds, balances the government's account. International reserves (i.e. the sum of TARGET2, deposits and bonds on the asset side of the central bank) adjust the rest of the world's account. Banks absorb all domestic private and public bonds available and extend credit without restriction. Banks also balance the market for domestic equity, the price of which depends on the price of foreign equity, which has a dominant effect. Foreign bonds and equity issued by the rest of the world equal their domestic demand.

*Table 7.1* Balance sheet structure of economic agents

| | | *Non-financial corporations* | | *Financial institutions* | | | |
|---|---|---|---|---|---|---|---|
| | | | | *Banks* | | *Banque de France* | |
| | | *Asset* | *Liabilities.* | *Asset* | *Liabilities.* | *Asset* | *Liabilities.* |
| $ANF_1$ | Produced non-financial assets | $p^F_{K_1} K^F_1$ | | | | | |
| $ANF_{12}$ | Inventories (12) + valuables (13) | $p^F_{K_{12}} K^F_{12}$ | | | | | |
| $ANF_2$ | Non-produced non-financial assets | $p^F_{K_2} K^F_2$ | | $p^B_{K_2} K^B_2$ | | | |
| $F_1$ | Monetary gold and SDRs | | | | | $p^{CB}_G G^{CB}$ | |
| $F_2$ | Bills and coins | $H^F$ | | $H^B$ | | | $H$ |
| | Refinancing between financial institutions | | | | $RF$ | $RF^{CB}$ | |
| | Bank reserves | | | $RES$ | | | $RES$ |
| | Govt. account at CB | | | | | | $D^{CBG}_L$ |
| | Target 2 | | | | | $TRGT2$ | |
| | Deposits | $D^F_A$ | | $D^B_A$ | $D^B_L$ | $D^{CB}_A$ | $D^{CB}_L$ |
| $F_3$ | Public securities | $p^{FG}_{B_A} B^{FG}_{B_A}$ | | $p^{BG}_{B_A} B^{BG}_{B_A}$ | | $p^{CBG}_{B_A} B^{CBG}_{B_A}$ | |
| | Foreign securities | $p^{FR}_{B_A} B^{FR}_A$ | | $p^{BR}_{B_A} B^{BR}_A$ | | $p^{CBR}_{B_A} B^{CBR}_A$ | |
| | Other securities | | $p^F_{B_L} B^F_L$ | $p^B_{B_A} B^B_A$ | $p^B_{B_L} B^B_L$ | $p^{CB}_{B_A} B^{CB}_A$ | |
| $F_4$ | Loans | $L^F_A$ | $L^F_L$ | $L^B_A$ | | $L^{CB}_A$ | |
| $F_5$ | [Domestic] Equity and inv. fund shares | $p^F_{E_A} E^F_A$ | $p^F_{E_L} E^F_L$ | $p^B_{E_A} E^B_A$ | $p^B_{E_L} E^B_L$ | $p^{CB}_{E_A} E^{CB}_A$ | $p^{CB}_{E_L} E^{CB}_L$ |
| | [Foreign] Equity and inv. fund shares issued by RoW | $p^{FR}_{E_A} E^{FR}_A$ | | $p^{BR}_{E_A} E^{BR}_A$ | | $p^{CBR}_{E_A} E^{CBR}_A$ | |
| $F_6$ | Insurance. pension funds and s.g.s.* | $A^F_A$ | | | $A^B_L$ | | |
| $F_7$ | Fin. derivatives and employee stock options | $X^F_A$ | | | $X^B_L$ | | |
| $F_8$ | Other accounts receivable/payable | $Z^F$ | | $Z^B$ | | $Z^{CB}$ | |
| F | Financial wealth | | $FW^F$ | | $FW^B$ | | $FW^{CB}$ |
| $B^{90}$ | Net worth | | $WLTH^F$ | | $WLTH^B$ | | $WLTH^{CB}$ |

| | | *Government* | | *Households* | | *Rest of the world* | |
|---|---|---|---|---|---|---|---|
| | | *Asset* | *Liabilities.* | *Asset* | *Liabilities.* | *Asset* | *Liabilities.* |
| ANF[1] | Produced non-financial assets | $p^G_{K_1} K^G_1$ | | $p^H_{K_1} K^H_1$ | | | |
| ANF[12] | Inventories (12) + valuables (13) | $p^F_{K_{12}} K^F_{12}$ | | $p^F_{K_{12}} K^F_{12}$ | | | |
| | | | | $p^F_{K_{13}} K^F_{13}$ | | | |
| ANF[2] | Non-produced non-financial assets | $p^G_{K_2} K^G_2$ | | $p^H_{K_2} K^H_2$ | | | |
| F[1] | Monetary gold and SDRs | | | | | | $p^{CB}_G G^{CB}$ |
| F[2] | Bills and coins | | | $H^H$ | | $H^R$ | |
| | Refinancing between financial institutions | | | | | | $RF^R$ |
| | Bank reserves | | | | | | |
| | Govt. account at CB | $D^{CBG}_A$ | | | | | |
| | Target 2 | | | | | | $TRGT2$ |
| | Deposits | $D^G_A$ | $D^G_L$ | $D^H_A$ | | $D^R_A$ | $D^R_L$ |
| F[3] | Public securities | | $p^G_{B_L} B^G_L$ | | | $p^{RG}_{B_L} B^{RG}_{BL}$ | |
| | Foreign securities | | | $p^{HR}_{B_A} B^{HR}_A$ | | | $p^R_{B_L} B^R_L$ |
| | Other securities | $p^G_{B_A} B^G_A$ | | $p^H_{B_A} B^H_A$ | | $p^R_{B_A} B^R_A$ | |
| F[4] | Loans | | $L^G_L$ | | $L^H_L$ | $L^R_A$ | $L^R_L$ |
| F[5] | [Domestic] Equity and inv. fund shares | $p^G_{E_A} E^G_A$ | | $p^H_{E_A} E^H_A$ | | $p^R_{E_A} E^R_A$ | |
| | [Foreign] Equity and inv. fund shares issued by RoW | $p^{GR}_{E_A} E^{GR}_A$ | | $p^{HR}_{E_A} E^{HR}_A$ | | | $p^R_{E_L} E^R_L$ |
| F[6] | Insurance. pension funds and s.g.s.* | $A^G_A$ | | $A^H_A$ | | $A^R_A$ | |
| F[7] | Fin. derivatives and employee stock options | $X^G_A$ | | $X^H_A$ | | | $X^R_A$ |
| F[8] | Other accounts receivable/payable | $Z^G$ | | $Z^H$ | | $Z^R$ | |
| F | Financial wealth | | $FW^G$ | | $FW^H$ | | $FW^R$ |
| B[90] | Net worth | | $WLTH^G$ | | $WLTH^H$ | | $WLTH^R$ |

*Table 7.2* Numerical balance sheet, France, 2019 (% of GDP)

| | | | *Non-financial corporations* | | *Banks* | | *Banque de France* | | *Government* | | *Households* | | *Rest of the world* | | |
|---|---|---|---|---|---|---|---|---|---|---|---|---|---|---|---|
| | | | *S11* | | *S12b* | | *S121* | | *S13* | | *S14* | | *S2* | | |
| | | | *Assets* | *Liabilities.* | *Assets* | *Liabilities.* | *Assets* | *Liabilities.* | *Assets* | *Liabilities.* | *Assets* | *Liabilities.* | *Assets* | *Liabilities.* | *A – L* |
| Non-Financial Assets | 1 | Produced non-fin assets excluding inventories | | | | | | | | | | | | | 334.2 |
| | 12/13 | Inventories + valuables | 17.5 | | | | | | 1.1 | | 6.3 | | | | 17.5 |
| | 2 | Non-produced non-fin assets | 93.7 | | 7.4 | | | | 38.6 | | 169.3 | | | | 309.0 |
| Financial instruments | 1 | Monetary gold and SDRs | | | | | 4.3 | | | | | | | 4,3 | 0 |
| | 21 | Bills and coins | 0.6 | | 0.5 | | | 10.2 | | | 3.4 | | 5.6 | | 0 |
| | 295 | Refinancing between FI | | | | −7.9 | 5.0 | | | | | | | 12.9 | 0 |
| | RES | Bank reserves | | | 22.2 | | | 22.2 | | | | | | | 0 |
| | G-CB | Govt. account at CB | | | | | | 1.1 | 1.1 | | | | | | 0 |
| | TGT 2 | Target 2 | | | | | 0.0 | | | | | | | 0.0 | 0 |
| | 2dep | Deposits | 28.3 | | 97.4 | 205.9 | 7.5 | 6.7 | 6.0 | 5.8 | 64.6 | | 47.7 | 33.1 | 0 |
| | 3e | Public securities | 1.2 | | 22.1 | | 17.4 | | | 99.2 | | | 58.5 | | 0 |
| | 3d | Foreign securities | 1.6 | | 63.3 | | 6.5 | | 1.1 | | 0.8 | | | 73.3 | 0 |
| | 3g | Other securities | | 27.6 | 42.5 | 67.6 | 5.0 | | 1.1 | | 0.8 | | 45.8 | | 0 |
| | 4 | Loans | 75.2 | 122.5 | 109.7 | | 0.2 | | | 8.3 | | 61.3 | 44.8 | 37.7 | 0 |
| | 5e | Domestic equity and investment fund shares | 194.0 | 333.3 | 84.6 | 104.1 | 0.7 | 6.1 | 25,1 | | 61.0 | | 78.1 | | 0 |
| | 5d | Foreign equity and investment fund shares | 72.9 | | 32.8 | | 0.1 | | 1.2 | | 3.8 | | | 110.8 | 0 |
| | 6 | Insurance, pension funds and s.g.s. | 1,8 | | | 92.5 | | | 0.2 | | 89.4 | | 1.1 | | 0 |
| | 7 | Fin. Derivatives and employee stock options | 0.0 | | | 1.7 | 0.0 | | −0.1 | | 0.0 | | | 1.8 | 0 |
| | 8 | Other accounts receivable/payable | 12.8 | | −3.1 | | 0.0 | | 0.5 | | 4.4 | | −14.7 | | 0 |
| *Financial balance* | | | | ***−95.1*** | | ***8.0*** | | ***0.6*** | | ***−77.1*** | | ***167.0*** | | ***−3.4*** | ***0*** |
| *Net worth* | | | | ***121.9*** | | ***22.4*** | | ***0.6*** | | ***14.8*** | | ***512.0*** | | ***−3.4*** | ***667.7*** |

Source: Authors' calculations using data from INSEE and Webstat (Banque de France)

## The main equations

### *Firms*

Firms have an accumulation rate of productive capital $\left(\frac{\Delta^{*}K_{1}^{F}}{K_{1-1}^{F}}\right)$ that depends on four variables, following a Kaleckian logic: the lagged profit rate related to total capital $\left(\frac{\Pi^{F}{}_{-1}}{p_{K1_{-1}}^{F}K_{1-2}^{F}+p_{K2_{-1}}^{F}K_{2-2}^{F}}\right)$ including the stock of land $\left(p_{K_2}^{F}K_{2}^{F}\right)$; the real interest rate[3] $\left(r_{L}^{F}-\pi_{Y}\right)$ and financial profitability $(r_{EA}^{F}-\pi_{Y})$, where $\pi_{Y}$ is the inflation rate, both with a negative sign; the debt structure here represented as the debt-to-own funds ratio $\left(\frac{L_{L}^{F}}{p_{EL}^{F}E_{L}^{F}+WLTH^{F}}\right)$, also with a negative effect. Financial profitability of equities held is the sum of revaluation and dividends received divided by the stock of equity of the previous period $r_{EA}^{F}=\left(\frac{E_{A-1}^{F}\Delta p_{EA}^{F}+Div_{r}^{F}}{p_{EA-1}^{F}E_{A-1}^{F}}\right)$. It is mainly driven by the rate of growth of equities' price. A version with the output gap was tested but is not shown in this version of the model.

$$\left(\frac{\Delta^{*}K_{1}^{F}}{K_{1-1}^{F}}\right)=0.02+0.1\left(\frac{\Pi^{F}{}_{-1}}{p_{K1_{-1}}^{F}K_{1-2}^{F}+p_{K2_{-1}}^{F}K_{2-2}^{F}}\right)-0.1\left(r_{L}^{F}-\pi_{Y}\right.$$
$$-0.02\left(r_{EA}^{F}-\pi_{Y}\right)-0.03\left(\frac{L_{L}^{F}}{p_{EL}^{F}E_{L}^{F}+WLTH^{F}}\right)$$

In financialized capitalism, firms tend to favor financial accumulation $\left(\frac{\Delta^{*}E_{A}^{F}}{E_{A-1}^{F}}\right)$ at the expense of productive accumulation. This translates into a financial accumulation rate that is an increasing function of the profit rate $\left(\frac{\Pi^{F}}{p_{K1}^{F}K_{1-1}^{F}+p_{K12}^{F}K_{12-1}^{F}+p_{K2}^{F}K_{2-1}^{F}}\right)$ and of financial profitability of equities held $\left(r_{EA-1}^{F}-\pi_{Y-1}\right)$, where (unlike the previous case) indebtedness as a ratio of own funds $\left(\frac{L_{L}^{F}}{p_{EL}^{F}E_{L}^{F}+WLTH^{F}}\right)$ plays a supporting role. A split between domestic $\left(E_{A}^{FFR}\right)$ and foreign equity $\left(E_{A}^{FR}\right)$ is also done.

$$\left(\frac{\Delta^* E_A^F}{E_{A-1}^F}\right) = 0.35\left(\frac{\Pi^F}{p_{K1}^F K_{1-1}^F + p_{K12}^F K_{12-1}^F + p_{K2}^F K_{2-1}^F}\right)$$

$$+0.02\left(r_{EA-1}^F - \pi_{Y-1}\right) + 0.01\left(\frac{L_L^F}{p_{EL}^F E_L^F + WLTH^F}\right)$$

$$p_{EA}^{FR} E_A^{FR} = p_{EA}^F E_A^F - p_{EA}^{FFR} E_A^{FFR}$$

Firms have an indebtedness behavior. In the medium term[4] their debt structure, as a ratio of total non-financial capital $\left(\frac{p_{BLL}^F BL_L^F}{p_{K1}^F K_1^F + p_{K12}^F K_{12}^F + p_{K2}^F K_2^F}\right)$, depends positively on the profit rate and negatively on the real interest rate[5] $\left(i_{10\,years} - \pi_Y\right)$. More than a debt behavior, it is an indebtedness norm, which reflects a given institutional relation between firms and banks. A split between bank debt $\left(L_L^F\right)$ and bonds $\left(B_L^F\right)$ is also made.

$$vc = \left(\frac{p_{BLL}^F BL_L^F}{p_{K1}^F K_1^F + p_{K12}^F K_{12}^F + p_{K2}^F K_2^F}\right) - 7.7\left(\frac{\Pi^F}{p_{K1}^F K_{1-1}^F + p_{K12}^F K_{12-1}^F + p_{K2}^F K_{2-1}^F}\right)$$

$$+3.2\left(i_{10\,years} - \pi_Y\right)$$

$$\Delta^* L_L^F = p_{BLL}^F \Delta^* BL_L^F - p_{BL}^F \Delta^* B_L^F$$

The change in firms' deposits as % of GDP $\left[\Delta\left(\frac{D_A^F}{p_Y Y}\right)\right]$ and the flow of inter-firm credits[6] as a share of firm's value added $\left(\frac{\Delta^* L_A^F}{VA^F}\right)$, i.e. credits granted by the firms to themselves, are the subject of a simplified model in which the real ten-year interest rate (with a negative sign) and the firms' indebtedness (as a liability) intervene, respectively.

$$\Delta\left(\frac{D_A^F}{p_Y Y}\right) = 0.004 + 0.6\Delta\left(\frac{D_{A-1}^F}{p_{Y-1} Y_{-1}}\right) - 0.06\left(i_{10\,yrs} - \pi_Y\right)$$

$$\left(\frac{\Delta^* L_A^F}{VA^F}\right) = 0.49\left(\frac{\Delta^* L_{A-1}^F}{VA^F{}_{-1}}\right) + 0.51\left(\frac{\Delta^* L_L^F}{VA^F}\right) - 0.25\left(\frac{\Delta^* L_{L-1}^F}{VA^F{}_{-1}}\right)$$

## Households

Household consumption $\left(C^H\right)$ depends on disposable income $\left(\frac{Y_d^H}{p_C{}^H}\right)$ and a wealth effect $\left(\frac{WLTH^H}{p_C{}^H}\right)$, where $p_C{}^H$ stands for the consumer price index. Apart from disposable income, household investment $\left(I_1^H\right)$ is a function of the real interest rate $\left(i_{10\,years} - \pi_I^H\right)$ with a negative effect and of the growth rate of the land price $\left(p_{K2}^{H}\right)$, which contributes to enhance the housing boom.[7] The price of land is itself a function of household investment and debt as a ratio of disposable income $\left(\frac{L_L^H}{Y_d^H}\right)$.

$$\Delta\ln\left(C^H\right) = 0.6\Delta\ln\left(\frac{Y_d^H}{pc^H}\right) + 0.08\Delta\ln\left(\frac{WLTH^H}{pc^H}\right) - 0.12vc_{-1}$$

$$vc = \ln\left(C^H\right) - 0.6 - 0.83\ln\left(\frac{Y_d^H}{pc^H}\right) - 0.06\ln\left(\frac{WLTH^H}{pc^H}\right)$$

$$\Delta\ln\left(I_1^H\right) = 0.4\Delta\ln\left(I_{1-1}^H\right) + 0.4\Delta\ln\left(\frac{Y_d^H}{p_I^H}\right) - 0.6\Delta\left(i_{10\,years} - \pi_I^H\right) - 0.4vc_{-1}$$

$$vc = \ln\left(I_1^H\right) - 1.1 - 0.5\ln\left(\frac{Y_d^H}{p_I^H}\right) + 0.9\left(i_{10\,years} - \pi_I^H\right) - 0.2\left(\frac{\Delta p_{K2}^H}{p_{K2-1}^H}\right)$$

$$\Delta\ln\left(p_{K2}^H\right) = 0.62\Delta\ln\left(p_{K2-1}^H\right) + 0.9\Delta\ln\left(I_1^H\right) - 0.15vc_{-1}$$

$$vc = \ln\left(p_{K2}^H\right) + 9.5 - 2.1\ln\left(I_{1-1}^H\right) - 1.5\ln\left(\frac{L_L^H}{Y_d^H}\right)$$

Household deposits $\left(D_A^H\right)$ are modeled in a simple way, as percentage of disposable income. Bank deposits depend on the ten-year real interest rate with a negative sign. Equity purchases $\left(p_{EA}^H E_A^H\right)$ are a function of the financial rate of return $\left(r_{EA}^H - \pi_C^H\right)$ and the ten-year real interest rate with a negative sign. Insurance purchases $\left(A_A^H\right)$ are related to the weight of the eldest (60 or older) in total population $DepRatio_{old}$, supplemented in the short term by a positive effect of the real ten-year interest rates and financial profitability.

$$\Delta\left(\frac{D_A^H}{Y_d^H}\right) = 0.5\Delta\left(\frac{D_{A-1}^H}{Y_{d-1}^H}\right) - 0.4\Delta\left(i_{10\,yrs-1} - \pi_{C-1}^H\right) - 0.2vc_{-1}$$

$$vc = \left(\frac{D_A^H}{Y_d^H}\right) - 0.9 + 1.04\left(i_{10\,yrs-1} - \pi_{C-1}^H\right)$$

$$\Delta\left(\frac{p_{EA}^H E_A^H}{Y_d^H}\right) = 1.8\Delta\left(r_{EA}^H - \pi_C^H\right) - 0.24vc_{-1}$$

$$vc = \left(\frac{p_{EA}^H E_A^H}{Y_d^H}\right) - 0.87 - 2.2\left(r_{EA}^H - \pi_C^H\right) + 3.1\left(i_{10\,years} - \pi_C^H\right)$$

$$\Delta\left(\frac{A_A^H}{Y_d^H}\right) = 0.27\Delta\left(\frac{A_{A-1}^H}{Y_{d-1}^H}\right) + 0.02\Delta\left(DepRatio_{old}\right)$$
$$+0.3\left(i_{10\,years} - \pi_C^H\right) + 0.14\left(r_{E_A}^H - \pi_C^H\right) - 0.15vc_{-1}$$

$$vc = \left(\frac{A_A^H}{Y_d^H}\right) + 2.7 - 0.13\left(DepRatio_{old}\right)$$

## Banks

Banks are accommodating in the current version of the model. They grant all credits requested, balance domestic private and public bonds, as well as domestic equities. Their financial accumulation rate $\left(\frac{\Delta^* E_A^B}{E_{A-1}^B}\right)$ depends on financial profitability lagged one period $\left(r_{E_{A-1}}^B - \pi_{Y-1}\right)$ with a split between domestic and foreign equities. The rate of accumulation of foreign securities $\left(\frac{p_{B_A}^{BR}\Delta^* B_A^{BR}}{p_{B_{A-1}}^{BR} B_{A-1}^{BR}}\right)$ depends on foreign real ten-year interest rates $\left(i_{10\,yrs}^* - \pi_Y^*\right)$. The flow of bank bond issuance $\left(p_{B_L}^B \Delta^* B_L^B\right)$ depends on the level of activity represented by GDP and the rise in land prices acting as a stimulus. Interest rates are treated exogenously with the ten-year interest rate on public bonds playing a leading role. Apparent (or implicit) interest rates are calculated for the various securities and are determined with simple margins with respect to the ten-year bonds interest rate. The price of public bonds $\left(p_{B_L}^G\right)$ varies inversely with respect to the one paid by the government $\left(r_L^G\right)$.

$$\left(\frac{\Delta^* E_A^B}{E_{A-1}^B}\right) = 0.03 + 0.4\left(\frac{\Delta^* E_{A-1}^B}{E_{A-2}^B}\right) + 0.04\left(r_{E_{A-1}}^B - \pi_{Y-1}\right)$$

$$\left(\frac{p_{B_A}^{BR}\Delta^* B_A^{BR}}{p_{B_{A-1}}^{BR} B_{A-1}^{BR}}\right) = 0.78\left(\frac{p_{B_{A-1}}^{BR}\Delta^* B_{A-1}^{BR}}{p_{B_{A-2}}^{BR} B_{A-2}^{BR}}\right) + 1.1\left(i_{10\,yrs}^* - \pi_Y^*\right)$$

$$\Delta\left(\frac{p_{B_L}^B \Delta^* B_L^B}{p_Y Y}\right) = 0.06\Delta\left(\frac{\Delta p_{K2-1}^H}{p_{K2-2}^H}\right) - 0.7vc_{-1}$$

$$vc = \left(\frac{p_{B_L}^B \Delta^* B_L^B}{p_Y Y}\right) - 0.1\left(\frac{\Delta p_{K2}^H}{p_{K2-1}^H}\right)$$

$$p_{B_L}^G = 0.22 + 0.7 p_{B_{L-1}}^G + 0.08\left(\frac{1}{r_L^G}\right)$$

## Rest of the world

Exports ($X$) and imports ($IM$) depend, respectively, on foreign $\left(Y^f\right)$ and domestic demand ($Y$) as measured by GDP in volume. Since the analyses are conducted for all goods services, it is more difficult to obtain satisfactory econometric results on price competitiveness. For imports the relative price effects could not be identified and only import prices ($p_{IM}$) could be isolated. Export and import prices (equations not shown here) are determined in standard fashion with a price maker/price taker arbitrage.

$$\Delta \ln(X) = 0.3\Delta \ln(X_{-1}) + 0.4\Delta \ln\left(Y^f\right) - 0.2\Delta \ln\left(\frac{p_X}{p_{X^*}}\right) - 0.14vc_{-1}$$

$$vc = \ln(X) - 1.7 - 0.6\ln\left(Y^f\right) + 0.5\ln\left(\frac{p_X}{p_{X^*}}\right)$$

$$\Delta \ln(IM) = 2\Delta \ln(Y) + 0.5vc_{-1}$$

$$vc = \ln(IM) - 1.8\ln(Y) + 0.2\ln(p_{IM}) + 8.5 - 0.01t$$

Capital inflows, in the form of bank deposits $\left(D_A^R\right)$, of loans granted $\left(L_A^R\right)$, and share purchases $\left(E_A^R\right)$, depend on the level of activity, variations in the real effective exchange rate ($REER$) and financial profitability for shares. Interest rate differentials could not be identified at this stage. Since the mid-2000s, purchases of government securities by the rest of the world have been part of quantitative easing policy. Capital outflows, of foreign shares and securities, depend on the demand made by domestic agents.

$$\left(\frac{\Delta^* D_A^R}{D_{A-1}^R}\right) = 4\left(\frac{\Delta Y}{Y_{-1}}\right) + 1.1\left(\frac{\Delta REER}{REER_{-1}}\right)$$

$$\left(\frac{\Delta^* L_A^R}{L_{A-1}^R}\right) = 0.24\left(\frac{\Delta^* L_{A-1}^R}{L_{A-2}^R}\right) + 2.3\left(\frac{\Delta Y}{Y_{-1}}\right)$$

$$\left(\frac{\Delta^* E_A^R}{E_{A-1}^R}\right) = 0.04 + 0.05\left(r_{EA}^R - \pi_Y\right) + 0.6\left(\frac{\Delta Y_{-1}}{Y_{-2}}\right)$$

## Prices, wages and employment

The general price level ($p_Y$) is determined by mark-up pricing from unit labor costs ($ULC$) with a short-term effect on demand pressure, measured (in the absence of a better indicator) by an output gap ($GAP$). A short-term effect of import price ($p_{IM}$) has also been added. Potential output $\left(va^{MP}\right)$ results from a simple production function used as a first approximation. Wage per worker in the market sector $\left(w^M\right)$ results from a wage-price-unemployment relation with an indexation slightly less than unity and a medium-term labor productivity $\left(\frac{va^M}{N^M}\right)$ effect. This wage per worker in the market sector serves as a reference for the evolution of that of the other sectors. Employment in the market sector $\left(N^M\right)$ adjusts with respect to medium-term employment resulting from the previous production function. Public employment is exogenous. Active population ($AP$ i.e. labor force) results from flexion of activity rates ($AP\,/\,TAP$) as a function of job creation ($N$).

$$\Delta\ln(p_Y) = 0.01 + 0.4\Delta\ln(ULC) + 0.3GAP + 0.03\Delta\ln(p_{IM-1}) - 0.4vc_{-1}$$

$$vc = \ln(p_Y) - 0.4 - 0.9\ln(ULC)$$

$$gap = \left(\frac{va^M - va^{pM}}{va^{pM}}\right)$$

$$\ln\left(\frac{va^{Mp}}{N^M}\right) = 0.8 + 0.5\ln\left(\frac{K_1^M}{N^M}\right) + 0.014t - 0.01t_{1992-2019}$$

$$\Delta\ln\left(w^M\right) = 0.005 + 0.5\Delta\ln\left(w_{-1}^M\right) + 0.4\Delta\ln\left(p_C^H\right) + 0.43\Delta\ln\left(\frac{va^M}{N^M}\right) - 0.38\Delta\ln\left(\frac{va_{-1}^M}{N_{-1}^M}\right) - 0.2vc_{-1}$$

$$vc = \ln\left(w^M\right) - 0.9\Delta\ln\left(p_C^H\right) + 0.1\ln(u) - 0.7\Delta\ln\left(\frac{va^M}{N^M}\right)$$

$$\Delta\ln\left(N^M\right) = 0.5\Delta\ln\left(N_{-1}^M\right) + 0.5\Delta\ln\left(va^M\right) - 0.08vc^*_{-1}$$

$$vc^* = \ln\left(N^M\right) - \left(\frac{\ln\left(va^M\right) - 0.8 - 0.5\ln\left(K_1^M\right) - 0.014t + 0.01t_{1992}}{1 - 0.5}\right)$$

$$\Delta\ln(AP) = 0.4\Delta\ln(N) + 0.4\Delta\ln(TAP) - 0.2vc_{-1}$$

$$vc = \ln(AP) - 0.37\ln(N) - 0.56\ln(TAP) - 0.002t$$

## Simulations and basic variants

### *Simulations on the past*

The model was run in dynamic simulation to reproduce the past starting in 1996, the year after which the dataset is homogenous.[8] Results are acceptable overall. We observe, however, an overestimation of prices and wages after 2012. We verify that the sum of financing capacities from the different agents is equal to 0 and that the central bank equilibrium is verified (rounded to the nearest decimal; Figure 7.1).

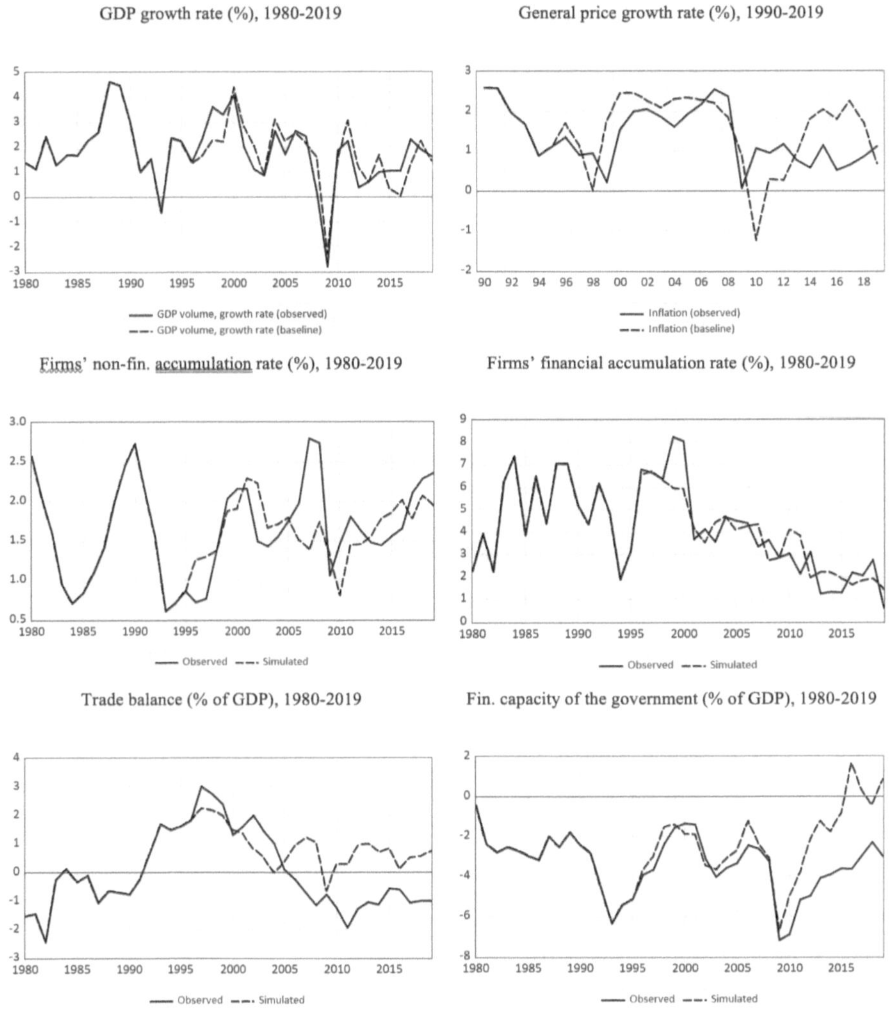


*Figure 7.1* Observed series vs simulations since 1996, selected variables.

## Basic variants

In order to study the properties of the model, certain basic variants are performed: a 1% of GDP increase in public investment (either one shot in a given year, or permanent each year), a 0.25% increase in the accumulation rate of firms, a 1% increase in the growth rate of household consumption and a 1% increase in the growth rate of wage per worker. These shocks were performed with respect to a fictitious baseline built over the period 2019–2030 abstracting from the COVID crisis. This is to ensure that the baseline

*Table 7.3* Impact of a 1% of GDP increase in public investment, one-off and permanent in 2021 (relative to the baseline)

| | *One-off* | | | | | | *Permanent* | | | | | |
|---|---|---|---|---|---|---|---|---|---|---|---|---|
| | *GDP volume* | *Price level* | *Firms investment* | *Trade balance % GDP* | *Public balance % GDP* | *Public debt % GDP* | *GDP volume* | *Price level* | *Firms investment* | *Trade balance % GDP* | *Public balance % GDP* | *Public debt % GDP* |
| 2020 | 100.00 | 100.00 | 100.00 | 0.00 | 0.00 | 0.00 | 100.00 | 100.00 | 100.00 | 0.00 | 0.00 | 0.00 |
| 2021 | 100.96 | 100.15 | 100.03 | −0.64 | −1.03 | −0.16 | 100.96 | 100.15 | 100.03 | −0.64 | −1.03 | −0.16 |
| 2022 | 100.02 | 100.18 | 100.15 | 0.03 | 0.04 | 0.84 | 100.95 | 100.32 | 100.18 | −0.60 | −0.98 | 0.62 |
| 2023 | 100.08 | 100.25 | 100.01 | −0.02 | 0.01 | 0.68 | 101.02 | 100.57 | 100.19 | −0.62 | −0.96 | 1.23 |
| 2024 | 100.08 | 100.33 | 100.01 | −0.02 | 0.01 | 0.59 | 101.07 | 100.89 | 100.20 | −0.64 | −0.95 | 1.71 |
| 2025 | 100.06 | 100.40 | 100.00 | −0.01 | 0.02 | 0.51 | 101.11 | 101.28 | 100.20 | −0.64 | −0.91 | 2.08 |
| 2026 | 100.05 | 100.44 | 99.98 | 0.00 | 0.02 | 0.46 | 101.13 | 101.71 | 100.18 | −0.64 | −0.88 | 2.36 |
| 2027 | 100.03 | 100.45 | 99.97 | 0.01 | 0.02 | 0.45 | 101.14 | 102.13 | 100.15 | −0.62 | −0.84 | 2.60 |
| 2028 | 100.02 | 100.43 | 99.95 | 0.02 | 0.02 | 0.49 | 101.13 | 102.54 | 100.09 | −0.60 | −0.81 | 2.84 |
| 2029 | 100.01 | 100.39 | 99.93 | 0.02 | 0.02 | 0.58 | 101.10 | 102.89 | 100.01 | −0.57 | −0.77 | 3.13 |
| 2030 | 100.00 | 100.34 | 99.91 | 0.03 | 0.01 | 0.69 | 101.07 | 103.17 | 99.91 | −0.54 | −0.74 | 3.52 |

is not affected by extreme shocks. The analysis of the COVID crisis and certain elements of response to it may be studied in the future.

The increase in public investment has the usual stimulus effects, a one-off or lasting increase in the volume of GDP depending on the nature of the shock, a limited or longer-lasting inflationist shift depending on the case, an imbalance in the trade balance and public finance and an increase in public debt limited to less than 1% of GDP in the case of a one-off shock or reaching nearly 4% of GDP over a ten-year period (Table 7.3).[9]

The increase in the accumulation rate of firms has similar effects than the shock to public investment, with differences due to the nature of the investment and the agents involved. With business investment, the recovery is gradual and inflationary pressures lower thanks to the increase in the production capacity that reduces demand pressure. As a consequence, the trade balance is less negatively affected than in the previous case. Growth improves public finances at medium term and reduces public debt, but at the price of an increase in firm indebtedness.

An increase in household consumption, and therefore a fall in their savings rate, also boosts growth with slight inflationary pressures. Firms' investment gets a little boost. The trade balance worsens in the short term but it recovers as growth falls. Public finances also improve slightly in the medium term.

An increase in the growth rate of wage per head in the market sector by 1% leads to more unfavorable effects. The wage-induced recovery and that of consumption is modest and ephemeral. The increase in unit labor costs yields a slippage in prices that erodes purchasing power and weighs on competitiveness. Weak growth limits, however, a further worsening of the trade balance. Thanks to inflation, the government balance and public debt are reduced. According to the results, the French economy would be profit-led, mainly due to the price-wage spiral and to the determination of investment highly dependent on profitability. Inflationary risks may be overestimated, and, although they may eventually be controlled, they cannot be ignored. This variant also illustrates that a little bit of wage-induced inflation contributes to reduce the public debt burden (Table 7.4).

## The weight of real estate and land

The impact of the increase in land prices can be illustrated with the help of a 10% permanent shock. The result is a recovery driven by a wealth effect on household consumption and a real estate boom sustained by rising property prices. The general price level increases somewhat, but the most negative element is the deterioration in the profitability of capital, which is linked to the rise in the land prices and significantly reduces the growth of firms' investments, thus the potential for future growth. Complementarily, a one-off shock to household investment boosts growth while maintaining the land boom at the expense of firms' investment (Table 7.5).

*Table 7.4* Impact of a 0.25% increase in the accumulation rate of firms, 1% growth rate of household consumption and 1% growth rate of wage per worker in 2021 (relative to the baseline)

| | *Firms' investment* | | | | | | *Firms' investment* | | | | | | *Firms' investment* | | | | | |
|---|---|---|---|---|---|---|---|---|---|---|---|---|---|---|---|---|---|---|
| | *GDP volume* | *Price level* | *Firms' investment* | *Trade balance %GDP* | *Public balance %GDP* | *Public debt %GDP* | *GDP volume* | *Price level* | *Firms' investment* | *Trade balance %GDP* | *Public balance %GDP* | *Public debt %GDP* | *GDP volume* | *Price level* | *Firms' investment* | *Trade balance %GDP* | *Public balance %GDP* | *Public debt %GDP* |
| 2020 | 100.00 | 100.00 | 100.00 | 0.00 | 0.00 | 0.00 | 100.00 | 100.00 | 100.00 | 0.00 | 0.00 | 0.00 | 100.00 | 100.00 | 0.00 | 0.00 | 0.00 | 100.00 |
| 2021 | 100.27 | 100.03 | 102.04 | −0.19 | −0.05 | −0.28 | 100.58 | 100.09 | 100.02 | −0.39 | −0.11 | −0.62 | 100.19 | 100.35 | −0.10 | −0.09 | −0.67 | 100.27 |
| 2022 | 100.30 | 100.05 | 102.29 | −0.20 | −0.03 | −0.31 | 100.51 | 100.19 | 100.11 | −0.32 | −0.06 | 0.60 | 100.24 | 100.88 | −0.09 | −0.15 | −0.47 | 100.30 |
| 2023 | 100.35 | 100.08 | 102.51 | −0.23 | −0.02 | −0.38 | 100.49 | 100.31 | 100.09 | −0.30 | −0.04 | 0.69 | 100.26 | 101.37 | −0.06 | −0.18 | −0.25 | 100.35 |
| 2024 | 100.39 | 100.12 | 102.72 | −0.26 | −0.01 | −0.49 | 100.47 | 100.47 | 100.06 | −0.27 | −0.02 | 0.86 | 100.25 | 100.71 | −0.03 | −0.18 | −0.88 | 100.39 |
| 2025 | 100.43 | 100.18 | 102.93 | 0.28 | −0.01 | −0.63 | 100.45 | 100.66 | 100.02 | −0.25 | −0.01 | 0.10 | 100.21 | 100.90 | 0.00 | −0.18 | −0.29 | 100.43 |
| 2026 | 100.47 | 100.25 | 103.14 | −0.31 | −0.02 | −0.81 | 100.42 | 100.84 | 100.97 | −0.22 | −0.04 | 0.37 | 100.17 | 100.93 | −0.02 | −0.17 | −0.49 | 100.47 |
| 2027 | 100.50 | 100.31 | 103.33 | −0.33 | −0.04 | −0.01 | 100.39 | 100.01 | 100.90 | −0.19 | −0.06 | 0.64 | 100.11 | 100.84 | −0.05 | −0.16 | −0.51 | 100.50 |
| 2028 | 100.53 | 100.38 | 103.52 | −0.35 | −0.06 | −0.23 | 100.34 | 100.14 | 100.81 | −0.15 | −0.08 | 0.89 | 100.06 | 100.67 | −0.07 | −0.14 | −0.37 | 100.53 |
| 2029 | 100.55 | 100.43 | 103.70 | −0.37 | −0.08 | −0.47 | 100.30 | 100.23 | 100.72 | −0.12 | −0.09 | 0.09 | 99.01 | 100.44 | −0.09 | −0.13 | −0.12 | 100.55 |
| 2030 | 100.57 | 100.47 | 103.87 | −0.39 | −0.10 | −0.71 | 100.24 | 100.27 | 100.61 | −0.08 | −0.10 | 0.23 | 99.97 | 100.18 | −0.10 | −0.11 | −0.77 | 100.57 |

Table 7.5 Impact of a 10% p=rmanent increase in the growth rate of land price and a one-off 10% increase in the growth rate of housing inv=stment in 2021 (relative to the baseline)

| | Land price (permanen_) | | | | | | Housing (one-offs) | | | | | |
|---|---|---|---|---|---|---|---|---|---|---|---|---|
| | GDP volume | Price level | Firms investment | Trade balance %GDP | Public balance %GDP | Public debt %GDP | GDP volume | Price level | Firms investment | Trade balance %GDP | Public balance %GDP | Public debt %GDP |
| 2020 | 100.00 | 100.00 | 100.0[illegible] | 0.00 | 0.00 | 0.00 | 100.00 | 100.00 | 100.00 | 0.00 | 0.00 | 0.00 |
| 2021 | 100.15 | 100.02 | 99.9[illegible] | −0.10 | −0.03 | −0.17 | 100.75 | 100.07 | 99.91 | −0.51 | −0.12 | −0.77 |
| 2022 | 100.40 | 100.09 | 99.5[illegible] | −0.27 | −0.05 | −0.48 | 100.87 | 100.13 | 99.71 | −0.57 | −0.07 | −0.91 |
| 2023 | 100.68 | 100.22 | 99.0[illegible] | −0.45 | −0.09 | −0.89 | 100.69 | 100.18 | 99.48 | 0.44 | −0.03 | −0.75 |
| 2024 | 100.93 | 100.42 | 99.5[illegible] | −0.61 | −0.14 | −0.32 | 100.43 | 100.26 | 99.35 | 0.24 | 0.00 | −0.52 |
| 2025 | 101.07 | 100.69 | 99.0[illegible] | −0.68 | −0.17 | −0.72 | 100.19 | 100.36 | 99.33 | 0.07 | −0.03 | −0.38 |
| 2026 | 101.08 | 101.03 | 97.6[illegible] | −0.67 | −0.18 | −0.06 | 100.02 | 100.45 | 99.39 | 0.05 | −0.06 | −0.31 |
| 2027 | 101.98 | 101.42 | 97.2[illegible] | −0.57 | −0.16 | =0.35 | 99.93 | 100.49 | 99.45 | 0.11 | −0.08 | −0.32 |
| 2028 | 100.80 | 101.82 | 96.9[illegible] | −0.41 | −0.12 | −0.61 | 99.90 | 100.47 | 99.48 | 0.12 | −0.08 | −0.32 |
| 2029 | 100.59 | 102.17 | 96.7[illegible] | −0.23 | −0.07 | −0.89 | 99.89 | 100.38 | 99.48 | 0.11 | −0.07 | −0.25 |
| 2030 | 100.37 | 102.45 | 96.4[illegible] | −0.05 | −0.02 | −0.98 | 99.90 | 100.24 | 99.45 | 0.09 | −0.05 | −0.08 |

## Unconventional monetary policy and fiscal policy

Two forms of unconventional monetary policy can be studied in this model: helicopter money and the cancellation of a part of the public debt held by the central bank.

### Helicopter money

Helicopter money can take several forms, either as a distribution of central bank money directly to households or businesses or as a distribution to the government. If we want to avoid a distribution of banknotes, the first form assumes that all households and firms have an account with the central bank. Although this is theoretically possible, it is not the case today. This is why we are only interested in the second form, i.e. via the State and its account with the central bank. Several steps have to be distinguished to account for helicopter money in the model.

The first is pure helicopter money distribution, i.e. the feeding of the State's account with the central bank for an amount equivalent to 1% of GDP and paid the first year.[10] This distribution alone does not have an impact other than increasing government wealth and diminishing that of the central bank. In a second step, in order to be able to use this helicopter money the government must transfer it to the accounts of commercial banks. The account with the central bank is debited, and the account with private banks is credited.[11] This transfer also has no impact on the real sector. In each case government wealth increases with respect to the baseline. It even increases slightly more thanks to the interest paid by banks to the government, and public debt decreases accordingly. Conversely, the central bank's wealth remains reduced by the same amount as before, while bank reserves (which can be interpreted as the central bank's indebtedness to private banks) increase.

In a third step the government uses helicopter money to finance additional public investment of the same amount (1% of GDP). Bank deposits are brought back to initial levels. We observe, unsurprisingly, a recovery effect with slight inflationary pressures of an identical size to the effects obtained in the case of public investment financed by public debt. However, the financing methods are different. In the current case, the government balance deteriorates by the same amount but public debt does not increase, given that expenditure is financed by the helicopter money transfer. Figure 7.2 illustrates this point. The graphs in percentage of GDP may seem paradoxical. Given the GDP increase the public balance as percentage of GDP worsens and simultaneously public debt as percentage of GDP falls. This recovery via investment without public debt has a counterpart. The wealth of the central bank worsens as much and stays at that level under the effect of the recovery. Symmetrically, government wealth increases given that the stock of capital increases without additional debt. It can be noted that bank reserves (i.e. central bank indebtedness to banks) initially increase but then fall (Figure 7.2).

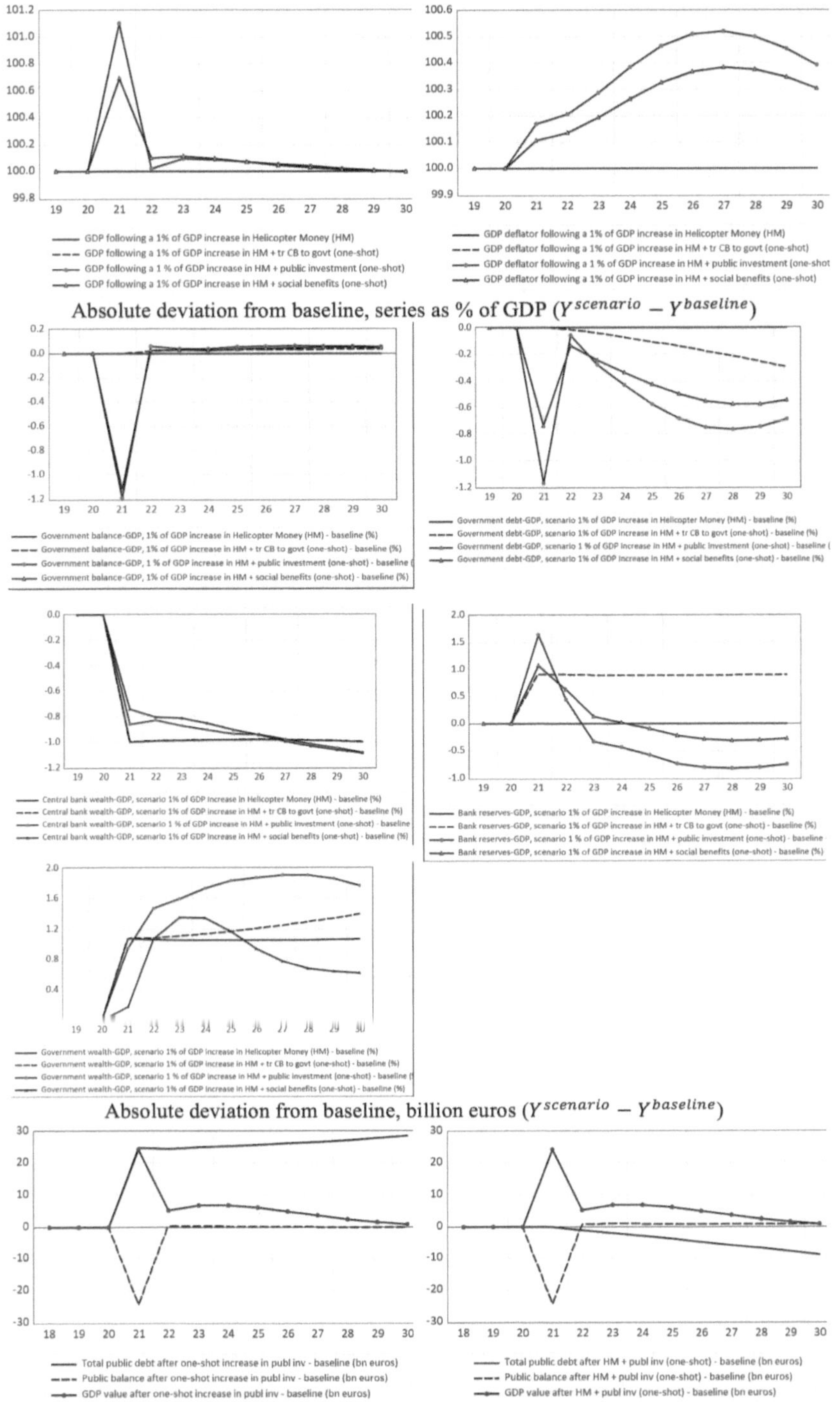


*Figure 7.2* Impact of helicopter money distribution of 1% of GDP, with a one-off increase in public investment or with social transfers in 2021.

Helicopter money to finance public investment is presented by its proponents (Couppey-Soubeyran, 2020) as a useful tool in a period of strong public indebtedness. The previous simulations could be completed by examining, not only a one-off shock but also a permanent increase in public investment in the context of the energy transition. The conclusions to be drawn would not be fundamentally different. There is no miracle. The recovery without public debt has as a counterpart a worsening of central bank wealth. This would not be a problem according to supporters of this policy. A central bank could still work with negative own funds. This could be the case if the procedure is punctual and limited, but more problematic in the context of a sustained policy. Financial markets could push up interest rates. The solutions proposed to restore the central bank's own funds are not convincing. The size of bank reserves would facilitate capital outflows or slippages in the securities or real estate markets. In the French case, as in the case of countries in the Eurozone without a central bank properly speaking, such policy would contradict European treaties. It could only be undertaken after a series of time-consuming negotiations whose outcomes would be more than uncertain.

Another possible use of helicopter money is to finance increased social transfers to households for an amount equivalent to 1% of GDP according to the same modalities as in the third step seen previously (the first two steps are identical). The results are similar to those under a recovery without public debt, but a worsening of central bank wealth.

## Cancellation of public debt held by the central bank

As a result of unconventional monetary policy, central banks hold a large amount of government securities, which constitute a significant part of public debt. One proposal put forward by some authors (Scialom and Bridonneau, 2020) is to cancel part of this debt in order to lighten budget constraints, thus providing room for maneuver to better finance the energy transition. This policy (cancellation of public debt equivalent to 15% of GDP) can be studied in the model in a simple way. A first gap-filling variable of −15% of GDP is introduced in the flow-stock equation generating the stock of public debt held by the central bank.[12] The same negative shock is introduced in the flow-stock equation generating the stock of total debt. Lastly, another gap-filling variable equation indicates that the cancellation concerns only public bonds. This partial cancellation of public debt held by the central bank has no effect on the real economy. Public debt falls but central bank wealth falls as much (Figure 7.3).

For the supporters of this policy, the reduction of public debt would loosen the constraints and would open the way to an increase in public investment (1% of GDP on a permanent basis) to finance the energy transition. As the simulations show, the combination of these two measures, partial cancellation of debt and increase in public investment, leads to a sustained recovery with rising inflationary pressures due to demand pressure and wage drift.

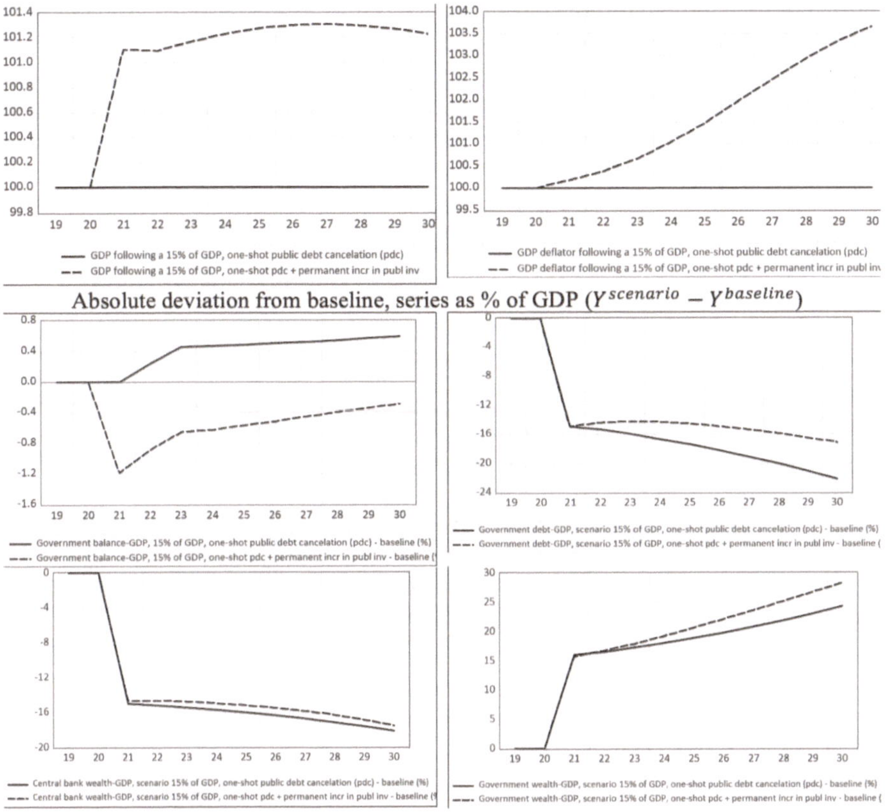


*Figure 7.3* Impact of a partial cancellation of debt held by the central bank, starting in 2021.

Thanks to the initial cancellation, public debt remains under control despite the increase in the public deficit. The counterpart of these evolutions is a persistent and marked deterioration of the central bank's wealth (−18% of GDP).

These results raise, in addition, the same reservations as those formulated about helicopter money. Insofar as the amounts of cancellation are high (more than in the previous case), it is difficult to believe that this marked deterioration of the central bank's own funds can remain without consequences. The risk of rising interest rates cannot be ignored. The ways in which the central bank can replenish its capital are not convincing, and accepting such policy within the Eurozone seems rather unlikely.

## Conclusion

Based on the accumulation accounts of INSEE and the financial accounts of Bank of France, a first version of an econometric SFC model of the French economy was presented. It is an aggregate model with a single product distinguishing five domestic agents (firms, households, banks, central bank, government) and the rest of the world with a complete representation of economic and financial accounts in flows and stocks. The structure of the model is close to that of existing SFC models with demand-led dynamics, an accumulation behavior of a Kaleckian type and an indebtedness norm. The dynamic simulations on the past over the period 1996–2019 provided acceptable results. The basic variants display the usual multiplier effects and a dominant profit-led logic. The dynamics of the housing sector and the land price boom seem to work at the expense of firms' productive investment. Finally, the effects of unconventional monetary policy were evaluated: distribution of helicopter money in favor of the government to finance additional public investment or social transfers, partial cancellation of the public debt held by the central bank. Stimulus without public debt has as a counterpart, a degradation of the wealth and own funds of the central bank that cannot be ignored. This is further reinforced in the case of partial debt cancellation because of the large amounts involved.

This first version of the model should be improved on several points, in particular: endogenizing interest rates and modeling of bond prices, better description of supply constraints and explicit treatment of the ECB currently integrated in the rest of the world, which makes monetary policy difficult to read.

## Notes

1 The complete working paper and the technical documentation are available on the website of the *Chaire Energie et Prospérité.*

2 The treatment of other changes in volume (OCV) and of revaluations is important, and rather technical. Without delving into the details, it suffices to say that for each item of the balance sheet an OCV or asset price must be computed in order to ensure stock-flow consistency.

3 $r_L^F$ is the apparent (or implicit) interest rate, calculated as the ratio of interests paid by firms and the stock of indebtedness from the previous period.

4 *vc* (bottom equation) stands for vector of cointegration, and is the medium-term relationship normalized to 0.

5 $i_{10\,years}$ is the interest rate on ten-year government bonds.

6 Given the presence of the *OCV* in the flow-stock equations, the flow of an instrument like inter-firm lending is not $\Delta L_A^F = L_A^F - L_{A-1}^F$ but rather $\Delta^* L_A^F = L_A^F - L_{A-1}^F - OCV_{L_A}^F$.

7 Note that the price index used as a deflator for disposable income and as the inflation rate in the real interest rate is the price index of households' investment $\left(p_I^H\right)$.

8 *Banque de France* provides the necessary data for the analysis of the financial accounts in two datasets. The first goes from 1978 to 2009 (discontinued) and the second from 1995 onwards. We kept the second dataset (which follows the SNA 2008 methodology) and adapted the methodology of the first one (SNA 1996) in order to fit before 1995.

9 GDP in volume, the price level and firms' investment are presented here as after-shock series multiplied by 100, divided by the baseline series. Trade and public balance as well as public debt are shares of GDP, so that the table shows the after-shock–baseline differences.

10 To account for this distribution of helicopter money in the model, it is necessary to feed the government's account with the central bank and add a negative gap-filling variable of the same amount on the accounting identity determining the variation of public indebtedness, in order to translate the fact that the government's account is increased thanks to helicopter money and not by indebtedness.

11 Here again the logic of the model requires the introduction of a gap-filling variable on the government's liability deposits, which are simply modeled as a function of government deposits held. This variable is negative to reflect the fact that these deposits have no reason to increase in the event of a helicopter money transfer.

12 This is introduced in the term OCV that closes the flow-stock equation and integrates, among others, the effects of the cancellation.

## References

Allard-Prigent C., Audenis C., Berger K., Carnot N., Duchêne S. and Pesir P. (2002), Présentation du modèle MESANGE Modèle Econométrique de Simulation et d'Analyse Générale de l'Economie, Document de travail de la Direction de la Prévision, Ministère de l'Economie et des Finances, mai.

Blanchard O., Giavazzi F. and Sa F. (2005), The US current account and the dollar, Brooking Papers on economic activity n°1.

Blanchard O. (2018), On the future of macroeconomic models, Oxford Review of Economic Policy, Rebuilding macroeconomic theory, vol 34, n°1–2, Spring-Summer.

Boyer R., Mazier J. and Olive G. (1974), Un nouveau modèle macroéconomique: STAR, Economie et Statistique, 61, pp 29–53.

Burgess S., Burrows O., Godin A., Kinsella S. and Millard S. (2016), A dynamic model of financial balances for the UK, Staff Working paper n° 614, September, Bank of England.

Couppey-Soubeyran J. (2020), La monnaie hélicoptère contre la dépression dans le sillage de la crise sanitaire, Institut Veblen, April.

Cripps F. (2016), Macromodel scenarios and implications for European policy in *Challenges for Europe in the world 2030*, Ed Eatwell J., McKinley T. and Petit P.; Ashgate, pp 81–126.

Dehove M., Fauqueur A., Gaudemet J.P., Husson M., Mathis J., de Monchy G. and Vallet D. (1981), Le modèle COPAIN : comportements patrimoniaux et intégration financière, Economie et Prévision, 48, pp 3–69.

Godley W. (1999), Seven unsustainable processes: medium term prospects and policies for the USA and the world economy, The Levy Economics Institute of the Bard College.

Godley W., Papadimitriou D.B., Dos Santos C.H. and Zezza G. (2005), The US and the creditors: can the symbiosis last? Strategic Analysis, The Levy Economics Institute of the Bard College.

Godley W. and Lavoie M. (2003), Two-country SFC macroeconomics using a closed model within a dollar exchange regime, Working Paper n°10, University of Cambridge.

Godley W. and Lavoie M. (2005–2006), Comprehensive accounting in simple open economy macroeconomics with endogenous sterilization or flexible exchange rates, Journal of Post-Keynesian Economics, 28(2) Winter, pp 241–276.

Godley W. and Lavoie M. (2006), A simple model of three economies with two currencies: the eurozone and the USA, Cambridge Journal of Economics, 10, 1093.

Godley W. and Lavoie M. (2007), Monetary Economics, Palgrave MacMillan.

Lavoie M. and Godley W. (2001–2002), Kaleckian growth models in a SF monetary approach framework: a Kaldorian view, Journal of Post-Keynesian Economics, 24(2) winter pp 277–312.

Obstfeld M. and Rogoff K. (2005), Global current account imbalances and exchange rate adjustments, Brookings Papers on economic activity n°1.

Reyes L. (2015), Economic policy and income distribution: the case of France since the early 1970s, PhD thesis, Paris 13 University.

Scialom L. and Bridonneau B. (2020), Crise économique et crise écologique: osons des decisions de rupture, Terra Nova, April.

Zezza F. and Zezza G. (2020), A SFC quarterly model of the Italian economy, Working Paper n° 958, June, Levy Institute

Wren-Lewis S. (2018), Ending the microfoundations hegemony, Oxford Review of Economic Policy, Rebuilding macroeconomic theory, vol 34, n°1–2, Spring-Summer.

# 8 A Stock-Flow Consistent Quarterly Model of the Italian Economy

*Francesco Zezza and Gennaro Zezza*

In this chapter, the authors show how to address the missing links between the real and financial sectors within a post-Keynesian framework, presenting a quarterly stock-flow consistent (SFC) structural model of the Italian economy. They set up the accounting structure of the sectoral transactions, describing the transaction matrix and balance sheet matrix, starting from the appropriate sectoral data sources. They describe their estimation strategy, present the main stochastic equations, and, finally, discuss the main channels of transmissions in the model.

## Introduction

Macroeconomists and policymakers need rigorous, albeit *realistic*, quantitative models to track the future paths and dynamics of some variables of interest, as well as to evaluate the effects of specific policies or external shocks. However, at the heart of all these models lies a standard macroeconomic module which, depending on the degree of sophistication and the research questions to be answered, represents *how* the economy works.

After the stagflation of the 1970s, "structural" models, developed following the Cowles Commission approach (Fair 2012), were abandoned by most central banks in favour of either dynamic stochastic general equilibrium (DSGE) types or micro-founded versions of investment—savings and liquidity preference—money supply (IS-LM) New Keynesian models (Hendry and Muellbauer 2018). It is now widely accepted that the models used by policymaking agencies have performed poorly, to say the least, in detecting the last two major recessions (2000–2001 and 2007–2008). The complete absence of a realistic monetary framework, along with the abstraction of banks and more generally of real-financial interactions, not only in DSGE but also in central banks' structural econometric models, made it impossible to detect the rising financial fragility that led to the Great Recession. On the contrary, research groups adopting modelling approaches that considered the flow of funds of institutional sectors, and possibly the interrelation of balance sheets with saving and investment decisions, have been acknowledged for producing timely projections of the crises (Bezemer 2010).

DOI: 10.4324/9781003253457-10

Following the financial crisis there have indeed been some advancements in neoclassical and New Keynesian policy models to better account for real-financial interactions but, as we discuss next, the step taken so far do not suffice. As the advent of the COVID pandemic implied a drastic structural break in macroeconomic time series, most macroeconometric policy models will need a thorough revision, opening another window of opportunity to discuss how to appropriately modify—or design—the next generation of policy models.

In this chapter, we present a quarterly SFC structural model of the Italian economy, developed within the SFC modelling approach pioneered by Wynne Godley (Godley and Lavoie 2007; Lavoie and Zezza 2011), which addresses the missing links between the real and financial sectors within a post-Keynesian framework. Our model follows the tradition of empirical SFC models developed by Godley and associates at the Levy Economics Institute of Bard College (Godley 1999; Papadimitriou, Nikiforos and Zezza 2013); it does not follow the New Cambridge approach, which considers a three-sector economy, as in Godley (1999), but expands the analysis of the private sector considering separately the interaction between households, nonfinancial corporations (NFCs), financial businesses, and the central bank.

In Section 2 we set up the accounting structure of the sectoral transactions, described in the "transaction" and "balance sheet" matrices. Section 3 presents our "closures," describing the behaviour of each institutional sector. We close the chapter with a brief overview of the main channels of transmissions in the model.

## Model Structure

The first advantage of the SFC approach is its ability to capture the interrelations in expenditure-saving decisions and their implications for financial markets. Consistency requires the identification of who-to-whom relationships between institutional sectors for payments/receipts, and for creditor/debtor relations, which may not be directly available from the data published in the nonfinancial and Financial Accounts of Institutional Sectors, but can sometimes be inferred from other statistics, such as the balance of payments or government accounts.

From this point of view, exploiting the information available in the accounts of the institutional sectors already implies an advantage over models based only on national account statistics that lack sectoral details. The accounts of institutional sectors became available in 1955 in the United States and in Italy in 1964[1] but are rarely, if at all, employed by macroeconomic modellers.

The choice of the model's level of detail can rely on the information available for such statistics coupled with the research question we want to address with the model. In our case, the model is meant to be used as a tool for evaluating policy scenarios. It therefore needs to have an adequate degree of detail for evaluating specific policy options, and be based on data at quarterly frequency, since annual data are released with too much delay to be useful for policy purposes.

Combining the information available from sectoral statistics, and following the procedure discussed in Zezza and Zezza (2019), we chose to disaggregate the balance sheet of all sectors as reported in Table 8.1.[2]

We split the stock of productive capital into nonresidential building (KNR) and other productive capital (KM) used in the model as determinants of investment functions based on a target capital-output ratio-and public capital (KG), linked to public investment. The latter can be used to test the impact government expenditure on capital account has on private sector productivity.

The relevance of stock measures for the determination of income and expenditure trajectories can be appreciated from the data in Figure 8.1, where we report the evolution of the stocks of housing and gross financial assets for the household sector over time, both measured relative to household disposable income.

It is well-known that in Italy investment in housing has always been considered a safer alternative to the purchase of financial assets in a household's portfolio, so that a portion of the value of existing homes should be considered as a source of future revenue for the retirement years. This is part of the reason why Italian institutions are less financially sophisticated than similar economies.[3]

As the chart in Figure 8.1 shows, the value of household housing wealth increased rapidly before the Great Recession, both because of real investment and because of the relative increase in the price of housing. It stabilized around 2009 and has decreased steadily, due to both the collapse in investment and the fall in the market price of homes. Household financial

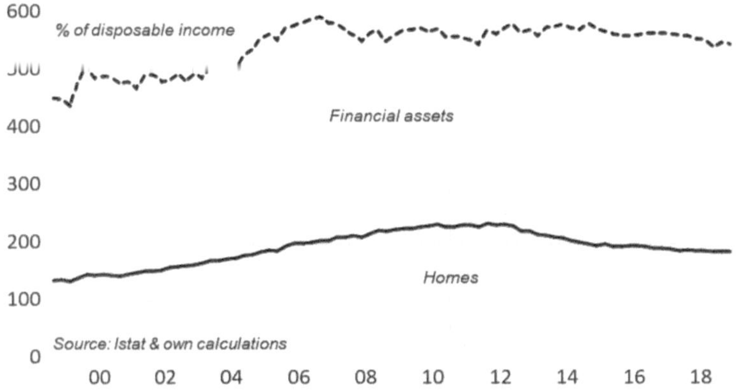


*Figure 8.1* Italy: household wealth.

*Table 8.1* Balance sheet of institutional sectors

| *Assets/liabilities* | *Sector* | | | | | | |
|---|---|---|---|---|---|---|---|
| | *HH* | *NFC* | *FC* | *CB* | *GVT* | *RoW* | *Total* |
| *Real assets* | | | | | | | |
| Capital (residential) | +KH | | | | | | +KH |
| Capital (nonresidential): Machineries | | +KM | | | | | +KM |
| Capital (nonresidential): Warehouses | | +KNR | | | | | +KNR |
| Capital (public) | | | | | +Kg | | +Kg |
| Financial assets | | | | | | | |
| Gold | | | | +GOLD | | −GOLD | 0 |
| Monetary base | $+MB_{hh}$ | | $+MB_{fc}$ | −MB | | $+MB_{T2}$ | 0 |
| CB refinancing | | | −ADV | +ADV | | | 0 |
| Bank deposits | $+DEPS_{hh}$ | $+DEPS_{nfc}$ | -DEPS | | $+DEPS_{gvt}$ | $+DEPS_{row}$ | 0 |
| Bank loans: cons. credit | −BLcc | | +BLcc | | | | 0 |
| Bank loans: mortgages | −Blmo | | +Blmo | | | | 0 |
| Bank loans to firms | | -BLfirms | +BLfirms | | | | 0 |
| Banks debt | $+BB_{hh}$ | | -BB | | | $+BB_{row}$ | 0 |
| Banks equities | +EB | | -EB | | | | 0 |
| Public debt | $+B_{hh}$ | $+B_{nfc}$ | $+B_{fc}$ | $+B_{cb}$ | -B | $+B_{row}$ | 0 |
| Firms equities | $+EN_{hh}$ | -EN | $+EN_{fc}$ | | $+EN_{gvt}$ | | 0 |
| Outgoing FDI | | +FDIo | | | | -FDIo | 0 |
| Incoming FDI | | −FDIi | | | | +FDIi | 0 |
| Foreign liabilities | $+F_{hh}$ | | $+F_{fc}$ | $+F_{cb}$ | | −F | 0 |
| Other net | $+ONFA_{hh}$ | $+ONFA_{nfc}$ | $+ONFA_{fc}$ | $+ONFA_{cb}$ | $+ONFA_{gvt}$ | $+ONFA_{row}$ | |
| Net financial assets | $NFA_{hh}$ | $NFA_{nfc}$ | $NFA_{fc}$ | $NFA_{cb}$ | $NFA_{gvt}$ | $NFA_{row}$ | 0 |

**Legend:** HH = households; NFCs = nonfinancial corporations; FC = financial corporations; CB = central bank; GVT = public sector; ROW = rest of the world.

**Notes: (+) signs stand for “assets” and (−) for “liabilities.”**

wealth has been less volatile. It still much higher than the stock of household liabilities (not shown in the chart), which has more than doubled between 1996 and 2009, rising to 55% of GDP, and has been slowly falling in the last years. One of the purposes of an SFC model like ours is to evaluate the impact of such changes in the market value of wealth on household expenditure and saving decisions.

For financial assets and liabilities, we integrated the information available in the Financial Accounts of Institutional Sectors (FAIS) with other monetary statistics published by the BoI[4] to achieve: (a) an adequate representation of the monetary aggregates relevant for monetary policy; (b) debtor-creditor relationship for each asset (while in the FAIS each sector often has the same asset on both sides of its balance sheet); and (c) an explicit representation of the major types of credit from both domestic and foreign financial institutions to the nonfinancial domestic sectors. For other financial instruments that we deemed less interesting for our purposes, we chose to use a residual category, other net financial assets (ONFA), trying to keep it to a relatively small size.

What an SFC model for Italy should capture is the dynamics of Italian public debt to evaluate its sustainability under the current eurozone rules. The evolution of Italian public debt is reported in Figure 8.2. It shows that the debt was slowly declining until the Great Recession, increased moderately relative to GDP with the crisis, and increased considerably with the crisis of confidence that started with the Greek crisis around 2011. The debt rose from 87% of GDP in the last quarter of 2011

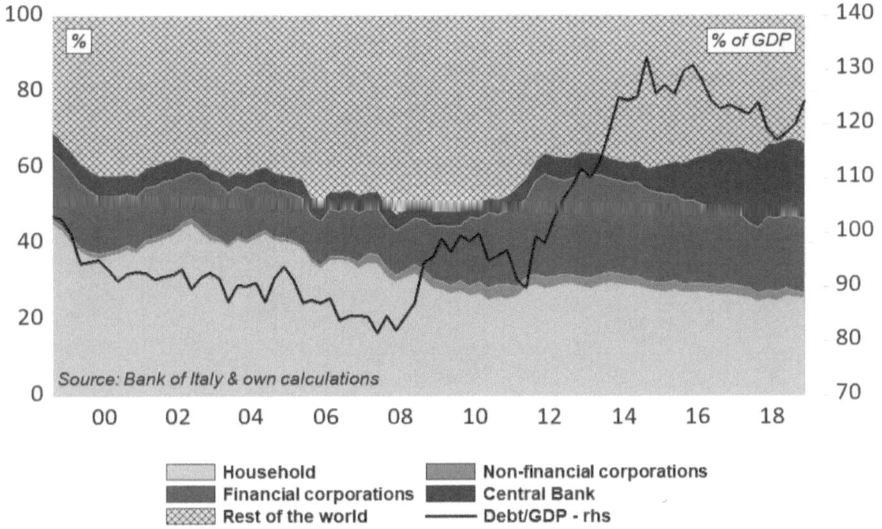


*Figure 8.2* Italy: government debt.

to 129% of GDP in 2015 and declined again with the start of the second phase of the European Central Bank's quantitative easing (QE), when the BoI—on behalf of the ECB—started purchasing large amounts of bonds from the market.

The chart in Figure 8.2 also shows that the share of public debt held directly by Italian households has been declining steadily, with households shifting a growing share of their portfolio towards assets issued by nonbank financial intermediaries, such as pension funds. The value of such assets in a household's portfolio has similar dynamics with the value of public bonds held by such intermediaries so that we chose to simplify the model's balance sheet; considering that households indirectly hold the public debt owned by these intermediaries, we removed their liabilities from the asset side of the household's balance sheet.

Other examples of the SFC approach's strengths over a simple model for flows are related to the determination of the composition of the household's portfolio and its relevance for financial markets and economic policy. In Figure 8.3 we report the major financial assets in a household's portfolio (after the consolidation mentioned above). We could summarize the dynamics in Figure 8.3 as a "search for safety" over the whole period: the share of very liquid assets (monetary base plus bank deposits) has been growing steadily from about 50% of GDP to over 70% of GDP, while the holding of riskier assets—such as banks' equities and bonds—has been declining. Households also steadily increased their holdings of foreign assets.[5]

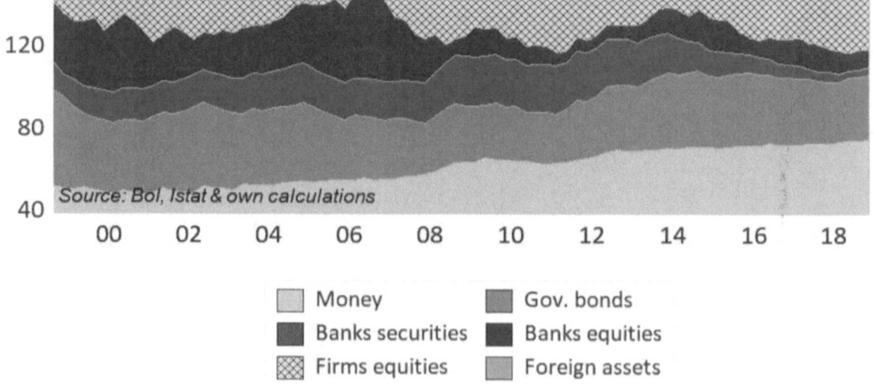


*Figure 8.3* Italy: household portfolio.

*Table 8.2* Italy: Transaction matrix

| | Sectors | | | | | | | |
|---|---|---|---|---|---|---|---|---|
| | *Production* | *HH* | *NFCs* | *FC* | *CB* | *GVT* | *RoW* | *TOT* |
| *Gross domestic product* | $+GDP$ | $-CONS$<br>$-GFCF_{hh}$<br>$-DINV_{hh}$ | $-GFCF_{nfc}$<br>$-DINV_{nfc}$ | $-GFCF_{fc}$<br>$-DINV_{fc}$ | | $-G$<br>$-GFCF_{gvt}$<br>$-DINV_{gvt}$ | $-XGS$<br>$+MGS$ | *0* |
| Wage income: domestic | −WB | +WAGES | | | | | −WAGESFROW | 0 |
| Wage income paid abroad | −WAGES2ROW | | | | | | +WAGES2ROW | 0 |
| Mixed income | −MIXY | +MIXY | | | | | | 0 |
| Operating surplus | −OPS | $+OPS_{hh}$ | $+OPS_{nfc}$ | $+OPS_{fc}$ | | $+OPS_{gvt}$ | | 0 |
| Indirect taxes | −INDTAX | | | | | $+INDT_{gvt}$ | $+INDT_{row}$ | 0 |
| Subsidies | +SUBS | | | | | $-SUBS_{gvt}$ | $-SUBS_{row}$ | 0 |
| *Memo: Income from production* | | $+INCP$ | $+OPS_{nfc}$ | $OPS_{fc}$ | | $INCP_{gvt}$ | $+INCP_{row}$ | |

Once the balance sheet of the model has been designed, it is easier to determine a consistent set of income flows between sectors. In Table 8.2 we report a simplified description of the main accounting relations between our institutional sectors, obtained by adding who-to-whom closures on the available data for nonfinancial transactions.

## The Model

Since the model is rather complex, made of more than 270 endogenous variables, this subsection only describes, sector by sector, the main mechanisms at work and their economic intuitions. A full description of the model is in Zezza and Zezza (2020).[6]

## Gross Domestic Product

As in the first row of Table 8.2, GDP at constant prices (*GDPK*, eq. 8.1) is given by the sum of the components of demand, namely, consumption (*CONSK*), investments and changes in inventories (*GFCFK* and *DINVK*, respectively), government expenditures (*GK*), and exports (*XGSK*) minus imports (*MGSK*).

$$GDPK = CONSK + GFCFK + DINVK + GK + XGSK - MGSK + \quad (8.1)$$

For variables measured at constant prices we use the published figures at chained 2010 prices, which have the property that the sum of the components of real GDP does not sum up to the total, so that a residual (*GDPKRES*) must be introduced to keep consistency between variables at current and constant prices. We need a similar residual variable when we consider detailed components of demand, as is the case for investment and exports. The components of GDP will be determined at constant prices and converted to current prices using their own deflators (rather than assuming a unique deflator).[7] Exports are split into goods and services. We checked whether model performance would improve by splitting imports along similar lines and decided against it.

Consistent with the measures of real wealth in Table 8.1, investment is split into housing, nonresidential, and machinery, which also includes other, smaller categories. As public investment is mainly nonresidential, we use the same deflator adopted for private nonresidential investment.

From the income side (the first column of Table 8.2), GDP is equal to the sum of wages paid domestically and to foreigners, mixed income, gross operating surplus, and indirect taxes and subsidies to production.

The level of employment is determined by real GDP and average labour productivity. Given the average unit wage, the wage bill is obtained. Wages accruing to domestic households are given by this wage bill, less wages paid to foreigners, plus wages earned abroad by residents. These income payments to/from the foreign sectors are not modelled yet, but the model could easily be extended to account for the role of immigrant workers, and possibly increase the level of detail of wages paid in the labour market.

Mixed income is simply obtained as a share of GDP. Indirect taxes and subsidies are modelled with an implicit ex post rate to GDP and allocated between European Union (EU) institutions and the government by calculating the amounts accruing to foreigners as the product of the corresponding implicit tax rates times the total payments and computing the government receipts residually.

Profits—or the gross operating surplus—is the residual category. It is allocated to the different institutional sectors according to exogenous shares, with NFCs' profits determined residually.

## Private Sector

### *Households*

Households collect their income from production—which is the sum of domestic salaries, mixed income, and operating surplus. These are determined in the production account, with the amount of profits accruing to households given by an exogenous share in total profits.

For all domestic sectors, primary income is given by income from production, plus income from capital obtained from other sectors, less payments made to other sectors (eq. 8.2). Given the balance sheet in Table 8.1, the household sector capital income received is the sum of interest (on their holdings of bank deposits, public debt, banks debt instruments, and foreign assets), dividends (on their stocks of firms' and banks' shares), and other net capital income. Households also pay interest incomes on the stock of loans—for both consumer credit and mortgages—and rent from land ownership to the government.

$$primary\ income = income\ from\ production + net\ capital\ income\ received\ /\ paid \tag{8.2}$$

To comply with the principles of SFC modelling, capital incomes are computed by multiplying the current interest rate to the opening (i.e., end-of-last-period) stock of wealth. For example, interest received by households is as in (8.4).

Notice that sometimes a residual variable is needed to keep consistency. This is because we computed a single interest rate—or rate of return—for each financial asset and obtained the flow of income by multiplying the appropriate interest rate with our measure of the opening stock. This implied a difference from the measure of income from capital published in the non-financial accounts of institutional sectors.

$$INTR_{hh} = \left(r_t^{deps} \cdot DEPS_{hh,\,t-1} + r_t^{b} \cdot B_{hh,\,t-1} + r_t^{bb} \cdot BB_{hh,\,t-1} + r_t^{f} \cdot F_{hh,\,t-1}\right) - DISC\_INT \qquad (8.3)$$

For the private sector, disposable income is given by adding net current transfers to primary income (8.4). For the household sector, it is obtained by adding pension payments and other net transfers to primary income and subtracting social contributions and tax payments. We determine total pension receipts by households as the sum of the payments made by the other sectors, which are determined through exogenous shares in total payment. Taxes are generated by the model from an average ex post implicit tax rate on the sum of household primary income and pensions received. Social contributions—paid to all other domestic sectors—are computed applying an implicit ex post rate on household income from production.

$$disposable\ income = primary\ income + net\ current\ transfers\ received\ /\ paid \qquad (8.4)$$

Private sector saving is the sum of disposable income and the variations in pension entitlements, minus final consumption (8.5). For the household sector, the variations in pension entitlements are completely determined by the payments of the other productive sectors, while final consumption (as obtained from the sectoral accounts) is given by consumption from the National Income and Product Accounts (NIPA) and a discrepancy.[8]

$$Saving = disposable\ income + variations\ in\ pension\ entitlements - final\ consumption \qquad (8.5)$$

Following Godley and Lavoie (2007) and the common practice in the SFC literature, we select the determinants of consumption to be coherent with a dynamic process of adjustment towards a stable stock-flow norm between household income and wealth. For the econometric specification,[9] we adopt a pragmatic approach, taking care of the order of integration of each variable in the models. In the case of consumption, we use an error correction approach, estimating separately the long-run coefficients linking real consumption per capita to real disposable income and wealth per capita, and a dynamic specification where we find that share prices also play a role.

Using the fully modified OLS (FMOLS) approach, we find cointegration among real consumption per capita, real disposable income per capita, and the opening stock of real wealth, as well as the interest rate on consumer credit after 2008. We find a structural break in the propensity to consume out of disposable income in the first quarter of 2009, with an increase in such propensity after that date.[10] Using symbols, the error correction term (CONSK_CE) is given by:

$$CONSK\_CE = \frac{CONSK}{POP} - f\left(\frac{YD_{hh}}{POP\rho p^{cons}};\ \frac{NFA\_HP_{hh}}{POP\rho p^{cons}} + \frac{\mathrm{KHK}}{POP};\ r^{blcc}\right) \qquad (8.6)$$

In the short run, the changes in real consumption per capita depend positively on disposable income $(YD_{hh})$ and changes in domestic share prices $\left(sp^{it}\right)$, and negatively on the interest rate on short-term loans to households $\left(r^{blcc}\right)$.

$$\Delta\frac{CONSK}{POP} = -\rho \cdot CONSK\_CE_{t-1} + \sum_{i=1}^{k}\beta_i \cdot \Delta\frac{CONSK_{t-i}}{POP_{t-i}} + \sum_{i=0}^{k}\gamma_i \cdot \Delta\frac{YD_{hh,\,t-i}}{POP_{t-i} \cdot p^{cons}_{t-i}} + \sum_{i=1}^{k}\delta_i \cdot \Delta SP\_IT_{t-i} + \sum_{i=1}^{k}\varphi_i \cdot \Delta r^{blcc}{}_{t-i} \tag{8.7}$$

For the short-run specifications we adopted the general-to-specific approach: starting from a general model in terms of dynamics, we tested the restrictions on nonsignificant parameters to find the final parsimonious model.

Finally, the private sector net lending position (8.8) is obtained by adding (subtracting) the transactions related to taxes and transfers on capital accounts and subtracting investments in real assets—which are split between gross fixed capital formation, changes in inventories, and the acquisitions of non-produced, nonfinancial assets.

$$\textit{Net lending} = \textit{saving} + \textit{net capital transfers received / paid} - \textit{real investment} \tag{8.8}$$

Household investments in dwellings and in inventories depend on exogenous shares in total housing investments and total changes in inventories, respectively. In the long run, real investment in new houses (eq. 8.9) reacts negatively to the existing stock of buildings (in real terms) and positively to the changes in disposable income in terms of the price of investments in new houses, which is consistent with a process of adjustment to a stable stock-flow ratio of housing wealth to income. The interest rate on mortgages also has a negative impact in the long term. We added three dummies to model structural breaks, as suggested by Eviews when running the appropriate tests.

We estimate the NIPA measure of the changes in inventories in real terms as a stock-flow adjustment towards a stable inventories-to-GDP ratio and link the sectoral account measure of real changes in inventories with the NIPA definition[11] to achieve accounting consistency. The stock of inventories at current prices is computed by multiplying the variable at constant prices by the GDP deflator. Finally, we differentiate our stock variable to obtain the relative flow.

$$\Delta GFCFK_h = f\left(\frac{YD_{hh,t-1}}{p^{gfcf}_{t-1}}; KHK; r^{blmo}\right) \tag{8.9}$$

We now turn to households' portfolio behaviour, i.e., how the changes in the net lending position translate into specular changes in the asset/liability structure of their balance sheet. As in all other sectors, net financial assets are determined (eq. 8.10) by cumulating net lending and net capital gains.[12]

$$\textit{Net financial assets} = \textit{opening stock of financial assets} + \textit{net lending} + \textit{net capital gains} \quad (8.10)$$

We define households' illiquid assets as the sum of their stocks of banks' equities and shares, government bonds, NFC shares, and foreign assets (eq. 8.11). Finally, we have a residual category, "other net financial assets," which is determined as a portfolio adjustment (eq. 8.12).

$$FASSETS_{hh} = BB_{hh} + EB_{hh} + EN_{hh} + F_{hh} \quad (8.11)$$

$$ONFA_{hh} = NFA_{hh} + BLCC + BLMO - (DEPS_{hh} + MB_{hh}) - FASSETS_{hh} \quad (8.12)$$

In the model, it is money—and thus *liquidity*—that links the past, the present, and the future, as in Keynes (1936). Thus, the household's first decision is about how much money they want to hold in liquid form (either banknotes or deposits at banks) in the future—which depends on economic activity, the unemployment rate, and a dummy for the sovereign debt crisis (eq. 8.13)—and how to split the cash between the two, which is done with a simple ratio determined by a trend and an autoregressive process (eq. 8.14).

$$\frac{DEPS_{hh} + MB_{hh}}{YD_{hh}} = f \quad (8.13)$$

$$\frac{\mathrm{MB_{hh}}}{\mathrm{DEPS_{hh}}} = \mathrm{f} \quad (8.14)$$

The next decision faced by households is how much debt they want to take on. In the model, households demand bank loans either to finance their housing investment through mortgages—the flow[13] of which (relative to disposable income) is driven by household residential investment, the interest rate on mortgages, the existing stock of mortgage debt, and mortgages write-offs (eq. 8.15)—or for consumption purposes, which depends on consumption relative to income and the interest rate on consumer credit (eq. 8.16)[14].

$$\frac{VBLMO}{YD_h} = f \quad (8.15)$$

$$\frac{BLCC - BLCC_{t-4}}{YD_h} = f \quad (8.16)$$

For the remaining demand for assets, our choice of methodology has been driven by what we may call a "pragmatic approach." This will be the focus of the next subsection.

***Households' Portfolios: Theory…***

Among the first proponents of the SFC approach was James Tobin (1969), whose portfolio theory of investment was later adopted by Godley—although from a post-Keynesian perspective—and integrated into SFC modelling (Godley and Lavoie 2007).

Suppose we have a closed system, with three financial assets (cash, bills, and bonds). A key assumption of SFC models is that households make a two-stage decision (Keynes 1936, p.166). First, they decide how much to save out of income. Second, they decide how to allocate their wealth (including the newly acquired wealth). The decision happens in the same time period, but they still do follow a hierarchical order: "The consumption decision determines the size of the (expected) end-of-period stock of wealth; the portfolio decision determines the allocation of the (expected) stock of wealth" (Godley and Lavoie 2007, p.103) Thus, the difference between disposable income and consumption is equal to the change in total wealth.

How shall households allocate their wealth between the different assets? Brainard and Tobin (1968) and Tobin (1969) proposed a simple theory, which added the transaction demand for money to the Keynesian story of liquidity preference.

$$\frac{H_d}{V^e} = \lambda_{10} + \lambda_{12} \cdot r^B + \lambda_{13} \cdot ERr_{BL} + \lambda_{14} \cdot \left(YD_r^e / V^e\right)$$

$$\frac{B_d}{V^e} = \lambda_{20} + \lambda_{22} \cdot r^B + \lambda_{23} \cdot ERr_{BL} + \lambda_{24} \cdot \left(YD_r^e / V^e\right)$$

$$\frac{(pBL \cdot BL)}{V^e} = \lambda_{30} + \lambda_{32} \cdot r^B + \lambda_{33} \cdot ERr_{BL} + \lambda_{34} \cdot \left(YD_r^e / V^e\right)$$

Or, in matrix form:

$$\begin{bmatrix} H_d \\ B_d \\ BL_d \cdot pBL \end{bmatrix} = \begin{bmatrix} \lambda_{10} \\ \lambda_{20} \\ \lambda_{30} \end{bmatrix} V^e + \begin{bmatrix} \lambda_{11} & \lambda_{12} & \lambda_{13} \\ \lambda_{21} & \lambda_{22} & \lambda_{23} \\ \lambda_{31} & \lambda_{32} & \lambda_{33} \end{bmatrix} \begin{bmatrix} 0 \\ \mathrm{r}^{\mathrm{B}} \\ \mathrm{ERr}_{\mathrm{BL}} \end{bmatrix} V^e + \begin{bmatrix} \lambda_{14} \\ \lambda_{24} \\ \lambda_{34} \end{bmatrix} YD_r^e$$

Households want to hold a certain share $(\lambda_{i0})$ of their wealth in the form of asset i, but this proportion is modified by the expected rate of return on this asset and by the level of expected (regular) disposable income. The 0 in the rate of return vector reflects the fact that cash does not bear interest. When making their portfolio allocations, households are concerned about the interest rate on bills $\left(r^B\right)$, which is determined at the end of the period and will generate the future interest payments, and by the expected return on bonds $(ERr_{BL})$.

The coefficients in each equation follow from the assumption that people make consistent decisions on wealth allocation. Thus, the sum of the constants must be unity, as the decision to hold one asset implies the decision to hold the remaining wealth in the other two. In the same way, the sum of the coefficients with respect to each argument of the portfolio equations must be zero: if a change in interest (or income) makes people wish to hold a higher proportion of cash, it implies that they want to hold a lower proportion of bills and bonds (and vice versa). This is the adding-up constraint (Tobin 1969): if there are $m$ assets, one needs to specify $m-1$ as the demand function (the last one being implied by the rest), thus assuring that any increase in a stock implies a corresponding decrease in some other, and the same applies to the relative rate of returns (i.e., an increase in one rate implies that, at least, there is a specular change in another).

### *Households' Portfolios: ... and Practice*

When dealing with real-world statistics, however, it is difficult to estimate from the data (given their structure, the available time span, the presence of structural breaks, etc.) the appropriate relations—if they exist—between the relative rate of returns and the demand and supply for different assets and liabilities. Nevertheless, the principles behind Tobin's theory shall hold. We will now illustrate the procedures we adopted to build the rate of return (RoR) matrix using our data for Italy.

We defined the growth rates of prices of financial assets $X$ ($ipX$) as the rate of change in their price over the last quarter (8.17). The return on assets $X$ ($raX$) is computed as the sum of the change in their price and the relative interest rate (8.18) and—for NFC shares only—we use the flow of dividends paid by NFCs relative to the existing stock of shares (8.19). We define the stock of each asset using the (estimated) portfolio ratios in total illiquid assets (8.20) and assume households to have adaptive expectations with respect to the RoR (four lags with diminishing weights, in eq. 8.20).

$$ipX = pX \,/\, pX_{t-1} - 1 \qquad (8.17)$$
$$raX = d(pX) \,/\, pX_{t-1} + rX \qquad (8.18)$$
$$raEN = d(pEN) \,/\, pEN_{t-1} + DIVPnfc \,/\, E_{t-1} \qquad (8.19)$$
$$X = rpX \cdot FASS_{t-1} \cdot (X_{t-1}) \qquad (8.20)$$
$$raX^{e} = 0.4 \cdot raX_{t-1} + 0.3 \cdot raX_{t-2} + 0.2 \cdot raX_{t-3} + 0.1 \cdot raX_{t-4} \qquad (8.21)$$

Finally, following the theoretical discussion made above, we estimated a system formed by banks debt instruments, banks equities, firms' equities, government bonds, and foreign assets, against their respective rates of returns.

Even though the estimation results are far from definitive, we did find some meaningful relations: first, there is a negative relation between the RoR on government bonds and foreign assets and, second, a negative one between banks' obligations and banks' shares, which is however less strong. Given the result of the system estimation, we found it sensible to only endogenize the equations for the portfolio ratios ($rp$) of bonds (8.22), banks' debt instruments (8.23), and foreign assets (8.24), and project the rest exogenously. Results are shown below.

$$rpB = f\left(raF^e; raBB^e\right) \quad (8.22)$$

$$rpBB = f\left(AR1,4; raEB^e; raB^e\right) \quad (8.23)$$

$$rpF = f\left(raB^e; raF^e\right) \quad (8.24)$$

### *Nonfinancial Corporations*

Recall that NFCs' profits are determined residually from total profits generated in production.

Firms' primary income, as before, is given by adding to the profits originated in production the incomes received (and paid) from capital, given the structure of their balance sheet. NFCs receive interest income on their stock of deposits and public debt, dividends from their holdings of foreign firms' shares, and other net capital incomes. They also pay interest incomes on their loans, dividends on the shares sold domestically and abroad,[15] and rent from land ownership to the government.

NFCs' disposable income is equal to the sum of primary income, other current net transfers, and social contributions received, after deducting the direct taxes paid domestically and abroad and the payments in pensions. Net current transfers are the sum of total transfers net of benefits (paid and received). We assume that NFCs pay direct taxes as a fixed share on their profits, with the amount paid abroad determined as a fixed share on the wages paid to foreigners and the amounts paid domestically determined residually. Pension payments and social contributions are determined through exogenous shares in households' total receipts/payments.

Again, NFCs' savings result from the addition of the revaluations in pension entitlements to disposable income, with the former given by an exogenous ratio for the share of NFC payments in total payments in pensions.

Finally, to obtain the NFCs' net lending position, we first need to add to savings the net transfers related to other transactions in capital accounts paid by the government, the other net transfers, and the taxes on capital transactions paid domestically and abroad. We then need to further subtract the firms' investment in gross fixed capital, changes in inventories, and other non-produced, nonfinancial assets. Firms' investment in physical capital is later split among (real) investment in machinery and nonresidential buildings through an exogenous fixed ratio in total investment, while investment in inventories is computed residually by subtracting other sectors' investment from total changes in inventories.

Portfolio adjustments for the nonfinancial business sector are meant to determine the additional demand for credit from banks (8.31)— meaning that firms will first use their own funds to finance investments and take on new debt to finance the gap. On the asset side, the stock of bank deposits is modelled as a ratio to the wage bill (8.25). This ratio has been increasing since the start of the eurozone crisis, but it will be projected exogenously in this version of the model.

The demand for government bonds is interpreted as an additional demand for liquid assets, and it is therefore modelled with respect to the stock of deposits (8.26). In other words, firms demand liquid assets with respect to their current expenses on labour, splitting their liquid assets between deposits and government bonds. In principle, a higher interest rate on bonds relative to the rate on deposits should increase the share of bonds in firms' portfolio, but the data are not congruent with this, so that this ratio will also be projected exogenously.

The flows of outgoing foreign direct investment (*VFDIO*) and incoming foreign direct investment (*VFDII*) are both projected exogenously as the result of domestic and foreign firms' strategies ruled by animal spirits (in eq. 8.27 and eq. 8.28, respectively).

Other net financial assets ($ONFA_{nfc}$, in eq. 8.29) are negative and growing in size, and therefore in the next version of the model they deserve a better treatment as additional sources of funding. For the time being, they are projected exogenously. Finally, new issues of equities (*VEN*, in eq. 8.30) are projected exogenously as an autonomous decision of firms.

$$DEPS_{nfc} = ratio_{nfc}^{deps} \cdot (WB_{t-1}) \quad (8.25)$$

$$B_{nfc} = ratio_{nfc}^{B} \cdot DEPS_{nfc,t-1} \quad (8.26)$$

$$FDIO = FDIO_{t-1} + VFDIO + p^{fdio} \cdot FDIO_{t-1} \quad (8.27)$$

$$FDII = FDII_{t-1} + VFDII + p^{fdii} \cdot FDII_{t-1} \quad (8.28)$$

$$ONFA_{nfc} = ONFA_{nfc,t-1} + VONFA_{nfc} + NKG\_ONFA_{nfc} \quad (8.29)$$

$$EN = EN_{t-1} + VEN + p^{en} \cdot VEN_{t-1} \quad (8.30)$$

$$BLFIRMS = BLFIRMS_{t-1} + \left(\Delta DEPS_{nfc} + \Delta B_{nfc} + \Delta FDIO + \Delta ONFA_{nfc} - \Delta NFA_{nfc}\right) - \Delta EN - \Delta FDII \quad (8.31)$$

***Financial Corporations***

Financial corporations' gross operating surplus is determined by their share in total profits, while adding net income from capital[16] yields primary income. Banks collect interest income on the outstanding stocks of loans issued to the private sector, the public debt held and the stock of foreign assets, dividends on their stock of NFCs' (domestic) shares, and other net capital incomes (net of FDIs). They also pay interest income on central bank advances, deposits, and the stock of liabilities issued. Finally, they pay dividends on their issued shares.

Adding the other current net transfers and social contributions received, and deducting the direct taxes paid and pension payments yields banks' disposable income.

As for the rest of the private sector, financial corporations' savings are the result of the addition of the revaluations in pension entitlements to disposable income, with the variations in pension entitlements given by an exogenous ratio times total payments in pensions.

Finally, banks' net lending position is obtained by adding (subtracting) the transactions related to taxes and transfers on capital accounts and subtracting investments in real assets—split as usual between gross fixed capital formation, changes in inventories, and the acquisitions of non-produced, nonfinancial assets. Banks' investment in machinery and nonresidential dwellings are determined by an exogenous ratio, while the change in inventories depends on exogenous shares in total changes in inventories. Recall that we removed the net lending position of the central bank from the accounts of monetary financial institutions.

We follow Godley and Lavoie (2007) in assuming that banks fulfil the demand for loans from household and nonfinancial firms and adjust their level of reserves accordingly, with the central bank accommodating. As we will examine in some detail when discussing the central bank, the model becomes more complex when QE starts, since banks will adapt their portfolio whenever cheap credit is available from central banks' QE operations.

The monetary base on the asset side of banks' balance sheets $\left(MB_{fc}\right)$ is split into two components (8.32): the reserve requirement ($MB_{fc}^{rr}$, in eq. 8.33)—which varies with the reserve ratio to deposits $\left(\alpha_1^{res}\right)$ and the share of sight deposits on total deposits $\left(\alpha_2^{rr}\right)$—and the residual liquidity $\left(MB_{fc}^{er}\right)$. Residual liquidity may be driven, on the one hand, by the demand for excess liquidity connected to financial instability, but on the other it has been the outcome of unconventional monetary policy (QE). As the ECB buys government bonds and other financial assets from banks in exchange for liquidity, the banking sector as a whole cannot help but accumulate such liquidity. We therefore model the "excess" stock of monetary base $\left(MB_{fc}^{er}\right)$ as the residual in banks' portfolio adjustment (8.34). Moreover, this increase in excess reserves translates mechanically into a worsening of the overall Target2 balance, since most QE operations involve cross-border transactions.

Consumer credit, mortgages, and loans to firms are all supplied by banks on demand. For firms' equities (eqs. 8.35 and 8.36), we assume that the financial sector is the residual buyer for the new emissions, while the evolution of the stock is linked to our spread measure. However, this has no implication on how the market price of equities is determined in the model. The issues of new bank equities ($VEB$), in turn, are projected exogenously as an independent decision of banks (8.37), and we assumed that the supply of equities is matched by households' demand.

We assume banks to clear the market for government bonds (eqs. 8.38 and 8.39). It should be noted, however, that most newly issued bonds have been purchased by the ECB through its QE operations, and this situation will last until the programme ends, implying that, in the current state of affairs, there is no market to clear. With respect to the demand for foreign assets ($F_{fc}$, eq. 8.40), we model the flow ($VF_{fc}$, eq. 8.41) as a function of the interest rate on government bonds $\left(r^b\right)$, the spread between Italian and German Treasuries (*SPREAD*), the (changes in) exchange rate against the US\$ $\left(xr^{it\_us}\right)$, and the flow of interest income paid by the foreign sector relative to the stock of assets.

Finally, as for all other sectors, the net change in other financial assets $\left(VONFA_{fc}\right)$ will be left exogenous, and the end-of-period stocks will be given by the usual accounting relationship (8.42).

$$MB_{fc} = MB_{fc}^{rr} + MB_{fc}^{er} \tag{8.32}$$

$$MB_{fc}^{rr} = \alpha_1^{res} \cdot \alpha_2^{sdeps} \cdot DEPS \tag{8.33}$$

$$\begin{aligned} MB_{fc}^{er} = {} & \Delta\left(NFA_{fc}\right) - \Delta\left(BLCC + BLMO + BLFIRMS + B_{fc} + EN_{fc} + F_{fc} + ONFA_{fc}\right) \\ & + \Delta(FC\_liab) - \Delta MB_{fc}^{rr} \end{aligned} \tag{8.34}$$

$$VEN_{fc} = VEN - \left(VEN_{hh} + VEN_{gvt}\right) \tag{8.35}$$

$$EN_{fc} = f\,(SPREAD) \tag{8.36}$$

$$EB = EB_{t-1} + VEB + p^{eb} \cdot EB_{t-1} \tag{8.37}$$

$$B_{fc} = B_{fc,t-1} + VB_{fc} + p^b \cdot B_{fc,t-1} \tag{8.38}$$

$$VB_{fc} = VB - \left(VB_{hh} + VB_{nfc} + VB_{row} + VB_{cb}\right) \tag{8.39}$$

$$F_{fc} = F_{fc,t-1} + VF_{fc} + p^f \cdot F_{fc,t-1} + DISC\_VF_{fc} \tag{8.40}$$

$$VF_{fc} = f\left(r^b, SPREAD, xr^{it\_us}, \frac{INTP_{fc,t-1}}{F_{t-1}}\right) \tag{8.41}$$

$$ONFA_{fc} = ONFA_{fc,t-1} + VONFA_{fc} + NKG\_ONFA_{fc} \tag{8.42}$$

## Public Sector

### *Central Bank*

The central bank only collects interest on the stocks of advances lent to banks and on the stocks of government bonds and foreign liabilities it holds. We assumed that all these interest streams are passed to the government sector so that the net lending position of the central bank is zero.

Following the current accounting conventions, some operations made by the central bank as part of the European System of Central Banks (ESCB) are treated as operations with the rest of the world (RoW), but the monetary liabilities in Target2 appear as part of the liabilities of the national central bank.

To model base money in a currency union, it is reasonable to assume that in normal times the demand for the monetary base, coming from households, banks, and foreign institutions, is accommodated by the central bank, as in equation (8.43a). The change in the monetary base would in turn be related to changes on the asset side, with the different components determined by the demand for liquidity coming from households, the reserve requirements needed by banks, and the part of external imbalances that are not covered by changes in other net assets vis-à-vis the RoW. Indeed, this is in line with the theoretical discussions of central bank monetary policy made by Godley and Lavoie (2007), Lavoie (2014), the Bank of England (McLeay, Amar and Thomas 2014), and the ECB itself (European Central Bank 2017).

$$MB = MB_{hh} + MB_{fc} + MB_{T2} \tag{8.43a}$$

In response to the Great Recession, however, the ECB started adopting "unconventional" monetary policies. Through its QE operations, the ESCB supplied central bank reserves well above the demand for liquidity stemming from the banking sector, inducing a sizeable increase in base money (and excess reserves). This mechanism started with the bank refinancing operations and was further enhanced with the launch of the asset purchase programmes (APPs).[17] When purchasing assets, the ECB supplies reserves to the banking system and,

> since banks are typically the only entities, apart from central government, that hold deposit accounts with the central bank, purchases are always settled through them, regardless of who the ultimate seller is. Thus, purchases conducted under the APP resulted in a mechanic, direct increase in base money.
>
> (European Central Bank 2017, p.64)

When running unconventional policies, it is thus the central bank, through its operations, that determines the amount of reserves in the system, instead of them being demand-driven through the net demand for credit. Most importantly, banks can do nothing to reduce the amount of reserves. Only if banks' demand for compulsory reserves increases (because of increases in deposits) should the stock of excess reserves diminish. Therefore, the total monetary base is fully determined by central banks' decisions to purchase assets (open market operations, targeted long-term refinancing operations [TLTROs], etc.).

In the presence of QE, thus, it is sensible to split the monetary base on the asset side of banks' balance sheets into two components (8.32). The first one is the reserve requirement (8.33), which varies with the reserve ratio to deposits $\left(\alpha_1^{res}\right)$ and the share of sight deposits in total deposits $\left(\alpha_2^{sdeps}\right)$. The second component is in turn represented by residual (excess) liquidity (8.34). While on the one hand this may have been driven by the demand for liquidity connected to financial instability, on the other it has been the outcome of unconventional monetary policy.

Thus, given that the ESCB has been purchasing Treasuries and other assets from the financial system in exchange for monetary base, so that some components of the monetary base are the mirror of QE operations rather than those arising from the demand for liquidity, we tentatively assume that the end-of-period stock of monetary base is determined by the asset side in the central bank's balance sheet (8.43), with net central bank financial assets determined exogenously, but taking into account net capital gains.

The value of gold reserves is computed considering the international price of gold, while the changes in the stock (i.e., net acquisition of gold) are treated as exogenous, and are relatively rare (8.44). A discrepancy ($DISC\_VGOLD$) is needed, as the revaluation of the stock of gold is not exactly equal to the theoretical estimate.

Changes in central bank advances (8.45) have been split into two components to better differentiate monetary operations and to disentangle the ECB's role from that of the Italian central bank. We subtract QE-related operations (mainly LTRO, $DADVQE1$) from total advances to get the Bank of Italy's ordinary operations ($DADVNET$), and both will be exogenously determined in the model.

We assume that the central bank's acquisition of government bonds (eqs. 8.46 and 8.47) is given partly by the second phase of the QE programme ($DBCBQE2$) and, for the rest ($DBCBNET$), by the central bank's standard operations, with both components determined exogenously. This assumption does not imply that the central bank is purchasing Treasuries on the primary market, nor that it is controlling the interest rate on Treasuries, which is governed by another equation in the model—one that links the interest rate on Italian bonds to the German rate, plus a spread that depends on financial conditions.

The net demand for foreign financial assets from the central bank (8.48) is currently left exogenous, as well as the net change in other financial assets, while the end-of-period stocks will be given by the usual accounting relationship.

$$MB = (GOLD + B_{cb} + F_{cb} + ONFA_{cb} + ADV) - NFA_{cb} \tag{8.43}$$

$$GOLD = GOLD_{t-1} + VGOLD + p^{gold} \cdot GOLD_{t-1} + DISC\_VGOLD \tag{8.44}$$

$$ADV = ADV_{t-1} + DADVNET + DADVQE1 \tag{8.45}$$

$$VB_{cb} = DBCBNET + DBCBQE2 \tag{8.46}$$

$$B_{cb} = B_{cb,t-1} + VB_{cb} + p^{b} \cdot B_{cb,t-1} + DISC\_VB_{cb} \tag{8.47}$$

$$F_{cb} = F_{cb,t-1} + VF_{cb} + p^{f} \cdot F_{cb,t-1} \tag{8.48}$$

$$ONFA_{cb} = ONFA_{cb,t-1} + VONFA_{cb} + NKG\_ONFA_{cb} \tag{8.49}$$

### *Government*

The public sector income from production is the sum of the indirect taxes collected and gross operating surplus minus subsidies to production.

Indirect taxes and subsidies paid by the government are computed residually from total payments after deducting foreign institutions' receipts.

To incomes from production, we add the transaction in capital incomes to get to government primary income. The government collects interest income on its stock of deposits, dividends from domestic shares held, and rental incomes from the private nonfinancial sector and pays interest on public debt to all other sectors.

Government disposable income is given by adding to primary income the direct taxes received, social contributions (determined residually from other sector receipts), plus the sum of other current net transfers and central bank seignorage, and finally deducting pension payments.

Public sector savings are the result of what is left of disposable income after the outlays in collective and individual consumption, which are determined as a fixed share in (real) total government expenditures.

Finally, the net lending position of the public sector is, as before, the difference between savings and investments, accounting for transfers and taxes on capital account, as well as government investments and changes in inventories, which are both determined by exogenous ratios.

When compared to those discussed above, the government sector's financial operations are quite straightforward. Indeed, the government holds deposits, mainly to pay out wages to public employees, and the flows are estimated as a function of government expenditures over deposits (eqs. 8.50 and 8.51).[18] We assumed that the government buys all the residual shares of domestic firms (eqs. 8.52 and 8.53) while the demand for ONFA is, as usual, left exogenous (8.54). Finally, it issues new bonds to cover the deficit (8.55).

$$DEPS_{gvt} = DEPS_{gvt,t-1} + VDEPS_{gvt} + DEPS\_WO_{gvt} \tag{8.50}$$

$$VDEPS_{gvt} = f(G) \tag{8.51}$$

$$VEN_{gvt} = VEN - \left(VEN_{hh} + VEN_{fc}\right) \tag{8.52}$$

$$EN_{gvt} = EN_{gvt,t-1} + VEN_{gvt} + p^{en} \cdot EN_{gvt,t-1} + DISC\_VEN_{gvt} \tag{8.53}$$

$$ONFA_{gvt} = ONFA_{gvt,t-1} + VONFA_{gvt} + NKG\_ONFA_{gvt} \tag{8.54}$$

$$VB = -NETLENDF_{gvt} + VDEPS_{gvt} + VEN_{gvt} + VONFA_{gvt} \tag{8.55}$$

### *The Rest of the World*

The RoW collects wages and incomes from trade and indirect taxes,[19] capital incomes in the form of interest, returns from FDI, and other capital incomes, while it pays interests on the issued liabilities and dividends in the forms of returns on FDI.

To primary incomes, we add the incomes from taxation, the other transfers in the current account, and the social contributions received, subtracting the pension payments to yield disposable income. Net lending, as usual, is determined by adding to the RoW's disposable income the taxes paid and received, and the other transfers on capital accounts.

At this stage of model development, we decided to treat the foreign sector as the residual buyer for some of our financial assets. This aspect will have to be improved in future releases. The RoW holds domestic banks' deposits as liquidity for trade (8.56). It buys the residual supply of domestic banks' securities (8.57), while the acquisition of new government bonds is currently left exogenous (8.58). Moreover, we assumed that the demands for foreign assets coming from the domestic sectors are completely matched (8.59).

Finally, the RoW's ONFA are determined as the sum of all other sectors (8.60), while the buffer stock is represented here by the Target2 balance (8.61).

$$DEPS_{row} = ratio_{row}^{deps} \cdot (XGS + MGS) \tag{8.56}$$

$$BB_{row} = BB - BB_{hh} \tag{8.57}$$

$$VB_{row} = d\left(B_{row} - p^{b} \cdot B_{row,t-1}\right) - DISC\_VB_{row} \tag{8.58}$$

$$VF = VF_{hh} + VF_{fc} + VF_{cb} \tag{8.59}$$

$$ONFA_{row} = -\left(ONFA_{hh} + ONFA_{nfc} + ONFA_{fc} + ONFA_{cb} ONFA_{gvt}\right) \tag{8.60}$$

$$\begin{aligned} MB_{T2} = {} & NFA_{row} - (DEPS_{row} + BB_{row} + B_{row} + FDII + ONFA_{row}) \\ & + (GOLD + FDIO + F) \end{aligned} \tag{8.61}$$

***Trade***

We now introduce the trade block of the model. We model imports of goods and services with an error correction model (ECM) depending, in the long run, on domestic demand and relative prices and, in the short run, on domestic demand only. We added a dummy for a structural break occurring in 2009Q2 (8.62). The imports deflator (eq. 8.65) is modelled as an ECM depending on foreign prices in local currencies (LPLC) and the exchange rate against the US$. We find a structural break in the growth rate of import prices with the introduction of the euro in 1999 and we use a dummy variable for 2009Q1 to account for the extraordinary drop in trade after the financial crisis; both breaks are found to be statistically significant.

$$\mathrm{MGSK} = \mathrm{f}\left(GDPK; \frac{p^{mgs}}{p^{gdp}}\right) \tag{8.62}$$

$$p^{mgs} = f\left(LPLC; xr; dum2009q1\right) \tag{8.63}$$

With respect to exports, considering the importance that export dynamics have always had for the Italian economy's performance, we decided to model separately the exports of goods (*XGK*) and services (*XSK*) (eqs. 8.64 and 8.65). Using the real exchange rate in our export equations does not provide useful results, since exports seem to react differently to changes in domestic prices, foreign prices, or the euro/dollar exchange rate. The reaction of export of services to foreign prices is unexpected and will require further investigation for a better specification in future work.

Since we model exports of goods separately from that of services, we need to obtain their deflators.[20] Starting from the former, the export deflator for goods (8.66) is modelled as an ECM depending on unit labour costs (*ULC*) in the long run and on foreign prices only in the short run. Contrarily, we find that the deflator of exports of services (8.67) depends solely on foreign prices in the long run, while it also depends on the exchange rate in the short run, with a significant effect following the euro's introduction.

$$XGK = f\left(LWDEM; xr^{it\_use}; LPLC; p^{gdp}\right) \tag{8.64}$$

$$XSK = f\left(LWDEM; xr^{it\_use}; p^{gdp} - LPLC; p^{gdp}\right) \tag{8.65}$$

$$p^{xg} = f\left(\frac{WAGEU}{PROD}; LPLC\right) \tag{8.66}$$

$$p^{xs} = f\left(LPLC; xr^{it\_use}\right) \tag{8.67}$$

***Labour Market***

The treatment of the labour market is rather rudimentary at this stage.

Population is projected exogenously, and the share of the working-age population is obtained through exogenous parameters, identifying those below the working age and retired people. Retired people are estimated from the difference between the population above 8.64, and those above 8.64 who are reported as employed or unemployed. The size of the labour force is also given by an exogenous participation rate. Our attempts to model the participation rate as a function of the state of the business cycle or other labour market indicators have not been successful yet. The participation rate has been increasing over time since the 1980s, from around 58% to the current 66%, but the increase in the employment rate has not been as substantial.

Employment (8.68) is determined from a simple relation to real GDP through average labour productivity (8.69), which we model as a function of the business cycle and of part-time workers' share in the labour force. For both the long- and short-run specifications we found the presence of a structural break related to the Great Financial Crisis (in 2008Q3).

$$EMP = GDPK \ / \ PROD \tag{8.68}$$

$$PROD = f\left(GDPK; ratio^{npti}; PROD; PROD\_CE; \text{"2008}q3\text{"}\right) \tag{8.69}$$

Unemployment (8.70) is thus a residual, and the unemployment rate (8.71) follows. We also compute the U6 measure of unemployment (8.73) by considering those marginally attached to the labour force (8.72) and those working part-time for economic reasons (8.74). While the first category is left exogenous at this stage of model development, we model the ratio of part-time workers in the labour force as a function of the business cycle and the unemployment rate (8.75). This variable enters our equation for the extended unemployment rate, but also that of productivity, so that increases in labour market fragmentation will translate into lower employment.

$$UNEMP = LF - EMP \tag{8.70}$$

$$UR = UNEMP \,/\, LF \tag{8.71}$$

$$LFP = \frac{LF \cdot ratio^{lfp}}{\left(1 - ratio^{lfp}\right)} \tag{8.72}$$

$$UR6 = \frac{(UNEMP + LFP + NPTI)}{(LF + LFP)} \tag{8.73}$$

$$NPTI = ratio^{npti} \cdot EMP \tag{8.74}$$

$$ratio^{npti} = f\,(UR; TREND; \text{"}2015q3\text{"}) \tag{8.75}$$

The level of employment, together with the average wage (*wageu*), determines the wage bill (8.76). The average wage, finally, is estimated as a function of domestic and foreign prices (through the imports deflator) and the past unemployment rate (8.77). Two dummies for 2003Q3 and 2005Q4 are introduced to consider two outliers (upward jumps in wages). The long-run elasticity of nominal wages to prices is one,[21] while import prices do not seem to have a long-run impact. An increase in the unemployment rate is found to have an impact on the level of wages (rather than on wage inflation, as in the Phillips curve). The short-run specification needs to be investigated further, since we find a negative short-run impact of price inflation on wage inflation.

$$WB = wageu \cdot EMP \tag{8.76}$$

$$wageu = f\,\left(p^{foi},\, p^{mgs},\, ur\right) \tag{8.77}$$

The consumption deflator (8.78) is linked to our main price index through an ECM mechanism with a long-run elasticity of unity. We included a dummy for 2009Q1, which is found to be statistically significant.

$$p^{cons} = f\left(p^{foi}; pmgs; dum2009q1\right) \tag{8.78}$$

Finally, there are a number of equations describing the interest rate, implicit interest rates, and rates of return for our assets, used to link our variables to the main rates and variables and give a system-wide dynamic. Of course, most of these specifications may well be improved, but it is not the purpose of this work to come out with the "best" econometric outcomes, but rather to capture the major interrelations among our sectors and overall financial dynamics.

## Model Properties

### *Validation against Historical Data*

In this section, we will show how the model performs in replicating historical data. The model is solved for the period 2000q1 to 2018q4. We will only look at the most important variables, show some of the problems that emerge, and discuss how these may be resolved.

Starting with GDP, Figure 8.4 displays the evolution of real GDP, in volumes and annual growth rates, showing that our estimate satisfactorily replicates historical data. The single components of GDP, in nominal values,[22] are displayed in Figure 8.5. We overestimate consumption and investment for the period 2013–2016—thus leading to a higher GDP growth rate in the baseline for the relative period—and accurately track the dynamics of the other components of demand, with all trends clearly captured by the model.

Model performance is not as satisfactory for aggregate financial balances, i.e., the net lending/borrowing position of the institutional sectors.[23] We closely track the government balance (except for the period 2012–2016) and only the overall dynamics with respect to other sectors. In particular, we underestimate net lending for the household and NFC sectors in the last part of the sample and overestimate it for financial firms during the same period. This may be due to accumulation of errors in previous lines of the transaction matrix that accumulate into net lending. In future research, the simulation error can be reduced with better econometric estimates.

With respect to the labour market, the unemployment rate, productivity level, and nominal wages are tracked satisfactorily.

The model's ability to track financial stocks of assets and liabilities depends on whether the relevant estimated equations refer to stocks or flows. In the latter case, a statistical discrepancy between the fitted value and the actual value arising, say, from an outlier, will imply a shift in the level of the stock that may not revert to its historical level even if no large discrepancies appear in the remainder of the sample. This is the case for our simulation of loans to firms, for instance.[24] Overall, the model replicates the dynamics of financial flows and those of most other stocks reasonably well.

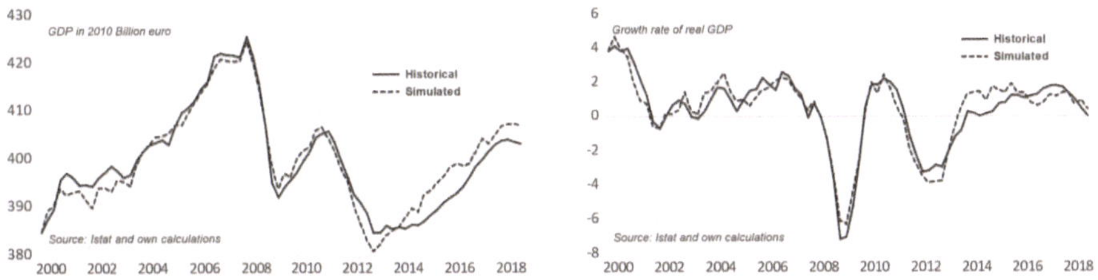


*Figure 8.4* Italy: real GDP.

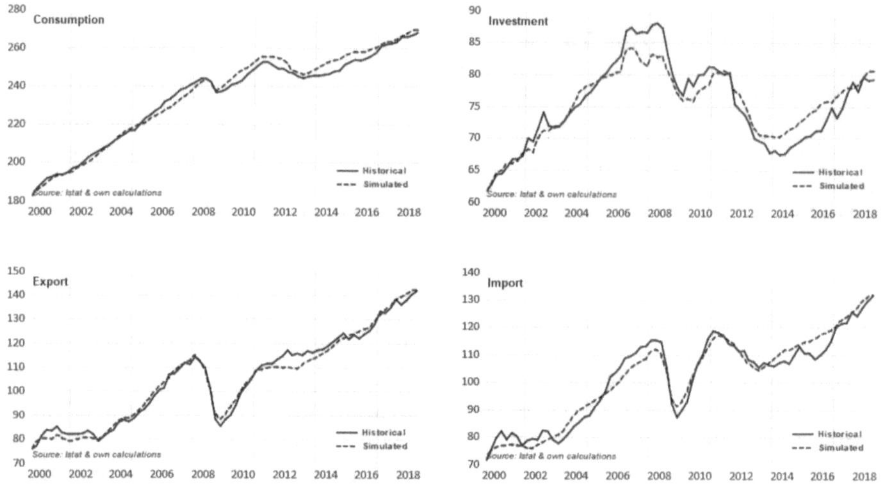


*Figure 8.5* Italy: Components of GDP. Billion euros.

Our price indicators—which include the deflators for all components of GDP—as well as our interest rates are all tracked in a satisfactory way in our in-sample simulation.

## Conclusions

In this chapter we have presented a new quarterly model for the Italian economy that consistently integrates real and financial markets following the empirical methodology pioneered by Wynne Godley known as "Stock-Flow Consistent approach."

However, Godley's empirical models have traditionally been much simpler, possibly for two reasons: the first is that, in the tradition of the "New Cambridge" approach, he was mainly interested in modelling the interrelation between the financial balance of the private sector as a whole and the financial balances of the public and foreign sectors. The other reason, connected to the first one, is that he often focused on countries with a large foreign deficit, which implies a leakage of aggregate demand that should be countered by an expansionary stance in the public sector, or else implies that aggregate demand can be sustained by the private sector only through increased borrowing from the other sectors, which will prove unsustainable in the long term.

The model presented here is an attempt to merge the SFC methodology for jointly tracking the real and financial sides of the economy to the methodology that was adopted for structural models by central banks around the world before the counter-revolution of rational expectations. Nowadays these structural models have evolved, incorporating microfoundations and rational expectations, which implies that monetary and financial markets can be treated separately. Given the failure of such models in projecting the dynamics that brought the Great Recession, we hope that the methodology suggested here can represent a starting point for a more robust alternative in structural modelling.

In our contribution we also show that the accounting structure of a detailed stock-flow model could—possibly should—be used by institutions producing financial and nonfinancial statistics for the institutional sectors to improve the quality of the data, which are currently affected by large discrepancies in measuring sectoral balances.

As the number of researchers interested in the construction of empirical SFC models is growing, in this chapter we have tried to show what type of practical problems arise and how they can be addressed using a pragmatic approach.

The strength of the model presented here is in the accounting consistency of all variables involved, as well as in the flexibility to handle changes in regimes, like those generated by the adoption of QE programmes from the ECB. The weaknesses to be overcome are related to the still-unsatisfactory treatment of portfolio management, since the Tobinesque approach from which we started was apparently not coherent with the dynamics of the different assets' rates of return. This will need to be addressed in future research.

Is it necessary to reach this level of complexity when building an empirical SFC model for a whole country? We plan to address this issue by comparing the properties of the current model with those of a simpler model. Intuitively, the structure of a model like the one we presented here needs a team for the regular updates of the databases, revision of the estimates, and overall model development, which, as mentioned, is a task that can be handled by institutions that regularly produce policy analysis, but not by a single independent researcher.

To conclude, we wish to note that the analysis of SFC models is usually completed by developing a medium-term out-of-sample projection to evaluate the model's multipliers and evaluate the model's response to the most important policy shocks. We performed this analysis in previous months with useful results, but given the current major shock affecting the Italian economy from the lockdown imposed to address the -19 epidemic, for which no macroeconomic data are yet available, we prefer to defer a description of policy experiments with this model to future research.

## Notes

1 Even though a first "national monetary balance sheet," produced by the BoI's research department led by Paolo Baffi, appeared in the 1948 Annual Governor's Report, see De Bonis and Gigliobianco (2012) for further details.

2 Data sources and the procedures used to estimate some model variables are reported in Zezza and Zezza (2020, appendix I).
3 See Gola et al. (2017).
4 See Zezza and Zezza (2020, appendix I) for details.
5 Which is the sum of short- and long-term instruments plus the shares of mutual funds issued by the RoW.
6 In what follows, we will use a K after the variable name (i.e., GDP*K*) to denote constant prices variables, otherwise variables are in nominal amounts. The subscripts "i" and "j" are used for institutional sectors and capital stocks, respectively.
7 For variables measured at constant prices we use the published figures at chained 2010 prices, which have the property that the sum of the components of real GDP does not sum up to the total, so that a residual (GDPKRES) must be introduced to keep consistency between variables at current and constant prices. We need a similar residual variable when we consider detailed components of demand, as is the case for investment and exports.
8 The discrepancy arises from the fact that we needed to seasonally adjust the data from the institutional accounts, while NIPA data were already seasonally adjusted.
9 For reasons of space we do not report the results of econometric estimates, and refer the reader to Zezza and Zezza (2020).
10 Real wealth per capita is not significant in the current specification, but we kept this variable, which has the right sign but a small magnitude, to respect the principle of convergence to a stable norm between wealth and income.
11 Inventories in national accounts are obtained residually and are not a good indicator for inventories in theoretical models. Therefore, we used a simple approach that ensures convergence to a stable stock-flow ratio of inventories to GDP. In future developments of the model, we will try to verify if inventories can be treated as a buffer when expectations on demand are introduced.
12 See Zezza and Zezza (2020, appendix I) for the details on the measurement and determination of capital gains.
13 We use V to denote flows, so that BLMO is the stock of mortgage loans, while VBLMO is the flow.
14 We found a positive relation between consumer credit and the relevant interest rate, which may suggest a Ponzi scheme.
15 With respect to dividends, we added the discrepancy from the X-12 procedure to NFC payments, $DIVP_{nfc}$.
16 When adjusting the series, we decided to add the discrepancies of the X-12 procedure to the interest received by financial corporations $\left(INTR_{fc}\right)$. This is so because financial institutions get almost half of the total interests paid and one should always try to get these discrepancies away from series that will enter the behavioural specifications' estimates, in particular those regarding the household and external sectors.
17 The main programmes adopted by the ECB consisted of two rounds of long-term refinancing operations (LTRO and TLTRO) and the APP, which substantially increased with the launch of the Public Sector Purchase Program (PSPP).
18 We computed an exogenous component for deposit write-offs to offset the discrepancies between the flow and the stock measures.
19 Paid only by NFCs.
20 It is worth noting, however, that the price elasticities that we found need more in-depth analysis.
21 The elasticity of wages to prices was larger than one, but since a test did not reject the hypothesis of a unit elasticity, we imposed this restriction.

22 We display here variables at current prices instead of constant prices so that the discrepancy is due to both the error in tracking the variable at constant prices and to the error in simulating prices.
23 Additional details are available from the authors upon request.
24 Deviations of simulated variables from their actual values have no impact when the model is used for simulation purposes, since such discrepancies are included automatically as additional exogenous variables, so that the baseline simulation replicates the data exactly.

## References


Bezemer, Dirk J. (2010). Understanding Financial Crisis through Accounting Models. *Accounting, Organizations and Society* 35(7), pp.678–688.

Bonis, Riccardo De, and Alfredo Gigliobianco (2012). The Origins of Financial Accounts in the United States and Italy: Copeland, Baffi and the Institutions, in Riccardo De Bonis and Alberto Franco Pozzolo (eds.) *The Financial Systems of Industrial Countries*, Berlin, DE: Springer, pp.15–49.

Brainard, William C., and James Tobin (1968). Pitfalls in Financial Model Building. *American Economic Review* 58(2), pp.99–122.

European Central Bank (2017). Base Money, Broad Money and the APP, *Economic Bulletin*, 6.

Fair, Ray C. (2012). Has Macro Progressed? *Journal of Macroeconomics* 34, pp.2–12.

Godley, Wynne (1999). "Seven Unsustainable Processes." *Levy Economics Institute Strategic Analysis.*

Godley, Wynne, and Marc Lavoie (2007). *Monetary Economics: An Integrated Approach to Credit, Money, Income, Production and Wealth.* Cheltenham: Palgrave Macmillan.

Gola, Carlo, Marco Burroni, Francesco Columba, Antonio Ilari, Giorgio Nuzzo, and Onofrio Panzarino (2017). Shadow Banking out of the Shadows: Non-Bank Intermediation and the Italian Regulatory Framework. *Questioni Di Economia e Finanza (Occasional Papers)*, no. 372.

Hendry, David F., and John Muellbauer (2018). The Future of Macroeconomics: Macro Theory and Models at the Bank of England. *Oxford Review of Economic Policy* 34(2), pp.287–328.

Keynes, John M. (1936). *The General Theory of Employment, Interest and Money.* London, UK. MacMillan.

Lavoie, Marc (2014). *Post-Keynesian Economics: New Foundations.* Cheltenham: Edward Elgar.

Lavoie, Marc, and Gennaro Zezza (2011). *The Stock-Flow Consistent Approach: Selected Writings of Wynne Godley.* Basingstoke: Springer.

McLeay, Michael, Radia Amar, and Ryland Thomas (2014) "Money Creation in the Modern Economy." *Bank of England's Monetary Analysis Directorate, Quarterly Bulletin Q1.*

Papadimitriou, Dimitri B., Michalis Nikiforos, and Gennaro Zezza (2013). A Levy Institute Model for Greece. *Levy Economics Institute Research Projects Report*, 1–31.

Tobin, James (1969). A General Equilibrium Approach to Monetary Analysis. *Journal of Money, Credit and Banking* 1(1), pp.15–29.

Zezza, Francesco, and Gennaro Zezza (2020). A Stock-Flow Consistent Quarterly Model of the Italian Economy. *Levy Economics Institute Working Paper Series No.958*, Working Paper.

Zezza, Gennaro, and Francesco Zezza (2019). On the Design of Empirical Stock–Flow Consistent Models. *European Journal of Economics and Economic Policies: Intervention* 16(1), pp.134–158.

# 9 The long decay of Argentina

## Could the 2010s have been different?

*Sebastian Valdecantos*

### Introduction (or the long decay)

A notorious thinker of the 19th century once said that "history repeats itself, first as tragedy, second as farce". The 2010s were, for the Argentinean economy, a new lost decade. But unlike the 1980s, where the country had to go through a debt crisis, a ridiculous war and two stabilization plans (one of them including a substitution of the national currency, which only lasted six years) that ended in hyperinflation and massive social unrest, the high macroeconomic instability of the 2010s did not end in a major social crisis.

After the peak registered in 2011, the per capita GDP has oscillated with a decreasing trend, being 10% lower in 2019 than it was ten years before. In line with the literature describing the contractionary effect of devaluations (Díaz-Alejandro 1963; Krugman and Taylor 1978), this downward trend of income seems to have been driven by the exchange rate devaluations that took place in 2014, 2016, 2018 and 2019. In parallel, the rate of inflation exhibited an accelerating trend that could only be contained when the nominal exchange rate was kept under control. This weak macroeconomic performance coincided with two antagonistic political regimes: while the second presidency of Cristina Fernández de Kirchner (2012–2015) attempted to establish a "social Keynesian" wage-led regime of accumulation,[1] the administration of Mauricio Macri (2016–2019) intended to lay the foundations of a finance-dominated accumulation regime[2] similar to the ones observed in the Pacific countries of the region, with Chile as the role model.

In light of the evolution of these variables it is clear that none of these two contrasting political economy approaches was able to achieve the macroeconomic stability required for the sustained growth of aggregate demand and employment. While macro-financial volatility and rising inflation became the norm, unlike the story of the 1980s, the systemic crisis that abruptly breaks out to make the adjustments that politics is normally not willing to do never ended up occurring. Although the currency crisis that took place in 2018 could have triggered a major social collapse, the government was able to control the situation with the aid provided by the IMF. The explosion of the incubating economic bomb was prevented (or put off) but the economy

DOI: 10.4324/9781003253457-11

kept on going through its process of slow decay, signalling either that the policy mixes implemented by the two governments were inconsistent or, possibly, that the roots of the problem were to be found deeper than what the scope of macroeconomics allows to dig.

In this chapter I propose to take the first way, i.e., to assume that the problem of Argentina's economy could have been solved through a more virtuous combination of macroeconomic policy tools. In particular, I try to test whether an alternative approach to foreign financing, capital flow regulation and portfolio allocation would have generated a more stable macroeconomic environment. I do this through an empirical stock-flow consistent (SFC) model to harness its accounting consistency, dynamic framework and holistic description of the economy. The technical details of the model can be found in Valdecantos (2020).

## The initial conditions: how Argentina began its 2010s

An interesting aspect of Argentina's balance of payments crisis of the 2010s is that it happened alongside a very small current account deficit (less than 1% of GDP) and low levels of external indebtedness (less than 20% of GDP), as shown in the right panel of Figure 9.1. Besides not implying high financing needs, these figures also suggest that whatever external financing the country required to sustain a moderate growth rate, they could have been found in international financial markets at reasonable prices. Other Latin American economies, whose external positions were significantly more vulnerable than Argentina's, found no problem in running persistent current account deficits through a continuous process of capital inflows made possible by the easy liquidity conditions in global financial markets facilitated by the expansionary monetary policies pursued by developed economies' central banks.

So, what are the reasons that made Argentina hit the external constraint way before the traditional external sector analysis would suggest that a

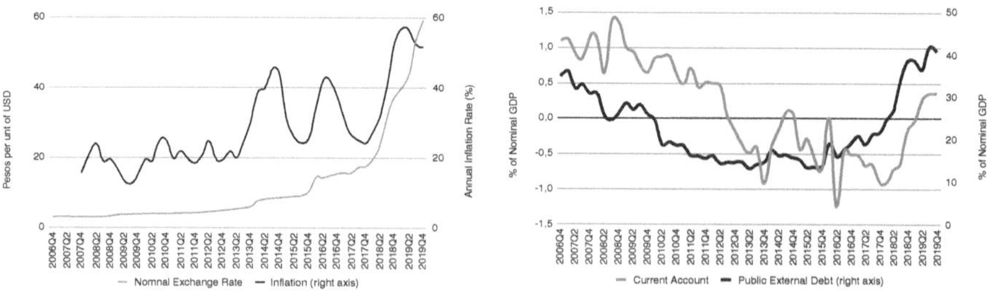


*Figure 9.1* Exchange rate instability with not so bad fundamentals.

Source: Self-elaborated based on Instituto Nacional de Estadística y Censos de la República Argentina (Argentinean National Statistics Institute).

balance of payments crisis is likely to happen? Is there any specific factor that made Argentina's macroeconomic situation different from its neighbours? One distinguishing aspect of Argentina's economy was an accelerating inflation (Figure 9.1 right panel), which by the beginning of the 2010s was averaging a 20% annual rate, way above most countries in the world, both developed and developing. This high inflation rate combined with an expansionary monetary policy (aimed at stimulating aggregate demand), drove the real interest rate down, thereby encouraging the private sector to place its wealth under the form of foreign exchange-denominated assets. Consequently, even though the Argentinean economy did not face a substantial current account deficit or pressing debt payments, it did suffer from a continuous leakage of foreign exchange through the financial account. While most Latin American countries were facing large current account deficits and financial account surpluses, Argentina exhibited a relatively balanced current account position with a persistent financial account deficit, which had to be compensated through the (always unsustainable) sale of the Central Bank's foreign reserves.

A new question then pops up. If it did not want to deploy a contractionary monetary policy that brought the real interest rate high enough to induce a change in the portfolio behaviour of the private sector, why did not the Argentinean government attempt to obtain the foreign exchange required to meet the private sector's demand for foreign assets through the issue of external debt when, given its low levels of indebtedness, it seemed to have plenty of room to do it? There are, in principle, two reasons that explain why it was not possible to increase the inflow of foreign financial capital. First, the government's reluctance to take external debt, mainly due to ideological reasons (which were also funded on the country's previous experiences with external debt-led growth processes). Second, Argentina had an open unsolved conflict with "holdout" creditors[3] which made it harder, though not impossible, to obtain external financing. Not being able to cope with the continuous deficit in the financial account and allowing for a nominal exchange rate devaluation not being a possibility (due to its inflationary effects), by the end of 2011 the Central Bank decided to impose capital controls on outflows (mainly financial, but to some extent also real), giving rise to a series of parallel (illegal) markets of foreign exchange and, therefore, a wide range of exchange rates. It was in that year, 2011, when per capita GDP was highest in Argentina's history. From then on, all the macroeconomic and social variables would persistently deteriorate. It was the beginning of Argentina's new lost decade.

## The failed quest for macro-financial stability

The approaches taken for the regulation of the financial account and the management of cross-border financial flows along the 2010s can be broadly characterized into two distinct strategies. Between 2012 and 2015, the government in place attempted to: (i) keep the nominal exchange rate stable; (ii) keep interest rates low to accommodate an expansionary fiscal policy; (iii) not to take external debt to prevent foreign meddling with domestic policy issues; (iv) prevent the leak of domestic savings arising from (ii) through tight capital controls on outflows (more specifically, the purchase of foreign exchange was strongly restricted). As previously mentioned, the results were unsuccessful, as domestic savings continued to leak through the parallel markets that, in turn, induced an increasing macroeconomic instability as the gap between the official exchange rate and its parallel versions grew larger. Some of the by-products of these multiple exchange rate markets were higher inflation expectations, lower incentives to invest and misaligned incentives between the Central Bank and the private sector.[4]

On the other hand, between 2016 and 2019 the new government coalition undertook a massive liberalization of the economy (which included the foreign exchange market and therefore the exchange rate) that resulted in a very fast increase in foreign indebtedness. Foreign investors were eager to purchase the bonds of a country that not only exhibited very low levels of indebtedness, but was now run by a market-friendly government. This coincided with a huge increase in the acquisition of foreign assets by the private sector, which was now able to channel its savings into foreign exchange-denominated assets with practically no restrictions. In order to attract foreign financial capital and to undermine the leak of foreign exchange, the Central Bank increased the issuance of short-term bills paying high interest rates. The dreamworld would only last two years. In 2018, global financial markets interpreted that Argentina's model was not sustainable and ceased lending to the country. In 2018, the Central Bank had to start liquidating its stock of foreign reserves, which was insufficient to prevent two devaluations in a matter of months. A major collapse could only be prevented by appealing to the IMF, which gave Argentina the largest bail-out in its entire history (57 billion USD). In a little more than a year, however, the IMF also convinced itself about the unsustainability of Argentina's trajectory and decided not to disburse the last instalment of the stand-by agreement. Devoid of any form of financing, suffering a continuous leak of foreign exchange and with almost no more Central Bank firepower, Macri lost the 2019 elections and left power, defaulting on the internal debt and reestablishing the capital controls whose removal had made up its main campaign slogan.

## An alternative approach to macro-financial stability

Could Argentina have implemented an alternative, more successful combination of economic policies leading to higher macro-financial stability? In order to address this question it is first necessary to imagine what is the sequence of events that would lead to that increased stability. The proposal is summarized in Figure 9.2, where three exogenous policy variables are

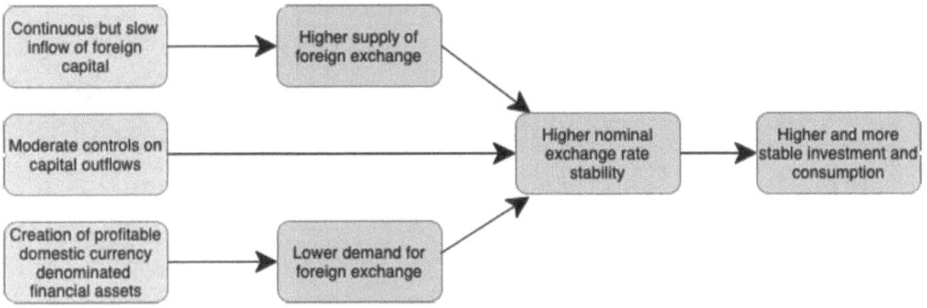


*Figure 9.2* The hypothetical path towards macro-financial stability.
Source: Self-elaborated.

changed (the three blocks on the left of the figure). The following analysis will be constrained to the period that ranges from 2012Q1 to 2018Q2, i.e., from the beginning of the second government of Fernández de Kirchner to the moment when the macroeconomic situation under the Macri administration gets out of control and the government appeals for a bail-out to the IMF.

First, instead of the erratic approach towards external indebtedness, a continuous but slow increase in the issuance of public external debt, as shown in the right panel of Figure 9.3, is proposed. The proposed trajectory for the external debt assumed a 1.5% quarterly growth for the outstanding stock of debt. As the figure shows, such an evolution of the external debt implies that all along the 2012–2015 period the government would have dealt with a higher supply of foreign exchange, which would have in turn provided it with a higher room of manoeuvre to relax the capital controls and reduce the pressure that was falling on the Central Bank's foreign reserves. On the other hand, this proposed trajectory of external debt would have implied a lower supply of foreign exchange after 2016. But considering that the excessive inflows of foreign financial capital those years was one of the main causes of the macroeconomic crisis of 2018, the proposed trajectory can be considered as a better option compared to the actual evolution of the external debt.

Second, instead of the extreme and also erratic approaches taken to regulate capital outflows observed in the 2010s, a middle ground trajectory is proposed. As observed in the left panel of Figure 9.3, capital controls on outflows were extremely high between 2012 and 2015, and then completely lifted after 2016.[5] Instead, a moderate level of capital controls on outflows all along the sample has been proposed. Although this relatively lower intensity of controls (compared to the actuals) would have implied a priori a higher demand for foreign exchange, it is expected that the higher inflows coming from the increasing external indebtedness would have compensated for that higher demand, leading to a more stable foreign exchange market.

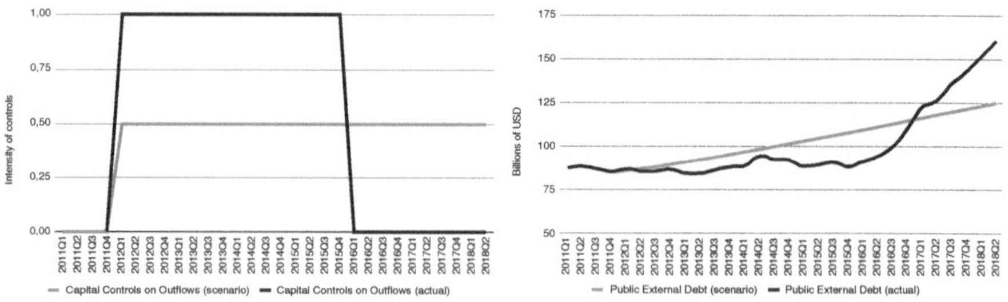


*Figure 9.3* Alternative trajectories for capital controls and external debt.
Source: Self-elaborated.

The simulations presented in the next section will shed light on this hypothesis. Regarding the period 2016–2018, the opposite effect is expected, i.e., lower indebtedness would have implied a lower supply of foreign exchange, but at the same time the higher capital controls would have reduced the demand for foreign exchange.

The last exogenous policy change proposed in Figure 9.2 consisted of the creation of profitable domestic currency-denominated assets such that the private sector reduces the amount of savings that are channelled to the acquisition of foreign assets. This would comprise a wide, though not necessarily complex, range of financial engineering techniques that go beyond (and might not even require) the setting of a positive short-term policy rate.[6] In order to keep the analysis simple and not make changes to the structure of the underlying model, this third element of the proposed policy mix is incorporated by a decrease in the parameter representing the elasticity of the private sector's demand for foreign assets to the evolution of the external debt. In other words, it is assumed that the strong relationship observed between external indebtedness and the domestic private sector's demand for foreign assets is weakened as more profitable (domestic currency-denominated) investment opportunities are created.[7]

As a result of the combination of these three policy changes it is expected that: (i) the demand for foreign exchange (from financial account transactions) is on average lower than it actually was; (ii) the supply of foreign exchange is on average higher than it actually was; (iii) these first two results lead to a higher exchange rate stability which, in turn, lead to; (iv) higher and more stable growth of private consumption and investment.

Before presenting the results of the proposed experiment a few words must be said about the channels of transmission at play in the model, with particular emphasis on the links between the exogenous policy variables that are being changed and aggregate demand. Private consumption, the largest component of aggregate demand, is described through a Keynesian equation where the main driver is the disposable income of formal workers and, to a lesser extent, the income of the owners of firms. Thus, exchange rate depreciations that are passed through prices (this effect is very strong in Argentina, as theoretically described by in the well-known works of Díaz-Alejandro [1963] and Krugman and Taylor [1978]) have a contractionary effect on demand. However, unlike the standard consumption equations used in the SFC literature, in the case of Argentina no wealth effect is included, as the empirical analysis carried out did not find evidence in favour of this specific channel.

Regarding private investment, a Kaleckian equation was estimated using the rate of profits and capacity utilization as its main determinants, both having a positive effect on investment but the impact of profits being stronger. In order to account for the specificities of the Argentinean economy this equation was augmented to include capital controls and the exchange rate, both of them expected to have a negative impact. The reason explaining the negative impact of capital controls on investment is that the impossibility of converting future profits into foreign assets discourages entrepreneurs from undertaking new investment projects. For its part, the exchange rate is expected to have a negative effect on investment because in Argentina exchange rate depreciations are normally characteristic of periods of macroeconomic volatility, which increase uncertainty and discourage firms from engaging in new investment projects.

The stage is now set to perform the counterfactual analysis proposed in this chapter.

## A reason to believe

The effect of the policy mix defined in the previous section on the most relevant endogenous variables of the model is plotted in Figure 9.4. The top left panel shows a downward trend in the demand for foreign assets, which implies a lower pressure on the nominal exchange rate, plotted in the top right panel. Even if compared to the actual evolution of the variables in 2012–2015 the scenario establishes a lower intensity of capital controls on outflows, the gradual shift in the portfolio of the private sector towards domestic currency-denominated assets combined with a higher supply of foreign exchange arising from the increased external indebtedness, which makes it possible to achieve a more stable trajectory of the nominal exchange rate. This, in turn, reduces the pace at which prices increase, thereby strengthening the purchasing power of households. As a result, consumption increases, also inducing an endogenous growth in investment through the channel of profits and capacity utilization mentioned above. However, the higher economic activity induces a larger demand for imported final goods and intermediate inputs, which worsens the trade balance and the current account, as shown in the bottom left panel. Still, the current account deficit resulting from this more vigorous economic growth does not seem to take unsustainable levels (as long as the country manages to keep on issuing debt in the international financial markets, which is one of the assumptions of the scenario).

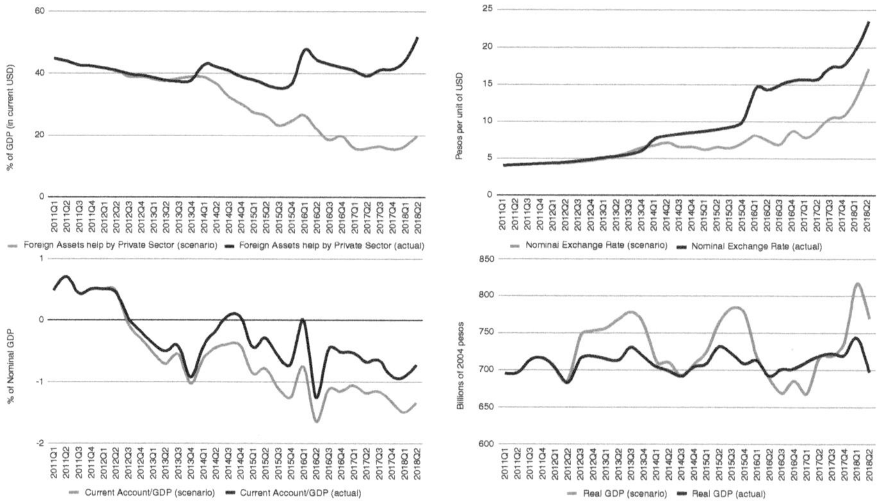


*Figure 9.4* Effects of the alternative policy mix.
Source: Self-elaborated.

The comparison of the results with the actual performance of the economy in the 2016–2018 period is also in line with the hypotheses. First, the fact that there is a higher intensity of capital controls limits the amount of private savings that are translated into foreign assets. This compensates for the relatively lower supply of foreign exchange arising from the slower trajectory of external indebtedness. Finally, the higher willingness of the private sector to purchase domestic denominated assets continues to relieve the pressure on the nominal exchange rate, compared to the actual course of events.[8]

The higher exchange rate stability, again, favours the growth of aggregate demand through strengthened households' purchasing power (mainly in 2016, where the economy actually suffered a sharp devaluation and therefore an acceleration of inflation). Despite some periods where output drops below its actual trajectory (see next section) the overall performance of the economy seems to be better with the alternative policy mix in the 2016–2018 period as well. This better performance is added to the fact that, given the exogenous policy decisions assumed in this scenario, the possibility of facing a currency crisis like the one the economy actually suffered in 2018 would have been lower, as the level of external indebtedness and the private sector's demand and actual possibilities of acquiring foreign assets would have been smaller as well.

From the results of these simulations it would seem that a combination of policies that yield higher macro-financial stability and, as a result of that, a higher and more sustainable aggregate demand could have been possible.

Thus, the conditions of possibility of the currency crisis that made the Macri administration appeal to the IMF could also have been prevented had both governments pursued a less erratic policy towards external indebtedness and cross-border financial flows, and designed financial instruments that encouraged the private sector to place its wealth in domestic currency-denominated assets. However, the results of the simulations show a cyclical behaviour of GDP that was not anticipated in our a priori reflections. In the next section we dig into these dynamics and analyse whether they undermine the conclusions with regard to the policy mix explored in this chapter.

## The cyclical behaviour of investment

Among the advantages of working with SFC models is the holistic description of the economic system and its multiple feedback effects, which capture the by-products of a specific shock or policy, many of which might not be anticipated prior to the simulations. When the behavioural equations of the model are estimated econometrically this holistic feature of SFC models becomes even more important as the results of the simulations can be given a quantitative interpretation. Under a given set of circumstances it might happen that a specific policy aimed at producing a specific effect on the key macroeconomic variables can end up producing a different result as a consequence of the joint interactions of the multiple feedback effects embedded in the model. The general equilibrium framework in which SFC models are constructed makes them suitable for a more careful analysis of the impact of a specific set of policies. In the particular case presented in this chapter, a partial analysis whose scope did not go beyond the domain of the analysis of the balance of payments would have been unable to capture the cyclical trajectory that GDP takes as a result of the proposed policy mix. So, what does the underlying SFC model have to say about the behaviour of output?

The exploration of the dynamics of the components of aggregate demand under the scenario show a higher and more stable private consumption along almost all the sample (due to the lower inflation rate), slightly higher exports before 2015 (because the lower capital controls induce exporters to liquidate a higher amount of their crop inventories) and mildly lower exports after 2016 (because of the higher capital controls compared to their actual intensity). Imports increase along the whole sample as a result of both higher aggregate demand and, to a lesser extent, a slightly more appreciated real exchange rate. This higher level of imports negatively affects the trade balance and the current account, as plotted in the bottom left panel of Figure 9.4. However, the component that explains the greatest part of the variations of GDP is private investment, whose dynamics and that of its main determinants are shown in Figure 9.5. In order to make the analysis easier, the figures plot each of the variables indicated in the vertical axis as a ratio to the actual trajectories.

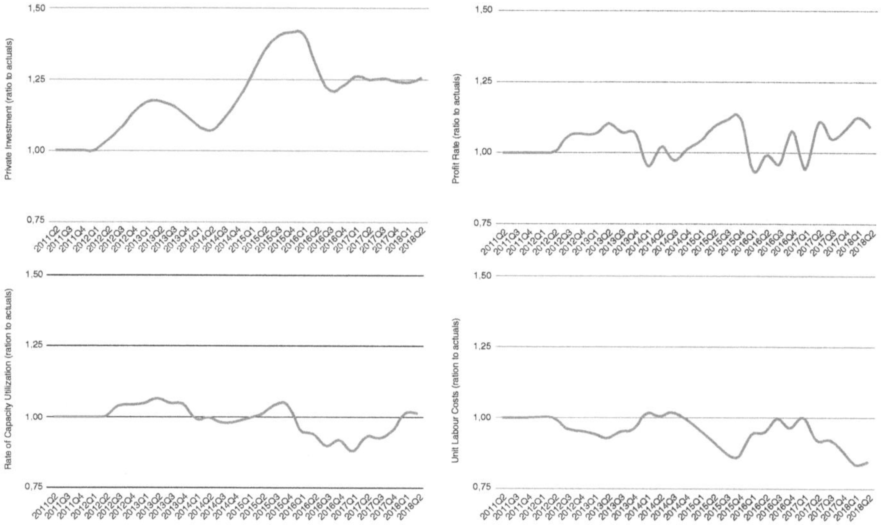


*Figure 9.5* The dynamics of investment and its determinants.
Source: Self-elaborated.

Private investment jumps in the first quarter of 2012 mainly due to the establishment of lower capital controls compared to the intensity they actually had. As a result of the higher investment aggregate demand increases, thereby inducing both a higher profit rate and a higher rate of capacity utilization (see top right and bottom left panels of Figure 9.5). Since these two rates are among the main determinants of private investment, their increase feeds back into the firms' decision about future capital accumulation, thereby increasing investment further in the subsequent periods.

However, after the initial increase the profit rate hits a peak and then starts to decline around mid-2013, though it is still higher with respect to the actual values. Decreasing profits negatively affect investment, which starts to fall as well, though being above the level observed in the original series. Declining investment also implies a reduction of aggregate demand and, therefore, capacity utilization. The reason why, towards the end of 2013, the trough of capacity utilization even reaches lower values than the ones actually observed is given by the fact that in the preceding upturn there was a process of more capital accumulation (compared to the actual values) that expanded the productive capacity of the economy. Thus, the first cycle of private investment can be summarized as follows. Investment is triggered by lower capital controls; it is then propagated by the feedback effects of the rate of profit and capacity utilization into investment until profits reach a peak and start to decline. The fall in the rate of profit changes the firms' behaviour, leading to a decrease in investment. This contractionary effect is then propagated by the feedback effects of both the rate of profit and capacity utilization into investment.

From the preceding analysis it is clear that the breakpoint in the investment cycle is given by the trajectory of the rate of profit. So, what is the main driver of profits or, more specifically, why is it that this rate reaches a maximum in mid-2013 instead of continuing to grow indefinitely? The answer can be found in the evolution of unit labour costs, which are plotted in the bottom right panel of Figure 9.5. The initial increase in output induces the commonly observed increase in labour productivity, since part of the new production is carried out with already employed workers. Given the nominal wages, which adjust to changes in employment and prices with a lag, the increase in labour productivity reduces unit labour costs thereby pushing profits up (as commented in the previous paragraphs). However, as output increases so does employment, putting upward pressure on nominal wages and, in turn, eroding the firms' profits. When these lower and eventually decreasing profits are combined with a growing stock of capital, in line with the expansion of investment, the rate of profit starts to decline. This is, indeed, what happens around mid-2013 and what gives the behaviour of investment (and GDP) a cyclical behaviour. Without explicitly looking for it the simulations performed in this policy proposal found a Marx-Goodwin-type cycle.

In the third quarter of 2014 private investment begins a new growth cycle thanks to the increase in the profit rate registered in the previous period which, in turn, is explained by a slight decrease in unit labour costs. The reason why unit labour costs stop their increasing trajectory is given by two processes. First, as aggregate demand was losing momentum so was employment and, therefore, nominal wage increases. Second, labour productivity, the other component of unit labour costs, starts to decline at a slower pace in line with the stabilization of real GDP, as observed in the bottom right panel of Figure 9.4. Although these changes in the trajectories of the variables of the unit labour costs and the profit rate seem negligible when looking at the figures, their changing signs end up having an impact on private investment giving rise to a new process of capital accumulation and growth of aggregate demand.

The sequence of causation underlying the cycle of investment is the same one observed before: given the prevalence of the exogenous forces triggering the initial increase of private investment (the establishment of lower capital controls), the resulting growth of aggregate demand implies in the short run both a higher rate of capacity utilization and a higher rate of profit (the latter being driven by the increase of productivity brought about by the rise of production relative to employment).

Unlike the previous cycle where the downswing phase was relatively smooth, in this case from the first quarter of 2016 a drastic slump is registered. In order to understand this effect it is important to recall that the exogenous policy mix proposed in this experiment assumes that capital controls are constant all along the sample, when in reality they were completely removed in this quarter (see left panel of Figure 9.3). Considering that higher capital controls discourage investment decisions, the fall of capital accumulation observed in the graph is now explained. In other words, the cyclical dynamics previously described are interrupted by an exogenous force that triggers the dynamics of the downswing: lower investment leads to a lower aggregate demand which, in turn, reduces capacity utilization and the rate of profit, thereby inducing a further decrease of investment.

Still, it is worth noting that across these two cycles investment seems to have an upward trend. Moreover, after the second cycle is over, investment seems to stabilize exhibiting no more cycles. The most likely explanation for this behaviour is that the multiple determinants of investment end up cancelling each other out, as can be seen when looking at the trajectories of the rate of profit (which is above its actual level) and the rate of capacity utilization (which tends to situate below its actual levels). A similar hypothesis can be posed for the determinants related to the financial sphere of the economy: while the higher capital controls (with respect to the actual values) discourage entrepreneurs from increasing investment, the higher exchange rate stability generates a more favourable environment for investment decisions. Ultimately, all these factors end up cancelling each other out to yield a constant level of investment, which is still higher compared to its actual trajectory presumably because aggregate demand and profits are higher on average, and also because the economy exhibits lower volatility.

## Conclusions

We began the discussion of Argentina's long decay by identifying the external constraint (whose main symptom is a persistent balance of payments crisis) and macroeconomic volatility as its main determinants. Not neglecting that the ultimate causes of these disequilibria are to be found in Argentina's (social and productive) structure and institutions, in this chapter we posed the question whether it would have been possible to tackle these problems through an alternative combination of macroeconomic policy tools. In particular, we aimed to test whether a more gradual process of external indebtedness combined with a less erratic capital regulation policy and the creation of a series of profitable domestic currency-denominated assets would have generated a more stable balance between the supply and demand of foreign exchange over the 2012–2018 period. The choice of the time frame for the simulations was not random: during these years two different governments with totally different political economy frameworks were in place, none of them being able to stabilize the economy. On the contrary, Argentina's macroeconomic performance went through a process of slow decay until it had to call for an extraordinary USD 57 billion stand-by agreement with the IMF in order to prevent a major currency crisis, with the likely social and political consequences observed not so long ago in the crises of 1989 and 2001.

The proposed experiment was made through an empirical SFC model to harness its accounting consistency, dynamic framework and holistic description of the economy. The results of the simulations show that, as expected in our hypotheses, there is a combination of the exogenous variables that would have produced the desired effects. In the 2012–2015 period, where tight capital controls were established and the government practically took no external debt, the simulations show that with the alternative policy mix the supply of foreign exchange would have been higher (both from higher exports and from capital inflows). The demand for foreign exchange would also have been higher as the softer capital controls included in the simulation would have allowed for more leakages, but these would have also been partially offset by the incentives of the private sector to rebalance its portfolio towards domestic assets. In the 2016–2018 period, on the other hand, there would initially have been a lower supply of foreign exchange due to the relatively lower acquisition of external debt, but the relatively higher capital controls and, again, the private sector's incentive to place a larger share of its wealth under the form of domestic assets would have reduced the demand for foreign exchange.

As in all counterfactual analyses an important caveat needs to be made. It should be recalled that the results obtained in the simulations are dependent on the change in the parameter of the portfolio equation representing the elasticity of the private sector's demand for foreign assets with respect to capital inflows. Unlike the other two elements that define the simulated scenario, the government does not directly define this parameter, which is mainly given by the various determinants of the private sector's portfolio choice. Thus, the simulations presented in this chapter assume that the government creates a series of financial investment alternatives (like the ones mentioned in the corresponding section) that effectively induce the private sector to modify its behaviour. In this sense, the evolution of the variables presented in the simulations should be rather interpreted as a possible trajectory in case the government would have taken a different approach towards external indebtedness and capital flow regulation being been successful at designing a new set of profitable domestic currency-denominated financial assets.

Besides showing that a more stable macro-financial environment could have been attained through a combination of policies like the ones simulated in the experiment carried out in this chapter, the results show that this would have led to a higher average level of aggregate demand. This higher level of economic activity would also have been desirable considering the actual trajectory of GDP exhibited a declining trend. The higher aggregate demand is explained partly by higher private consumption, which is strengthened due to the higher macroeconomic stability (which results in lower inflation and therefore a higher households' purchasing power). But the key driver of economic activity in the simulated scenario is private investment, which seems to follow cycles along the lines identified by Marx and Goodwin. Eventually, investment stabilizes at a higher level with respect to its actual trajectory, probably suggesting that the proposed policy mix produces more favourable conditions for entrepreneurs. These conditions are basically given by a more stable macroeconomy (less exchange rate volatility, inflation and abrupt output upheavals), which according to the simulations ends up outweighing the negative effect of establishing (moderate) capital controls. This is, probably, the key takeaway of the experiment carried out in this chapter, the good news being that macroeconomic policy can make a contribution to the stabilization of Argentina's economy.

A final remark regarding the SFC approach is worth making. Contemporary economies are so complex that a wide range of interactions and feedback effects are playing out all the time. When conducting a policy analysis like the one performed in this chapter it is important not only to make an accurate description of what is being tried to simulate, but also to account for the multiple effects that might interfere with the goals set by the researcher or policy-maker. The holistic nature of SFC models and their flexibility to add agents, assets, transactions and policy tools render them a powerful tool to perform these types of analyses. In the present chapter we saw that when attempting to obtain a specific result in a certain market (the foreign exchange market), this gave rise to by-products that affected other markets (the goods market, through the dynamics of private investment, and the labour market, through the dynamics of employment, productivity and wages). Even though these by-products were in line with the policy goals pursued in the simulations, it might well have not been the case. Phrased differently, not all the policies that have the desired effect on a specific market will prove to be consistent with the pursued effect at the general level. In order to be able to account for these multiple interactions and feedback effects across markets it is required to work within a general equilibrium framework. And in order to be reliable for policy analysis, that framework needs to be consistent in the accounting, to account for the dynamic interactions of the different processes described by the model (not just their contemporaneous effect) and to be grounded on strong empirical foundations. This is the proposal of empirical SFC models. The analysis presented in this chapter aimed at making a contribution to that agenda.

## Notes

1 Chena et al. (2018) label this way the attempt to deploy a set of policies that strengthened real disposable income—the main driver of private consumption—in a context where the wage bill could not grow any longer.
2 The notion of a finance-dominated regime of accumulation was not proposed by the government, but is a characterization based on the similarities between the orientation of the policies that were actually implemented and the features of

the finance-dominated regime as defined by Hein and Van Treek (2010) and Hein (2012). Among the main features of this regime, they distinguish a worsening of income distribution, higher household indebtedness to finance consumption, increasing shareholder power in the investment decision and the liberalization of capital markets.

3 The conflict arose as a result of a group of the so-called "vulture funds", who did not accept the debt restructuring proposed by Argentina in 2005 and decided to take the case to the courts in New York. In 2012, Judge Griesa ruled in favour of the creditors. For a brief timeline of Argentina's conflict with these hedge funds, see Moyer (2016).

4 For instance, exporters were encouraged to underinvoice their transactions to avoid liquidating the proceeds of their exports at the official (low) rate. Importers, for their part, were encouraged to overinvoice their purchases to acquire foreign exchange at the official rate (cheaper compared to the parallel rate).

5 The intensity of the capital controls variable is given by a dummy variable included in the estimations presented in Valdecantos (2020). The variable takes the value 0 from the fourth quarter of 2006 (the first observation for which it is possible to estimate the portfolio equations of the model) to the fourth quarter of 2011, as there were no impediments to the acquisition of foreign exchange. From the first quarter of 2012 to the fourth quarter of 2015 the variable takes the value 1, in an attempt to reflect the tight controls established during the administration of Fernández de Kirchner. From the first quarter of 2016 to the third quarter of 2019 the variable takes, again, the value 0 as there were no restrictions to the acquisition of foreign exchange during the administration of Macri.

6 A few recent examples of this can provide useful illustrations. The first one is the UVA-denominated time deposits, which can be acquired by any agent of the private sector. The UVA, which stands for "unit of purchasing power", is an index that tracks the evolution of prices. Thus, the time deposits placed in UVA earn the evolution of prices plus a specific rate of return, thereby always ensuring the saver a positive return. The second one is the so-called LEMIN, which can be acquired by mining companies in exchange for the foreign exchange that they liquidate after their exports have been invoiced and paid. These assets are denominated in pesos, but they are indexed to the evolution of the nominal exchange rate, thereby ensuring the firm that when it decides to sell it will always get an amount of pesos equivalent to the amount of dollars received from the exports.

7 Using balance of payments statistics Rua and Zeolla (2018) find evidence to support this strong relationship between external indebtedness and the private sector's demand for foreign assets. The estimations made in the model used for this chapter are in line with these results.

8 The reason why towards the end of the simulation period, i.e., in the first two quarters of 2018, the demand for foreign assets surges (although still being lower than what it actually was) is that, in an attempt to prevent the currency crisis that would unfold in April 2018, the Central Bank started to increase the interest rate. Given Argentina's economic history, instead of being correlated with a lower demand for foreign assets, higher interest rates tend to be accompanied by massive capital flights. This seems to reflect the failed attempts of the monetary authority to prevent currency crises. In terms of the modelling of the monetary policy tools this is problematic because equations obtained through econometric estimations might produce effects that go against the purpose of monetary policy. More specifically, since the empirical evidence shows a positive relation between interest rates and acquisition of foreign assets, simulating a policy where the Central Bank raises the interest rate in an attempt to prevent a currency crisis will, as a matter of fact, end up triggering it.

## References

Chena, P., D. Panigo, P. Wahren, and L. Bona. 2018. "Argentina (2002–2015): transición neomercantilista, estructuralismo á la Diamand y Keynesianismo social con restricción externa." Semestre Económico 21(47): 25–59.

Díaz-Alejandro, C. 1963. "A note on the impact of devaluation and the redistributive effect." Journal of Political Economy 71: 577–580.

Hein, E. 2012. The macroeconomics of finance-dominated capitalism and its crisis. Cheltenham: Edward Elgar Publishing.

Hein, E., and T. Van Treeck. 2010. "Financialisation and rising shareholder power in Kaleckian/Post-Kaleckian models of distribution and growth." Review of Political Economy 22(2): 205–233.

Krugman, P., and L. Taylor. 1978. "Contractionary effects of devaluation." Journal of International Economics 8(3): 445–456.

Moyer, L. 2016. "Argentina's debt settlement ends 15-year battle." New York Times, February 29.

Rua, M., and N. Zeolla. 2018. "Desregulación cambiaria, fuga de capitales y deuda: la experiencia argentina reciente." Problemas del Desarrollo 49(194). 5–30.

Valdecantos, S. 2020. "Argentina's (Macroeconomic?) Trap: Some Insights from an Empirical Stock-Flow Consistent Model" Levy Institute Working Paper No. 975. Annandale-on-Hudson, NY: Levy Economics Institute of Bard College.

# Part III

# Economic policy aspects

# 10 Central bank independence in an age of democratic values

*Louis-Philippe Rochon and Guillaume Vallet*

### *Introduction*

Central bank independence (CBI) is one of the sacrosanct postulates of mainstream monetary policy, one which is rarely, if ever, questioned in theory. For most central banks and central bankers, CBI is the only reliable framework to consider as its adoption, it is argued, gives central banks the ultimate ability to implement "sound" monetary policies in our democratic systems. Central banks, according to this view, are anointed and seen as institutions in charge of promoting a nation's prosperity. Indeed, the connection between "sound" monetary policies, on the one hand, and prosperity in democracies and CBI, on the other, rests on two fundamental arguments.

First, it is argued that in order to deliver a low and stable rate of inflation, central banks must be shielded from possible manipulations by the political elite who would want to co-opt the powers of the central bank to further their electoral goals, which more often than not are assumed to be inflationary, hence the expression "inflation bias". The mission of protecting a low and stable rate of inflation, institutionalized in the 1990s in inflation-targeting regimes, for instance, is further assumed to guarantee high employment and high and sustainable real economic growth.

This also relates to the so-called "New Consensus" framework (Walsh & Woodford 2005), namely, the "independence-price stability-inflation targeting" tryptic framework. Such a framework is alleged to enable central banks to reach price stability – to control inflation particularly – and thus to ensure central bankers' credibility and reputation.

To draw on this issue, the hazard hanging in the air refers to the "capture" argument: had central bankers not followed this tryptic framework, they would have been under the direct influence of politicians. Indeed, the latter are described as motivated purely and only by their eventual re-election – the so-called "electoral politics" (Tucker 2018, p. 103). In this context, they would try to exploit and hence benefit from the central banks' resources for their own sake. All in all, central bankers' commitment to price stability would be jeopardized because of the "intrinsic time inconsistency" model (Kydland & Prescott 1977).

DOI: 10.4324/9781003253457-13

Second, it is argued that independent central banks outperform less-independent central banks; in other words, that independent central banks deliver lower inflation than central banks that are not as independent. There is therefore a high degree of reverse causality between independence and inflation. Hence, the higher the degree of transparency and independence, the lower the rate of inflation.

Such a focus on inflation, which is usually presented as an "evil", is supposed to benefit society as a whole: low inflation would create a public good required for a "safe" economy underpinning the dynamics of democracy. In other words, low inflation would preserve the purchasing power of everyone, but especially the lower class, and as such would prevent income inequalities from rising. This explains why central bankers' expertise is sacralized because of their role towards the dynamics of democracy.

To elaborate on this idea, on the one hand, in an increasing complex world, the role of experts and technocrats (as agents, entirely devoted to their mission) is paramount to serving society (as an alleged principal, which sets its preferences). Mention should be made of two key approaches here. The first refers to M. Weber (2003). According to him, since capitalism is characterized by rationalization, it takes bureaucracy and thus experts such as central bankers to improve the functioning of both economic and political systems. Central bankers participate in "organizing" capitalism for the common good and the public good.

The second relates to W. Wilson's analysis (Wilson 1887). According to his view, there should be an increasing separation between politics and administration in a democracy, for the benefit of democracy itself. Since the substance of modern government has become increasingly complicated, elected representatives have delegated power and functions that are beyond their technical skills. There would be clear benefits in harnessing their "specific" and "unique" type of expertise to institutions alleged to serve democracy. Once again, this gives a prominent role to experts, and for this reason, there should be strong incentives to establish and nurture such expertise.

As a result of all this, in the realm of central banking, experts (central bankers) should be endorsed (anointed) with a clear and unique mission, with no external pressure (e.g. the aforementioned "electoral politics"). By virtue of this, they will do their best for the public good (low inflation; Tucker 2018). These are the roots of the social legitimacy of central banks' independence in democracy: "By delegating to an independent agency, political principals are placing trust in the institution and its sequence of leaders" (Tucker 2018, p. 111).

On the other hand, however, CBI challenges the specific relation between a people and its representatives (even unelected people such as central bankers), and, more broadly, the government of the people, for the people and by the people, to borrow Abraham Lincoln's famous expression. At stake is to rest on central banks' power to frame the economic and social structures of societies. Although officially defended *in theory*, as suggested above, CBI has been de facto largely questioned *in practice* by the actions of the central banks themselves: with the recent two crises, central banks have been mobilized to an extent rarely seen before.

At stake is also people's participation in democratic affairs as well as people's control over delegated powers. Likewise, Schumpeter (1990) also had this bias in mind when he emphasized that politicians are not faithfully concerned with the need to satisfy the rule "the government for the people".

In this contribution, we wish to expose the idea of CBI as a myth propagated by a profession that has accepted the idea, despite empirical evidence that shows there are no advantages, and by central bankers themselves, who position themselves or rather appointed themselves as gatekeepers.

The next section will briefly discuss the origins of the concept of CBI, while the following section will explore precisely how performing independent central banks are. Finally, the last section will explore the relationship between CBI and social responsibility.

## *A short history of an idea*

The modern notion of CBI originated, as best we think, six decades ago, with Milton Friedman, who in his 1962 essay entitled "Should There Be an Independent Monetary Authority?" asks whether the central bank should be organized with the "objective of a monetary structure that is both stable and free from irresponsible government tinkering" (p. 224). The idea gained traction with the great inflation in the 1970s. Today, it remains, at least in theory, a greatly defended idea, that, while it is slowly being criticized, will be difficult to abandon.

### Friedman and CBI

In his famous article, Friedman discussed three monetary arrangements, including a commodity standard, an independent central bank and legislated rules. In discussing the latter two in particular, Friedman rejected the idea of a truly independent central bank, and was critical of the idea than "in a democracy to have so much power concentrated in a body free from any kind of direct, effective political control" (1962, p. 227). "Money", he stated in the opening sentence, "was too important to be left to central bankers". We should be, he added, "fundamentally fearful of concentrated power".

Friedman concludes that an independent central bank with "wide discretion to independent experts" (p. 239) is not the answer. In fact, Friedman was mistrustful about the possibility that a single individual should benefit from such a great power as well as about the hazard of political bias: in line with the capture argument above, Friedman feared that politicians could choose central bankers not for their technical skills or their ability to serve society through their monetary policies, but because they could be political allies for their re-election.

For those reasons, Friedman defended strict monetary policy rules rather than CBI. This is of little surprise in light of Friedman's adaptative expectations framework: to him, monetary policy rules regarding the growth of money supply allowed for price stability and therefore predictability of monetary policies. In turn, emphasizing the relevance of rules that in turn contribute to price stability also strengthens the need for technocrats and experts separated from day-to-day politics, which gives them independence de facto. Indeed, only these "specific" and "unique" experts will have the right skills to follow the rules, and, because of that, these experts should benefit from a unique status apart from politics.

But in a way, this is a sort of independence. In fact, we argue that the emphasis on rules is what we could call "double-independence" because in this context, monetary policy becomes "self-governing", according to Le Heron (2007, p. 146). Hence, the reliance on monetary policy rules is based on this so-called "double independence": (1) independence from political manipulations, but also (2) independence from central bankers and other experts. As stated above, Friedman feared that so much power would be concentrated in the hands of monetary technocrats. Hence, relying on rules was judged to be "better" policy.

## CBI and the will of the people

Indeed, although the actual form of independence varies from one central bank to another, rules framing central banks' independence are alleged to be the legal tenet of a people's will. This model has even spread in the world since the collapse of the USSR and its satellites (Johnson 2016). With the status of independence, central banks are supposed to preserve the monetary order and, beyond that, the social order (Aglietta & Orléan 1982). Likewise, in line with Friedman's and New Classical authors' frameworks, following strict monetary rules and/or being independent enables central banks to not mislead people: therefore, in democracies, people can trust central banks to instantiate their adaptative and rational expectations. Or so the story goes.

The alleged condition for the existence of the effectiveness of the confidence people place in the central bank is that an independent central bank be transparent. Specifically, according to Eijffinger and Geraats (2006), transparency relates to five categories: political, economic, procedural, policy and operational transparency. On the whole, transparency refers to "the extent to which central banks disclose information that is related to the policymaking process" (Eijffinger & Geraats 2006, p. 3). In such a framework, central banks' transparency is crucial to the dynamics of democracies since it eases the understanding of monetary policy by the general public.

Therefore, CBI should be enshrined in the law. Indeed, the law frames independence in its different meanings: the modalities of appointment of central bankers (duration of mandates, their missions, etc.) and the objective as well as the limitations of monetary policy (especially in its relation to fiscal policy; see Cukierman et al. 1992; Crowe & Meade 2007). For central bankers, the CBI framework has gained ground since they have been directly incentivized to defend it. Central bankers defending low inflation through CBI build their reputation as "hawks" (Adolph 2013), which will be helpful for their future career in the private sector (particularly banking and financial sectors, see Diouf & Pépin 2017; Vallet 2019).

## *Moving away from CBI?*

As we asserted in the introduction, although CBI – and its associated monetary rules – is still the official model of most central banks, this has been slowly (and increasingly?) questioned, beginning at the end of the Great Moderation. According to Taylor (2013, p. 9),

> In my view, the same monetary policy considerations – working in reverse – are relevant for explaining the recent deterioration of performance. Monetary policy became much less rule like, starting in my view in the period from 2003 to 2005 when the policy interest rate was held far below levels that would have pertained in the 1980s and 1990s under similar conditions.

It is perhaps worth noting that the 2007 financial crisis, by far the most damaging crisis since the Great Depression, happened under the watch of CBI.

Likewise, the so-called "Covid turmoil", with its "great lockdowns" and its negative economic consequences, has compelled central banks to implement massive quantitative easing programmes. For instance, the European Central Bank launched on the 18th of March 2020 the Pandemic Emergency Purchase Programme (PEPP): the latter consisted of asset purchases of €750 billion, followed by €600 billion on the 4th of June, and again by €500 billion on the 10th of December of the same year. In particular, the PEPP led to the purchase of public sector securities, which questioned the traditional CBI framework existing so far. Indeed, the lines between monetary and fiscal policies have been blurred, and this will certainly last: in the Eurozone, the PEPP is not intended to soon.

More broadly, central banks have increasingly turned to new challenges aimed at enlarging their de facto mandates, such as environmental issues. Therefore, CBI is challenged: central banks seek to promote a differential treatment of environmental resources and to discourage the funding of "harmful industries" (Matikainen, Campiglio & Zenghelis 2017), in the context of global uncertainty related to climate change (Dietsch 2020). Such a "precautionary approach" (Chenet, Ryan-Collins & van Lerven 2019; 2021) aims to exert a new distributive impact benefitting the common good, and thus blurs the traditional lines of independence.

In a democracy, the choice of independence is supposed to be the outcome of a political process in which people, through the vote, have conferred the central bank the responsibility to act in their name and in their interest. Such a framework rests on a kind of "principal-agent" relationship in which the people are able to devise a single and stable preference (Alesina & Tabellini 2008). However, this framework should be questioned on several grounds:

- First, it is impossible for a "people" to devise a single and stable preference (Rochon & Vallet 2022). Democracies are made of different social groups that are in conflict over access to resources, and thus who politically organize to defend their particular, and often conflictual, interests, stances and preferences. In other words, a democracy is made of social conflicts (Touraine 1994). Moreover, not everyone is able to understand monetary policy (Pixley 2018): therefore, the framing of individual monetary preferences are unequal. The "contract" between central banks and the "people" is incomplete by design (Tucker 2018, p. 88) – contrary to the neoclassical model, there is neither perfect information nor complete contracts: the majority of the people do not understand the tricks of the trade of monetary policy (Pixley 2018). From this, we can assert first that the actual "principal-agent" relation is more complex than it appears at first sight. Second, and more importantly, central banks and central bankers are not neutral in the sense that their monetary policy serves some groups more than others: monetary policy is distributive by nature (Kappes & Rochon 2022).
- Second, the relationship between monetary policy and fiscal policy should be discussed more thoroughly because of the distributive nature of monetary policy. CBI emphasizes the "monetary dominance" model in which fiscal policy is neutralized for the benefit of the alleged monetary policy. By contrast, it is our belief that CBI should not oppose governments' objectives precisely to avoid creating a situation of conflict. Since governments' members are elected to concretize the democratic will of a people, the decisions of an independent central bank should be under supervision.

For these reasons, the status of independence of central banks should be consistent with the idea and the possibility of regular assessment and control over central bankers' decisions by the people. At stake is both the social legitimacy of central banks' policies and the democratic control of unelected people.

The above arguments suggest that the traditional model of CBI does not work anymore. This model should be superseded by a new framework of central banks resting on the social responsibility model.

## From independence to social responsibility

Three crucial arguments should be addressed at this stage:

1 Since CBI is about (insulated) power, it should be associated with control, transparency and accountability, or it should be replaced by "constrained discretion". For instance, Tucker (2018, p. 109) argues, "How a delegation is structured also matters, delivering a regime of constrained

discretion", which is consistent with a new framework for central banks' social responsibility (Rochon & Vallet 2022). Indeed, central banking is not only about respecting "neutral technics": central banks exert a distributive and even a "structural" power (Strange 1994); thus, they are not value-free (this reminds us of the dichotomy between efficiency and equity that Wilson (1887) put into light).

In addition, the impact of monetary policy on global welfare and well-being should always be addressed in central banking. The compatibility between monetary policy and constitutional principles should be ensured to prevent the monetary policy from serving bad purposes (military purposes for instance). To that end, central bankers must be appointed not for their political allegiance but for their ability to put their skills in line with these constitutional principles framing monetary policy.

2 The consequences of independence: If central banks exert distributive power, there are inevitably winners and losers. But in this case, who and which institutions compensate – or not – the losers in reference to democratic principles? This issue is about distributional justice, thus values and legitimacy. Because of the distributive nature of monetary policy, we ask whether insulated technocrats should have this power (Tucker 2018).
3 On the control of independent institutions' power. First, according to Tucker (2018), independent agencies such as central banks should become "trustee-independent" institutions (Tucker 2018). To gain trust implies to be in accordance with deep values and beliefs of a political community and to its main institutions. In particular, central banks are, in part at least, derivative of the legitimacy of the state (through a tie of transitivity): this is the crucial "hierarchical confidence" underpinning the legitimacy of money (Aglietta & Orléan 1982).

Moreover, moving to the "trustee-independent" framework emphasizes the role of deliberation and mitigation of insulated power. According to Tucker, trustees must be loyal to their mandate, not to their principal. However, this statement is criticizable: central bankers should also be more accountable towards people, and not only towards politicians: otherwise, there is a capture hazard of another kind – central bankers benefit from too much insulated power in relation to the management of public resources.

Against this backdrop, to promote a new model of central banks and social responsibility to frame the monetary decision-making process is required. This model would rest on the following two main features.

First, delegating power to independent agencies such as central banks should be controlled and tied to fiscal choices.

Likewise, Rochon and Vallet (2022) propose to create new internal bodies within central banks to mitigate central bankers' technocratic power, in order to improve the decision-making process of central banks whose mandates have broadened de facto and to give the people the chance to directly participate in public policies. Not only internal decisions in central banks should be taken by a committee, but the latter should be framed on a new basis: broadened challenges and mandates require new types of skills and expertise in central banking, with new people. To increase the likelihood of central banks to deal with monitorable objectives reinforces the social legitimacy of the institution.

In sum, it is not fair to delegate every decision to technocrats in democracy, and people should keep the right to be directly involved to some extent in the decision-making process affecting their day-to-day lives. CBI is questioned since it does not clearly contribute to people's welfare.

Second, the "incentives" model in use to select and reward the "best" central bankers is not satisfying anymore. We refer here to the career of central bankers, who are unelected individuals exerting distributive choices: so far, the "incentives" model has rested on the ability of the central banker to reach low inflation, for the reasons explained above. Orthodox literature often deals with "credible commitment" (to low inflation) in order to fulfil the principal's objectives in democracy. Indeed, reputation here is in line with the alleged bias of capture (a focus on inflation merely would ensure central bankers are neutral and serve the public good) as well as of moral hazard and adverse selection (central bankers must truly believe in what they are doing in relation to their reputation ("intrinsic motivation"); otherwise, they might not care about not hitting their target, pursuing other types of goal).

By contrast, with a mere focus on low inflation, the problem of adverse selection to select central bankers could occur. Instead, a new framework should promote the disconnection between central bankers' reputation and low inflation (in order to get rid of the idea of an "efficiency mandate", which reinforces the idea to delegate to technocrats such as central bankers; see Huber & Shipan 2002).

At this stage, it is worth reminding the aforementioned problem of incomplete contracts and asymmetry of information underpinning the principal-agent relationship between central banks and the people: Do people really know enough about monetary policy and central banks to be able to reward central bankers when they hit a low inflation target? If central bankers are supposed to serve the public good, their remit should be redesigned and their performance reassessed on a new basis: indeed, who are the true beneficiaries of low inflation, in the age of climate change and increasing social inequalities? As Tucker (2018, p. 102) summarizes, "society might have other reasons for valuing promises" and "they also rely on the culture of a society valuing and conferring regard for successful or dutiful public servants" (Tucker 2018, p. 107).

## Conclusion

In this short chapter, we wanted to take a critical look at CBI, from the point of view of its relationship to social responsibility within a democracy. What precisely is the role of central bankers, whose decisions have lasting distributive effects? Who benefits the most from their policies? Undoubtedly, the model of CBI as it has been existing so far will be increasingly questioned in the age of climate change and secular stagnation, which will require to reframe the nature of public policies serving the people.

## References


Adolph, Christopher (2013). *Bankers, bureaucrats, and central bank politics: The myth of neutrality*. Cambridge University Press.

Aglietta, Michel & Orléan, André (1982). *La Violence de la Monnaie*. Presses Universitaires de France, Paris.

Alesina, Alberto & Tabellini, Guido (2008). Bureaucrats or Politicians? Part II: Multiple Policy Tasks, *Journal of Public Economics*, 92, pp. 426–447.

Chenet, Hughes, Ryan-Collins, Josh & van Lerven, Frank (2019). Climate-Related Financial Policy in a World of Radical Uncertainty: Towards a Precautionary Approach. UCL Institute for Innovation and Public Purpose, *Working Paper Series*, IIPP WP 2019-13. At: https://www.ucl.ac.uk/bartlett/public-purpose/wp2019-13

Chenet, Hughes, Ryan-Collins, Josh & van Lerven, Frank (2021). Finance, Climate-Change and Radical Uncertainty: Towards a Precautionary Approach to Financial Policy, *Ecological Economics*, 183, 106957, https://doi.org/10.1016/j.ecolecon.2021.106957

Crowe, Christopher & Meade, Ellen E. (2007). The Evolution of Central Bank Governance Around the World, *Journal of Economic Perspectives*, 21 (4), pp. 69–90.

Cukierman, Alex, Webb, Steven B. & Neyapti, Bilin (1992). Measuring the Independence of Central Banks and Its Effect on Policy Outcomes, *World Bank Economic Review*, 6 (3), pp. 353–398.

Dietsch, Peter (2020). Legitimacy Challenges to Central Banks: Sketching a Way Forward, *Discussion Note 2020/2*, Council on Economic Policies. January. At: https://www.cepweb.org/legitimacy-challenges-to-central-banks-sketching-a-way-forward/

Diouf, Ibrahima & Pépin, Dominique (2017). Gender and Central Banking, *Economic Modelling*, 61, pp. 193–206.

Eijffinger, Sylverster C. W. & Geraats Petra M. (2006). How Transparent Are Central Banks?, *European Journal of Political Economy*, 22 (1), pp. 1–21.

Friedman, Milton (1962). *Should there be an independent monetary authority*? B.Y. Leland (Ed.), In Search of a Monetary Constitution, Harvard University Press, Cambridge, MA, pp. 219–243.

Huber, John D. & Shipan, Charles R. (2002). *Deliberate Discretion? The Institutional Foundations of Bureaucratic Autonomy*. Cambridge University Press, Cambridge, MA.

Johnson, Juliet (2016). *Priests of Prosperity. How Central Bankers Transformed the Post Communist World*. Cornell University Press, Ithaca and London.

Kappes, Sylvio and Louis-Philippe Rochon (2022). Monetary Policy and Income Distribution: Comparing the Mainstream and the Post-Keynesian Views, Working Paper.

Kydland, Finn E., and Edward C. Prescott (1977). Rules rather than discretion: The inconsistency of optimal plans. *Journal of Political Economy*, 85(3), pp. 473–491.

Le Heron, Edwin (2007). "The New Governance in Monetary Policy: A Critical Appraisal of the Fed and the ECB", In Arestis, Philip, Hein, Eckhard & Le Heron,

Edwin (eds.), *Aspects of Modern Monetary and Macroeconomic Policies*, Palgrave Macmillan, London, pp. 146–171.

Matikainen, Sini, Campiglio, Emanuele & Zenghelis, Dimitri (2017). The Climate Impact of Quantitative Easing, *Grantham Research Institute on Climate Change and the Environment*, May.

Pixley, Jocelyn (2018). *Central Banks, Democratic States and Financial Power.* Cambridge University Press, Cambridge, MA.

Rochon, Louis-Philipp and Vallet, Guillaume (2022). Masters of the Game: The Power and Social Responsibility of Central Banks and Central Bankers in a Democracy, Working Paper.

Schumpeter, Josef. A. (1990 [1942]). *Capitalisme, Socialisme et Démocratie.* Payot, Paris.

Strange, Susan (1994). The Study of International Political Economy, In Ursula, Lehmkuhl (ed.), *Theorien Internationaler Politik*, R. Oldenburg Verlag, München/Wien, pp. 310–330.

Taylor, John. B. (2013). The effectiveness of central bank independence vs. policy rules. *Business Economics*, 48(3), 155–162.

Touraine, Alain (1994). *Qu'est-ce que la Démocratie?* Fayard, Paris.

Tucker, Paul (2018). *Unelected Power.* Princeton University Press, Princeton, NJ.

Vallet, Guillaume (2019). "This is a Man's World: Pouvoir et Autorité Genrés dans le Milieu des Banques Centrales", *Revue de la régulation*, 25 (1) [available on line: DOI: 10.4000/regulation.14738].

Walsh, Carl, E. & Woodford, Michael (2005). Interest and Prices: Foundations of a Theory of Monetary Policy, *Macroeconomic Dynamics*, February, pp. 462–268.

Weber, Max (2003 [1919]). Le Savant et Le Politique, La Découverte, Paris.

Wilson, Woodrow (1887). The Study of Administration, *Political Science Quarterly*, 2 (2), pp. 197–222.

# 11 Foreign exchange accumulation and the advent of the monetary policy quadrilemma

*Thibault Laurentjoye*

## 1 Introduction

The tremendous accumulation of official foreign exchange (hereafter, FX) reserves over the last decades is one of the most striking features of the international economy. An increase in the ratio of international reserves to GDP (cf. Table 11.1) has been observed mostly in emerging markets across Asia and Latin America, as well as certain advanced economies such as Japan and Switzerland. This follows a change in the perceived role and use of international reserves held by central banks, which has gone from mainly passive and residual to active and strategic. It is now accepted that "foreign exchange intervention in the spot market can counter a sharp depreciation of overshooting of [a country's] currency" (People's Bank of China 2019) and that FX reserves provide "insurance against external turbulence" (Central Bank of Brazil 2019).

Research on the topic was initially driven by the work of practitioners – economists working in central banks, think tanks or international organisations – and more recently translated into macroeconomic theory. A new consensus is emerging, whereby using reserves as a policy tool can improve monetary policy autonomy in a flexible exchange rate regime or help maintain a fixed peg (Basu et al. 2020, Bianchi & Lorenzoni 2021). This newly found policy role for international reserves has deep consequences for the conduct of monetary policy in an open setting. By adding reserves to the list of policy tools, one can turn the famous monetary policy trilemma into a quadrilemma – as has been emphasised implicitly by Frenkel (2007) and explicitly by Aizenman (2013, 2019).

This chapter offers a twofold contribution to support the case for the quadrilemma. The first contribution is a logical characterisation of the quadrilemma in the form of a single equation which includes exchange rate variations, interest rate differential, capital controls and the level of reserves. The second contribution consists of a nominal stock-flow consistent (SFC) model with two countries, characterised by perfect capital mobility and imperfect asset substitutability, to study the pure effect of international investors' portfolio reallocation following unanticipated changes in the

DOI: 10.4324/9781003253457-14

*Table 11.1* FX reserves to GDP in selected countries

| *Country* | *2020* | *2000* | *Change* |
|---|---|---|---|
| Switzerland | 144% | 19% | (+125%) |
| China | 142% | 63% | (+79%) |
| Singapore | 107% | 83% | (+23%) |
| Czech Republic | 68% | 21% | (+46%) |
| Thailand | 51% | 26% | (+26%) |
| Israel | 43% | 18% | (+25%) |
| Peru | 36% | 17% | (+19%) |
| Malaysia | 32% | 28% | (+4%) |
| Iceland | 30% | 4% | (+25%) |
| Japan | 28% | 7% | (+26%) |
| Republic of Korea | 27% | 23% | (+5%) |
| Hungary | 27% | 24% | (+3%) |
| Republic of Poland | 26% | 16% | (+10%) |
| Brazil | 25% | 5% | (+20%) |
| China, P.R Mainland | 23% | 14% | (+9%) |
| India | 22% | 22% | (0%) |
| Colombia | 22% | 9% | (+12%) |
| Norway | 21% | 16% | (+4%) |
| Denmark | 20% | 9% | (+11%) |
| Mexico | 19% | 5% | (+14%) |
| South Africa | 16% | 7% | (+9%) |
| Chile | 16% | 19% | (−3%) |
| Turkey | 13% | 9% | (+4%) |
| Indonesia | 13% | 11% | (+2%) |
| Sweden | 11% | 7% | (+4%) |
| Argentina | 10% | 8% | (+2%) |
| United Kingdom | 8% | 3% | (+5%) |
| New Zealand | 7% | 7% | (−1%) |
| Canada | 6% | 4% | (+1%) |
| Australia | 3% | 5% | (−2%) |
| United States | 1% | 1% | (+0%) |

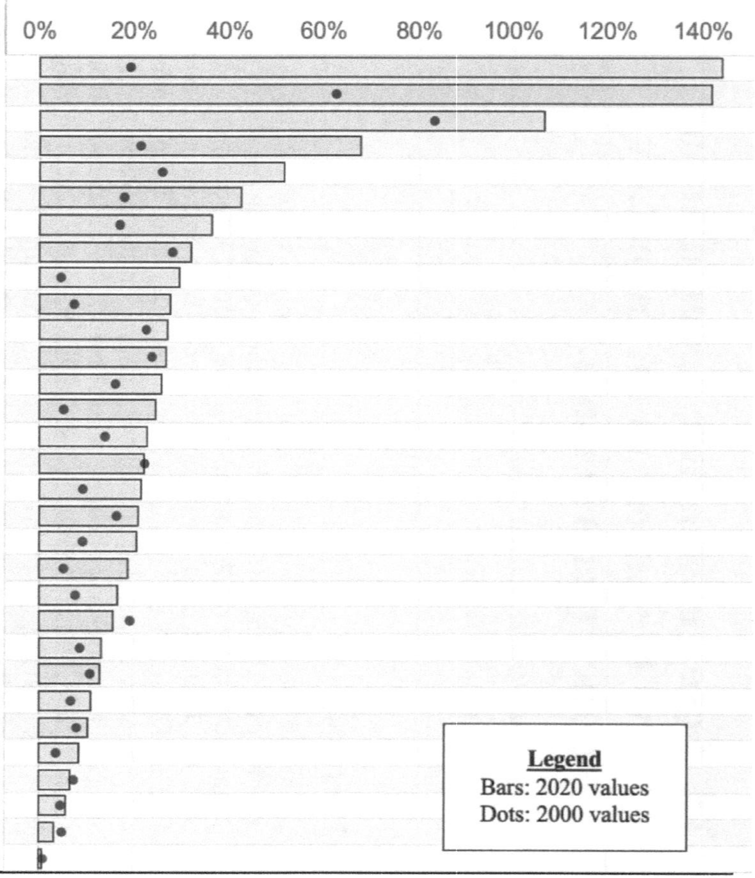

policy rate of the domestic economy. The model is run several times, varying the direction of the monetary policy shock and the relative size of the two countries. Two constraints on reserves are highlighted, one in the short run and one in the long run – albeit less significant – which define the limit between the classical trilemma and the quadrilemma.

The rest of this chapter is organised as follows. The next section provides a non-exhaustive survey of the literature on the rise of FX reserves in the recent decades. Section 3 reviews the monetary policy trilemma and highlights some of its shortcomings. Section 4 discusses recent developments in international economics, namely, the quadrilemma versus dilemma controversy, as well as the implications of the use of dominant currencies in pricing and financing processes. Section 5 presents the monetary policy quadrilemma in the form of a single equation. Section 6 contains a modelling attempt to display the most unorthodox application of the quadrilemma, that is, the trilemma 'breach'. The model highlights the existence of asymmetric constraints on FX reserves in the short run, as well as a long-term inversion of FX reserve variations when flows are solely driven by investors' portfolio reallocation.

## 2 The rise of FX reserves as a policy tool

The question of FX reserves has been around for centuries, if not longer. In the context of metallic standard systems, countries with insufficient reserves were expected to devalue their currency against gold to restore their trade balance or increase interest rates to attract capitals. During the Bretton Woods era, insufficient reserves would provoke "balance-of-payment crises" which later became "currency crises" (Krugman 1979, Obstfeld 1984). However, in neither of these contexts were reserves given an active role to play in terms of policy making; they were merely regarded as a residual determined passively by trade, income and capital flows.

An evolution occurred at the end of the 1990s and early 2000s, whereby reserves acquired a more active and strategic role (Aizenman 2019). This paradigm shift followed a decade of violent currency crises in Asia and Latin America: Mexico in 1994–1995, Thailand, Indonesia and South Korea in 1997–1998, Brazil in 1999, Argentina in 2001. Calvo and Reinhart (2002) talk about "fear of floating" to describe the behaviour of emerging countries whose currencies officially float freely but who effectively intervene on FX markets to limit exchange rate fluctuations. Using daily data from Mexico and Turkey, Domaç and Mendoza (2004) show that FX interventions can indeed reduce short-term exchange rate volatility, which can prove pivotal in achieving inflation targeting in countries where the pass-through from exchange rate to inflation is high.

Aizenman and Lee (2007) provide an early discussion of the potential reasons behind the accumulation of FX reserves, which they call "motives". The first one is the precautionary motive, which corresponds to a self-insurance usage of reserves to avoid financial disruption linked with current account deterioration, sudden stops of capital inflows or speculative attacks. Then comes the mercantilist motive, whereby reserve accumulation aims to neutralise appreciating forces in the FX market, often as part of a broader strategy of export-base growth. Using a sample of 58 countries, advanced as well as emerging, the authors compare the importance of the two motives and conclude to an overall greater relevance of the precautionary motive. Notably, they find the degree of capital account liberalisation to be statistically significant and positively correlated with the ratio of international reserves to GDP across the sample. According to the authors, this implies that "capital market developments are a robust factor behind the recent build-up in international reserves, if not the single most important factor" (p. 200).

According to Arslan and Cantú (2019), the precautionary motive was progressively superseded by goals associated with monetary and exchange rate policies. Aizenman et al. (2015) investigate the changing nature of the hoarding of international reserves in the aftermath of the Great Financial Crisis using principal component analysis on data consisting of 95 countries – of which 22 advanced – from 1999 to 2012. Their results highlight changes in the determinants underpinning reserve accumulation after the financial crisis. The volatility in commodity prices that characterised the late 2000s led many countries, in particular emerging ones, to use their reserves to cushion these shocks, which constitutes another declination of the precautionary motive. Aizenman et al. (2015) also point to the existence of significant differences in average hoarding between regions, measured by regional fixed effects, which they attribute to implicit rivalry between countries of the same region. The authors use as a potential explanation the existence of a "keeping up with the Joneses" effect first identified by Machlup (1966) and adapted to reserve accumulation by Cheung and Qian (2009).

Drawing on a survey of 21 central banks, Patel and Cavallino (2019) identify multiple operational objectives of FX intervention: influencing the level of the exchange rate, smoothing its trend path, limiting its volatility, limiting the pressure caused by international investors and providing liquidity when the market is too thin. The end goals associated with these operational objectives include smoothing commodity prices, maintaining external competitiveness as well as reducing FX speculation and funding shortages. As far as the implementation of FX intervention is concerned, spot market interventions remain the most common form although the use of forwards and derivatives has been on the rise – Brazil being an extreme case, where all FX intervention has been taking place in the form of FX swaps since 2013 (Central Bank of Brazil 2019). According to Patel and Cavallino, the main reason to use derivatives is to economise reserves and keep them for specific uses such as funding gaps. This confirms earlier results by Aizenman et al. (2015), who found a negative correlation between international reserve accumulation and access to swap lines after the Great Financial Crisis.

In parallel with the benefits stated above, accumulating FX reserves also comes at a cost. Dutt (2021) lists three forms of concerns. The first one is the financial cost of hoarding reserves, since reserves can be invested in assets whose return is lower than the cost of central bank liabilities or can be invested in higher yielding assets. However, this cost must be compared with the gains coming from reduced financial instability and the associated lower risk premium. The second concern stems from the possibility of moral hazard since reserves can create a false feeling of safety and foster excessive risk-taking in the domestic economy. The third concern is of a more political nature: in the absence of a designated supranational institution acting as an international lender of last resort, there is a risk that access to FX refinancing facilities such as swap lines be given on a somewhat arbitrary basis or in a way interfering with the sovereignty of peripheric countries. It is therefore not possible to isolate a 'pure cost' of holding international reserves, since costs and benefits are intertwined. Within the scope of the present chapter, I will assume that the accumulation of FX reserves over the course of several decades indicates that, overall, the benefits of this accumulation outweigh its cost(s).

## 3 Cracks in the trilemma

The dominant approach to monetary policy theory in an open setting relies on the famous trilemma coming from Mundell (1963) and Fleming (1962). In its classical form, the trilemma or impossible trinity states that a country (or any geographical entity) cannot pursue an independent monetary policy while maintaining a fixed exchange rate in a context of freely moving capitals. Another way of stating the trilemma is to offer a choice between three configurations:

- Floating autonomy characterised by flexible exchange rates, high capital mobility and autonomous monetary policy – the USA, Japan, India, Norway, Sweden and the Euro area taken as a whole belong to this category.
- Monetary alignment characterised by fixed exchange rates, high capital mobility and constrained monetary policy – member countries of the Euro area fall within this category, as well as countries pegged to external currencies such as Singapore or Denmark.
- Financial autarky characterised by fixed exchange rate, low or non-existent capital mobility and autonomous monetary policy – this configuration was encountered during the Bretton Woods era from 1944 to 1971, and more recently in China during most of the 1990s and 2000s.

An obvious caveat of the classical formulation of the trilemma is the reference to 'monetary policy' as if it were an unambiguous term, whereas in both theory and reality, monetary policy is vastly heterogeneous. As far as macroeconomic theory is concerned, monetary policy used to refer to changes in the quantity of money and had come to signify changes in interest rates only a few decades ago. Yet, not all countries use interest rates in the same way: some central banks use corridor systems consisting of multiple rates (e.g. the ECB) while others mostly rely on a single rate approach (e.g. the Bank of England or the National Bank of Switzerland). Certain central banks, such as the Monetary Authority of Singapore, do not even use interest rates as an official policy tool. Instead of talking about 'monetary policy', it would therefore be preferable to refer to precise policy measures, such as interest rate targeting or FX intervention.

The internal articulation of monetary policy frameworks also varies greatly across countries. For instance, Denmark uses interest rates as a tool to maintain a fixed exchange rate vis-à-vis the euro which is itself a way of importing price stability (Danmarks Nationalbank 2021a). By comparison, Singapore uses FX intervention as a way of keeping the nominal effective exchange rate within a crawling band, as exchange rate targeting is seen as a better way of stabilising prices than interest rate policy (Monetary Authority of Singapore 2021).

Notwithstanding this semantic caveat, the trilemma is still widely accepted as the most relevant way of framing challenges posed to monetary policy makers in an open economy (Obstfeld 2015, Obstfeld et al. 2017) although the way it is used has evolved over time. Notably, its interpretation has become more nuanced. For instance, the choice of exchange rate regimes has gone from a choice between two extremes, hard peg and pure floating, to considering intermediate arrangements, such as managed floating, crawling bands and pegs.[1] The mobility of capital can be measured using the Chinn-Ito index (Chinn & Ito 2006), which goes from zero to one. Monetary policy autonomy can be assessed by regressing interest changes in a given country on changes in interest rates in the core countries (Aizenman et al. 2016).

Lavoie (2014) introduces a distinction between capital mobility and asset substitutability. Capital mobility is related to technical and political factors, such as the development of financial markets, their degree of connection abroad and the absence of capital controls. Asset substitutability pertains to investors' preferences, as reflected in their portfolio allocation and reaction to price and yield changes. Lavoie insists that perfect capital mobility does not mean that yields will necessarily align, since investors treat various assets as imperfect substitutes.

It is possible to express imperfect asset substitution using a general interest-parity relationship:

$$r_{DOM} = r_{FOR} - \Delta xr^{e}_{DOM} + \rho \tag{11.1}$$

where $r_{DOM}$ is the domestic interest rate, $r_{FOR}$ the foreign interest rate, $\Delta xr^{e}_{DOM}$ the expected change in the domestic exchange rate xr (expressed as the number of foreign currency units per domestic currency units) and ρ a variable capturing the effects of imperfect asset substitution.

To understand the kind of pattern followed in the real world by the variable ρ from equation [11.1], the best option is to look at interest rate differentials between two financially integrated countries sharing similar economic fundamentals and linked with a fixed exchange rate. The case of Denmark, which has been conducting a fixed exchange rate policy since 1982, initially against the Deutsche Mark and then against the euro,[2] seems very relevant in that respect.

Denmark is widely considered a very robust economy. Its current account surplus amounts to 7.5% of GDP on average since 2013, which is on par with Germany. Its public debt is highly rated by all agencies and stood at respectively at 33.3% and 42.2% of GDP at the end of 2019 and 2020, while Germany's public debt stood at 59.7% and 69.8%. Furthermore, Denmark is completely financially integrated with its European neighbours due to its belonging to the European Union, and it has demonstrated several times its ability to maintain a peg with Germany than the Eurozone.

Figure 11.1 shows the spread on the ten-year bond yields between Denmark and Germany from January 2006 to November 2021. A positive value indicates that the Danish yield was higher than the German yield. The average spread over the period is 0.139%, which means investors received on average this additional yield as a premium for holding Danish ten-year government bonds. This fact is quite hard to reconcile with the traditional

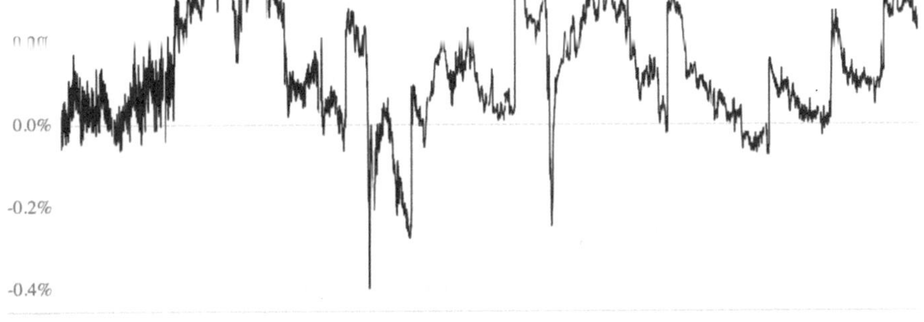


Source: investing.com, author's calculations.

*Figure 11.1* Ten-year bond spread between Denmark and Germany.

uncovered interest rate parity, even in its augmented version including a risk premium (Obstfeld 2015) since Denmark is, if anything, even more robust than Germany from an economic and financial perspective.

Another striking feature of the spread over the period is its volatility. Although the spread has been positive most of the time, it ventured a few times under zero, reaching as low as −0.4% on 1 December 2011, −0.28% on 27 August 2012 and 0.25% on 12 February 2015 – at the height of a speculative episode which triggered a rare and significant use of reserves by the Danmarks Nationalbank. When in positive territory, the spread went many times above 0.2% and stayed there for around a year in 2015–2016.

From these observations, it follows that the variable ρ for Denmark is slightly positive on average and oscillates between −0.1% and 0.4% most of the time. This seems hard to reconcile with the uncovered interest-parity approach underpinning the classical trilemma.

## 4 Beyond the trilemma: quadrilemma or dilemma?

Several authors have questioned the relevance of the trilemma for the globally financialised world of the early 21st century. Interestingly, the two main suggestions to revise the trilemma are going in apparently opposite directions (Dovonou 2021) since one camp argues the post-Bretton Woods era is characterised by the presence of financial stability which turns the trilemma into a quadrilemma (Aizenman 2013) while the other claims that the existence of a global financial cycle renders exchange regimes ineffective to hinder the transmission of monetary policy from centre to periphery, thus turning the trilemma into a dilemma (Rey 2013).

### 4.1 The quadrilemma approach

According to Aizenman (2013, 2019), the trilemma originated in the context of the Bretton Woods system, characterised by limited international capital mobility, fixed exchange rate regimes and autonomous national monetary policies, while since the end of Bretton Woods in 1971, former member countries have opened their financial account and most of them have opted for flexible exchange rate regimes. Both these factors have proved to be quite destabilising.

In the case of floating currencies, uncertainty created by violent fluctuations in the exchange rate have incentivised central banks to use FX intervention to smooth the exchange rate path and reduce its volatility, thus moving from free to managed floating. In the case of countries with pegged currencies – whether fixed or crawling – the accumulation of foreign reserves has contributed to the maintenance of the peg, China in the 1990s and 2000s being a prime example.

Unlike the Bretton Woods era, which saw no major financial crisis, the post-Bretton Woods era has been ridden with financial instability, which was made possible by the high degree of financial integration between countries facilitating the circulation of 'hot money' flows, sudden stops and international credit spillovers. According to Aizenman, "concerns about financial stability morphed the trilemma into a quadrilemma" (Aizenman 2019, p.449). Although Aizenman identifies financial stability as the fourth corner of the trilemma, alongside exchange rate stability, financial integration and autonomous policy, in practice he uses foreign reserves as a measurable proxy.

Andaiyani et al. (2020) provide an application of the quadrilemma to Indonesia, using data covering the years 1983–2017, which they further break down into the two sub-periods before and after 1999. The authors find that FX reserves have significantly contributed to the overall macroeconomic adjustment process following monetary policy changes, but they argue that reserves could have played a greater role.

The fundamental insights of the quadrilemma – although not the term 'quadrilemma' itself – can be found earlier in Roberto Frenkel (2007) who states:

> In a context of free capital mobility, [... t]he condition for combining control of the exchange rate with the preservation of monetary autonomy is the existence of an excess supply of international currency at the exchange rate targeted by the central bank. That is, the conditions in the current account and capital account are such that the local currency would appreciate if the bank did not intervene to hold down the exchange rate. In this context, *the monetary authority can set the exchange rate by purchasing the excess supply in the currency market* and can control the interest rate by sterilizing the monetary effects of this intervention, which it does by issuing treasury or central bank bonds in the money market. The central bank has two instruments for achieving its two goals: *intervention in the foreign currency market to set the exchange rate* and intervention in the money market to determine the interest rate.
>
> (Frenkel 2007, p.30, italics mine)

Frenkel goes on to suggest that in a context of international reserve scarcity, an asymmetry appears between surplus and deficit countries – the former being able to escape the trilemma due to their ability to regain reserves, while the latter cannot.[3]

Even the most ardent proponents of the trilemma have admitted that the use of international reserves could have implications on the conduct of monetary policy in an open setting. For instance, Obstfeld (2015) notes that the accumulation of large stocks of FX reserves has acted as a stabilising factor for capital flows, thereby improving trilemma trade-offs.

In its famous manual, Blanchard (2017) first presents the usual view that "under fixed exchange rates, the central bank gives up monetary policy as a policy instrument" (p.424) before moving to more realistic considerations in the appendix of chapter 19:

> with imperfect capital mobility, a country has some freedom to move the domestic interest rate while maintaining its fixed exchange rate. This freedom depends primarily on three factors: [...] the willingness of investors to shift between domestic and foreign assets, [...] the degree of capital controls, [...] the amount of foreign exchange reserves it holds.
> (Blanchard 2017, p.430)

Economists affiliated to the Modern Money Theory (MMT) approach usually support flexible exchange rate arrangements as a central feature of monetary sovereignty. It is therefore all the more remarkable to read the following excerpt from Wray (2015):

> Above we argued that a floating exchange rate provides the greatest domestic policy space, while a fixed exchange rate normally reduces that space – unless, like China, sufficient foreign currency reserves are accumulated to remove any doubt that the peg can be maintained.
> (p.176)

The ability of reserves to improve monetary policy space is also emphasised by Bianchi & Sosa-Padilla (2020). Using a model of endogenous sovereign default, the authors find that "when the government issues debt to accumulate reserves, this does not necessarily lead to increases in spreads" (p.2). This is because accumulated reserves can be useful to mitigate higher borrowing costs when borrowing conditions are particularly adverse. As a result, the authors conclude that "a government that increases its debt, but accumulate reserves at the same time, may not see increases in the cost of borrowing" (p.2).

## 4.2 The dilemma approach

Another major claim regarding the evolution of the trilemma comes from Hélène Rey (2013, 2016) according to whom the existence of a global financial cycle hinders the ability of variable exchange rate regimes to insulate countries from external shocks, which can only be sheltered by using capital controls or prudential measures. From this, Rey (2013) concludes that the monetary policy trilemma has morphed into a dilemma, whereby the only choice lies between foregoing autonomous monetary policies or implementing measures to reduce capital mobility.[4]

Rey's approach can be found in several complementary papers. To measure the global financial cycle, Rey (2013) highlights the existence of co-movements of capital flows within a sample of 49 countries. She also identifies the global financial cycle as being tightly and negatively related to the VIX – which is an index calculated using the prices of S&P 500 options to generate a 30-day forward projection of volatility. Rey (2016) further identifies three mechanisms or (sub)channels: an "international credit channel" operating through collateral constraints, a "risk-taking channel" that relies on the synchronisation and compression of risk premia around the world and a "fear of floating channel" stemming from potentially disruptive central bank reactions.

Using a cross section of 858 risky asset prices distributed on five continents, Miranda-Agrippino and Rey (2015) show that 25% of the variance of risky returns can be explained by a "global factor" for which they effectively use the VIX as a proxy. Passari and Rey (2015) regress stock market returns and domestic credit to GDP market returns on a combination of explanatory variables including the VIX and a classification of exchange rate regimes divided into four categories ranging from hard peg (1) to free float (4), across four periods (1990–2013, 1990–2007, 2000–2007, 2007–2013) and the same 49 countries as Rey (2015).

A major flaw of the dilemma approach comes from the sample of countries used, which is heavily skewed in favour of developed countries. Out of 49 countries used by Passari and Rey (2015), 20 of them are European, and while Asian countries include China and Indonesia, India is not included. Furthermore, most of the European countries either belong to the Eurozone or have been pegged to the euro – like Denmark. As a result, category 1 consists mostly of the Eurozone, as well as a few other countries such as China during the de facto fixed peg period, and Argentina during the currency board era. The sampling bias is even more pronounced in Miranda-Agrippino and Rey (2015), which does not include Asian emerging countries or any Latin American country at all. As a result, the 'global financial channel' ought to be renamed 'first-world financial channel'.

Perhaps unsurprisingly, Rey's dilemma conjecture has since been refuted in several works. Using a sample of 40 emerging markets over the period 1986–2013, Obstfeld et al. (2017) find that countries with fixed exchange rate regimes are more likely to experience financial vulnerabilities than those with relatively flexible regimes. Using a sample spanning across 161 countries from 1970 to 2013, and multiple specifications, Ligonnière (2018) obtains several key results. First, he finds that monetary policy autonomy is mainly driven by financial openness and the exchange rate regime – which invalidates the dilemma claim. Second, he finds that the addition of FX reserves as a control variable improves the quality of the estimation, which supports Aizenman's quadrilemma claim. Finally, Ligonnière finds that the sensitivity to the global financial cycle depends less on the fluctuations of the VIX than on the presence of global investors and global banks in the different countries.

### 4.3 Dominant currency paradigm

A last branch of the recent international macroeconomic literature highlights the existence of a "dominant currency paradigm" (Gopinath et al. 2020,

Gopinath & Itskokhi 2021) and analyses the implications of financing and price setting using the currencies of core countries, particularly the US dollar. While the traditional Mundellian approach is based on producer currency pricing (also known as local or exporter currency pricing), this new approach acknowledges the dominance of a small number of currencies in global financing and pricing practices. As far as the monetary policy trilemma is concerned, the implications of borrowing and setting prices in dominant currencies are twofold. First, the use of dominant currency renders domestic monetary policy less effective, as it cannot influence the financing conditions of agents borrowing in external dominant currencies. Second, exchange rate depreciation can prove problematic when domestic liabilities are denominated in a foreign currency, as their value expressed in domestic currency will increase.

The effect of dominant currency practices on the theoretical choice of an n-lemma is not clear-cut. On the one hand, it could be argued that dominant currency usage underpins a theoretical move towards the dilemma, since changes in the interest rates associated with the domestic currency have less effect on domestic financing conditions – thereby crippling the trilemma. On the other hand, the use of dominant currencies in pricing and financing processes strengthens the case for peripheric countries to accumulate international reserves as a way of insuring themselves against external financial instability, by becoming their own international lender of last resort. Using their "integrated policy framework", Basu et al. (2020) find that FX intervention makes sense in the context of dominant currency pricing, especially when the debt in external currency is high.[5]

In light of the previous considerations, I believe the case for turning the trilemma into a quadrilemma is much stronger than the case for the dilemma. This is not to say that Rey's approach should be dismissed altogether, but as far as the characterisation of an n-lemma is concerned, the quadrilemma approach appears more relevant.

## 5 A statement of the quadrilemma

Let us now turn to a synthetic exposition of the quadrilemma. As a starting point, the central bank intervenes on the spot market to influence the exchange rate. Noting xr, the exchange rate defined as the number of unit of foreign currency per unit of domestic currency, CA the sum of the current and capital accounts[6] (see IMF 2009), NFI the net financial inflows – i.e. the financial account excluding changes in official reserves – and FXR the amount of official FX reserves, we have the following relation:

$$\Delta \mathrm{xr} = \alpha \ (\mathrm{CA} + \mathrm{NFI} - \Delta \mathrm{FXR}) \tag{11.2}$$

where $\alpha$ is a positive function, meaning that in the absence of FX intervention by the central bank, a net inflow will lead to exchange rate appreciation, while a net outflow will provoke an exchange rate depreciation. Due to the minus sign, an increase in the FX reserves will lead to a lower exchange rate, while pushing the exchange rate up will necessitate a reduction in reserves.

This describes the relationship between exchange rate and reserves in most exchange rate regimes. For instance, a perfectly fixed peg ($\Delta xr = 0$) involves allowing FX reserves to fluctuate without restriction to match the net inflows or outflows. On the other hand, adopting a perfectly floating regime involves leaving the reserves untouched ($\Delta FXR = 0$). Intermediate possibilities include managed floating, where reserve variations are used to smooth exchange rate fluctuations, or crawling peg, where a targeted variation of the exchange rate will determine the extent of reserve use.

As a second step, I assume that at any point NFI are, among other things, a function of the differential between national and foreign interest rates ($r_{DOM} - r_{ROW}$) where $r_{DOM}$ is the vector of domestic interest rates, $r_{ROW}$ is the vector of foreign interest rates and NFI is a decreasing function of the interest rate differential – no assumption is made about the slope and intercept of NFI.

Finally, I note β the degree of mobility of capital between countries: $\beta = 1$ means that capitals flow freely between countries, while $\beta = 0$ corresponds to a situation where capital controls prevent investors from entering or leaving the country at short notice.

Combining the previous elements, we obtain the following equation to identify the monetary policy quadrilemma:

$$\Delta xr = \alpha \left(CA + \beta .NFI\ (i - i^*)\ -\ \Delta FXR\right) \tag{11.3}$$

According to equation [11.3], and assuming for the sake of simplicity that CA = 0, it is possible to maintain a fixed exchange rate, i.e. $\Delta xr = 0$, if at least one of the following conditions is satisfied:

a The exchange rate is insensitive to net FX flows, i.e. $\alpha() = 0$.
b Capital controls are enforced, i.e. $\beta = 0$.
c Capital flows are insensitive to interest rate differentials, i.e. $k(\ ) = 0$.
d Domestic interest rates adjust so that $NFI\ (i - i^*) = 0$, which is tantamount to saying monetary policy is constrained.
e Reserves can vary to compensate for new FX flows, i.e. $\Delta R = \beta.NFI\ (i - i^*)$.

Options (a) and (c) are usually ruled out, due to the implicit assumption that price elasticities of supplies and demands for financial assets are different from zero. Therefore, possibilities (b), (d) and (e) remain to stabilise the exchange rate: capital controls, interest rate adjustment and the use of reserves. We can therefore establish the following quadrilemma:[7]

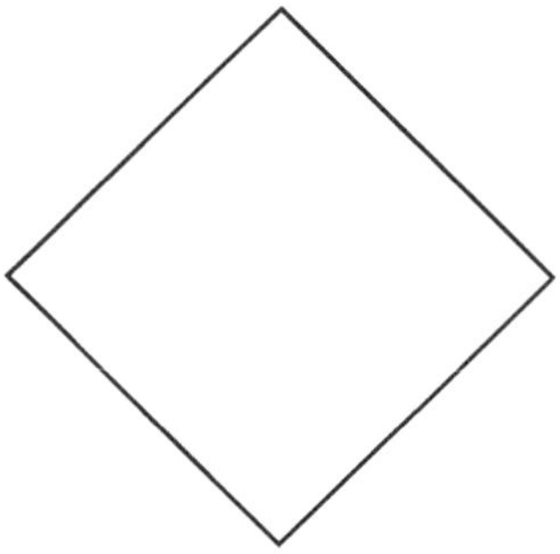


*Figure 11.2* Quadrilemma.

Three of the four corners can be simultaneously met, which means:

- There is scope for leading an autonomous interest rate policy in the context of a fixed peg, even in the absence of capital controls, as long as FX reserves are sufficient (particularly in the case of net outflows).
- If there is a constraint on FX reserves, one of the other dimensions will have to give in, which reactivates the classical trilemma.

## 6 A simple modelling of the quadrilemma

> In a context of free capital mobility, the central bank can simultaneously control the exchange rate and the interest rate. This runs directly counter to what is claimed by the so-called "trilemma" of an economy open to capital movements. Here we argue that this trilemma is false in certain circumstances and, consequently, is false as a general theorem.
>
> (Frenkel 2007, p.30)

In this section, I provide a simple model[8] to display the most extreme application of the quadrilemma, that is, the possibility of bypassing the trilemma altogether, in line with Frenkel's quote above. I use a two-country SFC model[9] consisting of two countries linked by a fixed exchange rate arrangement: domestic economy (DOM) and rest of the world (ROW). The exchange rate is normalised to 1 and does not appear explicitly in the equations. The structures of the stocks and flows of the two-country economy are illustrated by the matrices in Tables 11.2 and 11.3.

*Table 11.2* Balance sheets

| *Balance sheets* | | | | | | | | | |
|---|---|---|---|---|---|---|---|---|---|
| | *DOM* | | | | *ROW* | | | | |
| | Households | Firm | Government | Central bank | Households | Firms | Government | Central bank | Sum |
| DOM bills | $+B^{DOM}_{HH_{DOM}}$ | | $-B^{DOM}$ | | $+B^{DOM}_{HH_{ROW}}$ | | | $+B^{DOM}_{CB_{ROW}}$ | 0 |
| ROW bills | $+B^{ROW}_{HH_{DOM}}$ | | | $+B^{ROW}_{CB_{DOM}}$ | $+B^{ROW}_{HH_{ROW}}$ | | $-B^{ROW}$ | | 0 |
| DOM ccy | $+M^{DOM}_{HH_{DOM}}$ | | $+M^{DOM}_{GOV_{DOM}}$ | $-M^{DOM}$ | | | | | 0 |
| ROW ccy | | | | | $+M^{ROW}_{HH_{ROW}}$ | | $+M^{ROW}_{GOV_{ROW}}$ | $-M^{ROW}$ | 0 |
| Balance | $-V_{DOM}$ | | $+D_{DOM}$ | $NW_{CB_{DOM}}$ | $-V_{ROW}$ | | $+D_{ROW}$ | $NW_{CB_{ROW}}$ | 0 |
| Sum | 0 | | 0 | 0 | 0 | | 0 | 0 | 0 |

*Table 11.3* Dependent variable: stock market returns

| *Income – expenditure transactions* | *DOM* | | | | *ROW* | | | | |
|---|---|---|---|---|---|---|---|---|---|
| | *Households* | *Firms* | *Government* | *Central bank* | *Households* | *Firms* | *Government* | *Central bank* | *Sum* |
| Consumption | $-C_{DOM}$ | $+C_{DOM}$ | | | $-C_{ROW}\cdot$ | $+C_{ROW}$ | | | |
| Government expenditure | | $+G_{DOM}$ | $-G_{DOM}$ | | | $+G_{ROW}$ | $-G_{ROW}$ | | |
| Trade | | $+X_{DOM}$ | | | | $-IM_{ROW}$ | | | |
| | | $-IM_{DOM}$ | | | | $+X_{ROW}$ | | | |
| GDP | $+Y_{DOM}$ | $-Y_{DOM}$ | | | $+Y_{ROW}$ | $-Y_{ROW}$ | | | 0 |
| Interest payments | $+B^{DOM}_{HH_{DOM}}$ $*r_{DOM}$ | | $-B^{DOM}$ $*r_{DOM}$ | | $+B^{DOM}_{HH_{ROW}}$ $*r_{DOM}$ | | | $+B^{DOM}_{CB_{ROW}}$ $*r_{DOM}$ | 0 |
| Taxes | $+B^{ROW}_{HH_{DOM}}$ $*r_{ROW}$ | | | $+B^{ROW}_{CB_{DOM}}$ $*r_{ROW}$ | $+B^{ROW}_{HH_{ROW}}$ $*r_{ROW}$ | | $-B^{ROW}$ $*r_{ROW}$ | | 0 |
| | $-T_{DOM}$ | | $+T_{DOM}$ | | $-T_{ROW}$ | | $+T_{ROW}$ | | |
| CB profits | | | $+Div_{DOM}$ | $-Div_{DOM}$ | | | $+Div_{ROW}$ | $-Div_{ROW}$ | 0 |
| Flow of funds transactions | | | | | | | | | |
| DOM bills | $-\Delta B^{DOM}_{hh_{DOM}}$ | | $+\Delta B^{DOM}$ | | $-\Delta B^{DOM}_{hh_{ROW}}$ | | | $-\Delta B^{DOM}_{CB_{ROW}}$ | 0 |
| ROW bills | $-\Delta B^{ROW}_{hh_{DOM}}$ | | | $-\Delta B^{ROW}_{CB_{DOM}}$ | $-\Delta B^{ROW}_{hh_{ROW}}$ | | $+\Delta B^{ROW}$ | | 0 |
| DOM ccy | $-\Delta M^{DOM}_{hh_{DOM}}$ | | $-\Delta M^{DOM}_{gov_{DOM}}$ | $+\Delta M^{DOM}$ | | | | | 0 |
| ROW ccy | | | | | $-\Delta M^{ROW}_{hh_{ROW}}$ | | $-\Delta M^{ROW}_{gov_{ROW}}$ | $+\Delta M^{ROW}$ | 0 |
| Balance | 0 | | 0 | 0 | 0 | | 0 | 0 | 0 |

## 6.1 Model specification

The equations governing production in both countries are standard. Production (Y) is the sum of household consumption (C), government expenditure (G) and the trade balance (X – IM). Household consumption is a function of their disposable income (YD) and lagged wealth $\left(V_{(-1)}\right)$. Government. expenditure is a constant. Exports are determined by the other country's imports, which are a linear function of production.

$$Y_i = C_i + G_i + X_i - IM_i \tag{11.4}$$
$$C_i = \alpha_{1i} * YD_i + \alpha_{2i} * V_{i(-1)} \tag{11.5}$$
$$G_i = \bar{G}_i \tag{11.6}$$
$$X_i = IM_j \tag{11.7}$$
$$IM_i = \mu_i * Y_i \tag{11.8}$$

where, for each country i, $\alpha_{1i}$ is the propensity to consume out of disposable income, $\alpha_{2i}$ the propensity to consume out of wealth, $\mu_i$ the propensity to import and j denotes the other country.

Since firms do not retain any earnings, the value of production goes to households in the form of income. Household gross income (YG) is therefore the sum of production and interest income on domestic and foreign debt. Disposable income (YD) equals gross income minus income tax (T), itself a linear function of gross income (noting θ the income tax rate):

$$YG_i = Y_i + r_{i(-1)} * B^i_{hh_i(-1)} + r_{j(-1)} * B^j_{hh_i(-1)} \tag{11.9}$$
$$T_i = \theta * YG_i \tag{11.10}$$
$$YD_i = YG_i - T_i \tag{11.11}$$

When noting amounts of monetary and financial assets, the main letter relates to the type of asset: M in the case of currency (money), and B in the case of bills. The superscript pertains to the issuer. Since each type of asset can be issued by one issuer (the central bank in the case of currency, the government in the case of bills), only the country is mentioned. The subscript indicates who holds the asset: household or government in the case of currency, household or central bank in the case of bills. The number between brackets indicates the extent of the lag. Therefore, $B^i_{hh_i(-1)}$ is the amount that households of country i held in the form of their government's bills at the end of the previous period, and $B^j_{hh_i(-1)}$ the amount they held in the form of foreign government's bills. $r_{i(-1)}$ is the yield on domestic bills and $r_{j(-1)}$ the yield on foreign bills, both in the previous period.

The variation of households' wealth is equal to the difference between their disposable income and consumption. Households in each country allocate their wealth between domestic bonds, foreign bonds and domestic currency. The share of wealth allocated to each type of asset (e.g. bills issued by the government of country k) follows a Tobinesque process, whereby it is equal to the sum of a fixed proportion ($\lambda^{k,0}$) and variable increments depending on the respective yields on domestic ($\lambda^{k,r_i}$) and foreign bills ($\lambda^{k,r_j}$):

$$\Delta V_i = YD_i - C_i \quad (11.12)$$

$$B^k_{HH_i} = V_i * \left( \lambda^{k,0}_{HH_i} + \lambda^{k,r_i}_{HH_i} * r_i + \lambda^{k,r_j}_{HH_i} * r_j \right) \quad (11.13)$$

$$M^i_{HH_i} = V_i - B^i_{HH_i} - B^j_{HH_i} \quad (11.14)$$

The modelling of the endogenous money process associated with interest rate targeting[10] relies on a distinction between fundamental and market government debt – respectively noted $D_i$ and $B_i$, with i representing the country. Fundamental government debt, or government financing needs, is equal to the sum of past government deficits. It differs from market government debt, which is the sum of government bills issued on demand, held by households of both countries and the central bank of the other country. The two variables B and D can differ in size, based on portfolio preferences and the financing needs of the government. The difference between market and fundamental government debt corresponds to the balance of the government at its central bank ($\Delta M_{GOV}$). When market debt is greater than fundamental debt, the government holds excess funds as central bank reserves. When fundamental debt is greater than market debt, the government incurs an overdraft at its central bank. We assume that both reserves and the overdraft yield zero interest.[11] Finally, both central banks transfer their interest income earned on their international reserves to their government in the form of a dividend (Div).

$$\Delta D^i = G_i - T_i + r_{i(-1)} * B^i_{(-1)} - Div_i \quad (11.15)$$

$$\Delta B^i = B^i_{HH_i} + B^i_{HH_j} + B^i_{CB_j} \quad (11.16)$$

$$\Delta M^i_{GOV_i} = \Delta B^i - \Delta D^i \quad (11.17)$$

$$Div_i = r_{j(-1)} * B^j_{CB_i(-1)} \quad (11.18)$$

The current account of country i ($CA_i$) is the sum of the trade account and the international income account, i.e. net interest income. The financial account of country i ($FA_i$) is the sum of the changes in foreign households and central bank holdings of domestic bills, minus the changes in domestic households' holdings of foreign bills.

$$CA_i = X_i - IM_i + r_{j(-1)} * \left( B^j_{HH_i(-1)} + B^j_{CB_i(-1)} \right) - r_{i(-1)} * \left( B^i_{HH_j(-1)} + B^i_{CB_j(-1)} \right) \quad (11.19)$$

$$FA_i = \Delta B^i_{HH_j} + \Delta B^i_{CB_j} - \Delta B^j_{HH_i} \quad (11.20)$$

Since the central bank of ROW has no exchange rate target, it does not intervene on the FX market, thus keeping its foreign reserves constant. The burden of adjustment falls entirely onto DOM's central bank.

$$\Delta B^{DOM}_{CBROW} = 0 \quad (11.21)$$

$$\Delta B^{ROW}_{CBDOM} = CA_{DOM} + FA_{DOM} \quad (11.22)$$

By assumption, the two countries have always had a fixed exchange rate arrangement and their current accounts have always been equal to zero in the past. Initial foreign reserves are assumed to come from a currency exchange between the two central banks at an indefinite point in the past. The two countries have therefore initially the same amount of FX reserves, regardless of their relative size.[12]

Monetary authorities of DOM target both the domestic interest rate and the exchange vis-à-vis the rest of the world, while the monetary authorities of ROW target the foreign interest rate. Sterilisation of FX reserves by DOM occurs as a by-product of these policy stances. For example, a reduction in DOM's interest rate leads to investors, both domestic and foreign, selling DOM's securities to buy ROW securities instead. On the one hand, DOM's central bank commits to buying as many domestic securities as needed to stabilise the interest rate at its new, low level. On the other hand, its commitment to maintaining a fixed exchange rate leads DOM's central bank to sell as many FX reserves as needed. As a result, the size of DOM's balance sheet does not change, but its composition does: foreign securities are replaced with domestic ones.

## 6.2 Country configurations and portfolio setups

Three configurations are considered, corresponding to different relative sizes of the two countries. In the first scenario, the two countries are the same size and have perfectly symmetric portfolio coefficients ('Symmetry DOM/ROW') with no home bias in the holding of bills. In the second scenario, DOM is half as big as ROW ('Small DOM'), while the opposite happens in the third scenario, where DOM is twice as big as ROW ('Big DOM'). Note that, due to stock consistency, it is impossible to maintain symmetry in portfolio coefficients when the two countries are not the same size. It is a mathematical necessity that the biggest country – DOM or ROW depending on the scenario – must hold proportionately more of its bills than it does the other country's bills.

In the symmetric scenario, the households in each country start with a total portfolio of 100, which breaks down into 44 held in bills of their country, 44 held in bills of the other country and 12 held in currency – to simplify, it is assumed that households cannot hold the other country's currency. In the asymmetric scenarios, the 44-44-12 breakdown in household portfolio still applies to the small country, but the households of the big country whose total portfolio is twice as big hold 132 in the form of bills of their country, 44 in bills of the small country and 24 in their country's currency.

In all the scenarios, the central bank of each country starts with FX reserves of 12, held in the form of the other country's bills. Since we assume that DOM unilaterally pursues a fixed exchange rate, DOM's reserves vary to absorb net flows consecutive to changes in its interest rate, while ROW's reserves remain constant. As far as the public sector's balance sheet is concerned, a difference between the symmetric and asymmetric scenarios stems from the amount of government reserves at the central bank. Keeping the weight of currency in the households' portfolio equal between the two countries, while assuming the same amount of FX reserves in the two countries, implies that the net position of the government of the larger country with its central bank must be lower than the position of the government of the small country.

## 6.3 Introducing the shocks

In all the iterations of the model, interest rates in DOM and ROW are initially set to 2%. Two types of shocks are considered, both consisting of unanticipated variations in DOM's interest rate: the first one is an increase to 3%, and the second one is a reduction to 1%.

When DOM decreases its interest rate, investors from both countries react by selling DOM bills, buying ROW bills and increasing their holdings of currency. Since households can hold currency only from their own country, the decrease in the holdings of DOM bills by ROW investors fully translates into a higher demand for ROW assets – bills or currency – while the decrease in the holdings of DOM bills by DOM investors will only partly give way to capital outflows, since their demand for DOM currency will increase too.

The initial shock on DOM's FX reserves is therefore entirely due to the financial account, through changes in holdings of assets:

$$\Delta B^{ROW}_{CB_{DOM}} = FA_{DOM} = -\Delta B^{ROW}_{HH_{DOM}} - \Delta B^{ROW}_{HH_{ROW}} - \Delta M^{ROW}_{HH_{ROW}} \quad (11.23)$$

In the case of an increase in DOM's interest rate, the opposite happens: investors will buy DOM bills, sell ROW bills and reduce their holdings of currency. This leads the government of DOM to issue additional public debt to accommodate the demand – otherwise, the interest rate would have to decrease to its initial level.

The transmission of the shock happens through the same channel across all configurations, i.e. regardless of the relative size of the two

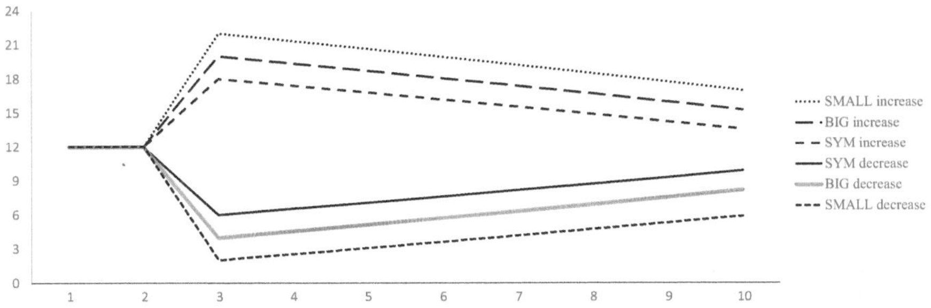


*Figure 11.3* FX reserves of country DOM across the various scenarios.

countries – only the magnitude differs. Figure 11.3 shows the evolution of DOM's FX reserves in the six scenarios – each corresponding to a different shock/configuration combination:

***Short-term effects***

In the short run, a rise in the interest rate of DOM brings about an increase in DOM's FX reserves, while a reduction in its interest rate provokes a decrease in its FX reserves. The initial shock is larger in the case when DOM is a small country – although interestingly the effect is stronger when DOM is the big country, compared to the symmetric configuration.

In none of the scenarios is the initial FX reserve variation big enough to deplete the reserves. This is due to a combination of several factors, which can be identified by combining equations (11.23) and (11.13):

$$B^{ROW}_{CB_{DOM}} \geq \lambda^{ROW,\, r_{DOM}}_{HH_{DOM}} * \Delta r_i * V_i + \lambda^{DOM, r_{DOM}}_{HH_{ROW}} * \Delta r_i * V_j \qquad (11.24)$$

The effect of the shock on DOM's FX reserves depends on investors' sensitivity to changes in yields, the change in interest rates and the level of wealth in the two countries. In other words, in the short run the trilemma can be bypassed as long as reserves are high enough, considering the change in interest rate, the degree of asset substitutability and the level of wealth in the two countries.

If the initial FX reserves are not sufficient to cushion the capital outflows, DOM will either have to let its interest rate increase or resort to external refinancing from ROW's central bank, for instance, in the form of swap lines.

### 6.4 Longer-term effects

As can be seen on Figure 11.3, the initial effect quickly reverses: a negative interest rate variation gives way to an increase in FX reserves, and vice versa. This is because the interest rate differential starts having an impact on the current account – while the initial financial account effect was a one-off. After a reduction in DOM's interest rate, DOM will pay less to ROW than it will receive, while the opposite will be the case following a rise in its interest rate. This means that in the long run, the pure effect of portfolio reallocation is the opposite of the short-run effect: an interest rate reduction would end up 'paying for itself' while an interest rate increase would eventually lead to the depletion of FX reserves.[13]

We therefore seem to observe an 'overshooting' of FX reserves – whereby a sharp initial variation in FX reserves is followed in the longer run by slower variations in the opposite direction – somewhat reminiscent of the exchange rate overshooting identified by Dornbusch (1976). However, Dornbusch relies on strict uncovered interest parity and short-term price stickiness of real goods and services – while this model makes no assumption on interest rate parity or price rigidity[14] – and Dornbusch's exchange rate tends towards an equilibrium value in the long term – while in this model, the level of FX reserves does not converge when solely determined by investors' preferences.

Table 11.4 reports the changes in selected variables across all scenarios and shocks. In each case, the first figure indicates the absolute change in each variable (with the associated percentage between brackets underneath), while the second figure shows the incremental variation over the next five periods (i.e. from t+1 to t+6, t being the period at which the shock occurs). This allows to see which variables keep on going in the same direction and which ones change trajectory once the initial effect of the shock wears off.

### 6.5 Reflections on the limits of the model

This model can be considered a reasonable approximation as far as short-run analysis is concerned, but is far less robust for longer-run analysis.[15] The model focuses on the effect of interest rate changes on portfolio allocation, which is the phenomenon underpinning interest rate parity arbitrage. To keep the rest of the model simple while performing multi-dimensional analysis, I considered only nominal variables, and production does not include a gross capital formation component. If we accept the idea that, in actual reality, changes in central bank interest rates affect financial decisions much earlier than decisions pertaining to the production of real goods and services, then this model is most reliable in the short run. In the long run, the model can be considered interesting insofar as it shows what the pure long-run effect of portfolio changes would be, in the absence of effects of monetary policy on the real side of the economy.

*Table 11.4* Selected variable changes across scenarios and shocks

| | | *1% decrease in DOM interest rate* | | *1% increase in DOM interest rate* | |
|---|---|---|---|---|---|
| *Variable* | *Scenario* | *Shock effect* | | *Further 5 periods* | |
| **DOM households' holdings of DOM bills** | **Symmetry DOM/FOR** | ↓4.00 (*−9.1%*) | ↑4.00 (*+9.1%*) | ↓9.00 (*−0.2%*) | ↑0.13 (*+0.2%*) |
| | **Small DOM** | ↑4.00 (*−9.1%*) | ↑4.00 (*+9.1%*) | ↓0.08 (*−0.2%*) | ↑0.12 (*+0.3%*) |
| | **Big DOM** | ↓8.00 (*−6.1%*) | ↑8.00 (*+6.1%*) | ↓0.41 (*−0.3%*) | ↑0.53 (*+0.4%*) |
| **DOM households' holdings of ROW bills** | **Symmetry DOM/FOR** | ↑2.00 (*+4.5%*) | ↓2.00 (*−4.5%*) | ↓0.10 (*−0.2%*) | ↑0.11 (*+0.3%*) |
| | **Small DOM** | ↑2.00 (*+4.5%*) | ↓2.00 (*−4.5%*) | ↓0.10 (*−0.2%*) | ↑0.11 (*+0.3%*) |
| | **Big DOM** | ↑4.00 (*+9.1%*) | ↓4.00 (*−9.1%*) | ↓0.16 (*−0.3%*) | ↑0.15 (*+0.4%*) |
| **DOM households' holdings of DOM currency** | **Symmetry DOM/FOR** | ↑2.00 (*+16.7%*) | ↓2.00 (*−16.7%*) | ↓0.03 (*−0.2%*) | ↑0.03 (*+0.3%*) |
| | **Small DOM** | ↑2.00 (*+16.7%*) | ↓2.00 (*−16.7%*) | ↓0.03 (*−0.2%*) | ↑0.03 (*+0.3%*) |
| | **Big DOM** | ↑4.00 (*+16.7%*) | ↓4.00 (*−16.7%*) | ↓0.09 (*−0.3%*) | ↑0.08 (*+0.4%*) |
| **DOM Foreign Exchange Reserves** | **Symmetry DOM/FOR** | ↓6.00 (*−50.0%*) | ↑6.00 (*+50.0%*) | ↑2.72 (*+45.3%*) | ↓3.00 (*−17.3%*) |
| | **Small DOM** | ↓10.00 (*−83.3%*) | ↑10.00 (*+83.3%*) | ↑2.72 (*+135.7%*) | ↓3.52 (*−16.0%*) |
| | **Big DOM** | ↓8.00 (*−66.7%*) | ↑8.00 (*+66.7%*) | ↑2.94 (*+73.5%*) | ↓3.31 (*−16.6%*) |
| **ROW households' holdings of DOM bills** | **Symmetry DOM/FOR** | ↓4.00 (*−9.1%*) | ↑4.00 (*+9.1%*) | ↓0.09 (*−0.2%*) | ↑0.13 (*+0.3%*) |
| | **Small DOM** | ↓8.00 (*−18.2%*) | ↑8.00 (*+18.2%*) | ↓4.00 (*−0.1%*) | ↑0.09 (*+0.2%*) |
| | **Big DOM** | ↓4.00 (*−9.1%*) | ↑4.00 (*+9.1%*) | ↓0.10 (*−0.2%*) | ↑0.14 (*+0.3%*) |
| **ROW households' holdings of ROW bills** | **Symmetry DOM/FOR** | ↑2.00 (*+4.5%*) | ↓2.00 (*−4.5%*) | ↓0.10 (*−0.2%*) | ↑0.11 (*+0.3%*) |
| | **Small DOM** | ↑4.00 (*+3.0%*) | ↓4.00 (*−3.0%*) | ↓0.17 (*−0.1%*) | ↑0.21 (*+0.2%*) |
| | **Big DOM** | ↑2.00 (*+4.5%*) | ↓2.00 (*−4.5%*) | ↓0.11 (*−0.2%*) | ↑0.12 (*+0.3%*) |
| **ROW households' holdings of ROW currency** | **Symmetry DOM/FOR** | ↑2.00 (*+16.7%*) | ↓2.00 (*−16.7%*) | ↓0.03 (*−0.2%*) | ↑0.03 (*+0.3%*) |
| | **Small DOM** | ↑4.00 (*+16.7%*) | ↓4.00 (*−16.7%*) | ↓0.03 (*−0.1%*) | ↑0.03 (*+0.2%*) |
| | **Big DOM** | ↑2.00 (*+16.7%*) | ↓2.00 (*−16.7%*) | ↓0.03 (*−0.2%*) | ↑0.03 (*+0.3%*) |

## 7 Conclusion

The addition of FX reserves to the macroeconomic policy toolkit turns the monetary policy trilemma into a quadrilemma. After discussing some of the literature on FX reserves, the dilemma approach, the dominant currency paradigm, I have put forward a presentation of the quadrilemma based on a single equation encompassing the four dimensions to consider: exchange rate fixity, absence of capital controls, autonomous interest rate policy and constraints on FX reserves.

To illustrate this claim, I have used a simple SFC model, which has highlighted different dynamics in the short run and in the long run. In the short run, the model shows that the trilemma does not hold in the case of an increase in the domestic interest rate, as long as the government is willing to issue public debt on demand.

In the case of an interest rate decrease, provided the central bank is willing to intervene on both foreign and domestic markets, it is possible to bypass the trilemma if the initial level of FX reserves is sufficient to absorb the capital outflows immediately resulting from the change in interest rate – the other determining factors being the change in interest, investors' sensitivity to changes in relative yields and the level of wealth in the two countries.

In the longer run, the initial financial account, stock-related effect is superseded by a current account, flow-related phenomenon, due to the change in net interest income occasioned by the interest rate differential. This leads to a progressive reversal of net financial position between the two countries. However, this is the consequence of looking at the pure effect of portfolio reallocation in the long term, to the exclusion of other channels such as investment or effects on prices. The long-run conclusions of the model need to be taken with caution.

More research is needed in the field of international monetary policy to understand the conditions of application of the quadrilemma. Let me make a few suggestions:

- Adding more sectors and features to the model used here, especially to make it more realistic in the long run.
- Comparing local and dominant currency pricing and financing.
- Analysing the difference between sterilised and non-sterilised interventions, in relation with initial current account imbalances.
- Investigating the use of swap lines and other alternatives to FX reserve accumulation.
- Allowing for exchange flexibility to assess the existence of exchange rate overshooting in a context of imperfect asset substitutability.

## Notes

1 This "bipolar" view of exchange rate regime choice (Fischer 2001) could explain at least partly why reserves have not been given a more prominent role in international monetary policy theory: under pure floating exchange rate regimes, reserves are supposed to remain constant as exchange rate determination is left

to the market, while in hard peg contexts, the discretionary use of reserves is deemed impossible regardless of the degree of international capital mobility. As a result, reserves have no real role to play one way or the other.

2 Although the official fluctuation band associated with the Exchange Rate Mechanism II (ERM 2) is ±2.25%, in practice over the last decade the National Bank of Denmark has effectively enforced fluctuation bands in the vicinity of ±0.35%, which means a very tight peg.

3 This asymmetry was also noted by several authors, including De Grauwe (1997).

4 It is worth mentioning that Bianchi and Lorenzoni (2021) consider a "prudential use" of FX reserves, which they see as a substitute for capital controls.

5 In any case, the degree of currency dominance varies across space and time: the more dominated a country, the more constrained the trade-off between policy objectives, while countries with dominant currencies shall face less constraints.

6 I assume that all the transactions are monetary, i.e. none of them takes place in kind as this would skew the equality.

7 This quadrilemma is formulated in terms of policy tool availability, whereas Aizenman's quadrilemma is formulated in terms of policy objectives (Aizenman 2013, 2019). Note that I use 'interest-rate policy' instead of 'monetary policy'. 'Constraint on FX reserves' can be economic (low or depleted reserves), political (unwillingness to make an active use of reserves) or legal.

8 The model, entirely coded in visual basic, is available on request.

9 The main influence for this model is Chapter 6 from Godley and Lavoie (2012). The pioneers of SFC modelling are Allen and Kenen (1980) and Godley and Cripps (1983), although SFC modelling really took off under Godley & Lavoie's lead in the late 1990s and the 2000s. The last decade has witnessed the emergence of a significant SFC literature. Important recent developments include Caiani et al. (2016), Raza et al. (2019), Byrialsen and Raza (2020), Mazier (2020), Godin and Yilmaz (2020), Valdecantos (2020).

10 This form of endogenous money, associated with changes in the holding of domestic bonds by the central bank, must be distinguished from endogenous money arising from credit lending by commercial banks – which is absent from this model.

11 Denmark offers an example of this type of arrangement: the Danish government issues more debt than it needs for strictly financing motives and saves the excess amount at the Danish central bank (Danmarks Nationalbank 2021b).

12 It is also a logical necessity when dealing with the symmetric scenario described further.

13 Note that the slope of the change in FX reserves is the same across all country configurations associated with a given shock. This is because the initial level of FX reserves is identical across all scenarios, and so is the interest rate differential for each type of shock.

14 Although I could have assumed price rigidity, the nominal approach followed is compatible with price flexibility and a cross-elasticity of demand to price algebraically equal to −1.

15 This is also in line with Patel and Cavallino's (2019) survey finding that an average FX intervention is seen as reaching its highest effect in the short term (two to eight weeks) before declining.

## References

Aizenman, Joshua (2013). The impossible trinity — From the policy trilemma to the policy quadrilemma, *Global Journal of Economics*, Vol. 2, No 1, pp. 1–17.

Aizenman, Joshua (2019). A modern reincarnation of Mundell-Fleming's trilemma, *Economic Modelling*, Vol. 81, pp. 444–454.

Aizenman, Joshua, Cheung, Yin-Wong, & Ito, Hiro (2015). International reserves before and after the global crisis: Is there no end to hoarding? *Journal of International Money and Finance*, Vol. 52, pp. 102–126.

Aizenman, Joshua, Chinn, Menzie D. & Ito, Hiro (2016). Monetary policy spillovers and the trilemma in the new normal: Periphery country sensitivity to core country conditions, *Journal of International Money and Finance*, Vol. 68, pp. 298–330.

Aizenman, Joshua & Jaewoo Lee (2007). International reserves: Precautionary versus mercantilist views, theory, and evidence, *Open Economies Review*, Vol. 18, No. 2, pp. 191–214.

Allen, Polly R. & Kenen Peter B. (1980). *Asset Markets, Exchange Rates, and Economic Integration*, Cambridge University Press.

Andaiyani, Sri, Hidayat, Ariodillah, Muthia, Fida &Widharosa, Nona (2020). Trilemma to quadrilemma: An empirical study from Indonesia, *Jurnal Ekonomi Pembangunan*, Vol. 18, No. 2, pp. 119–128.

Arslan, Yavuz & Cantú, Carlos (2019). The size of foreign exchange reserves, in *Reserve Management and FX Intervention*, BIS Papers, No. 104, pp. 1–23.

Basu, Suman, Bow, Emine, Gopinath, Gita, Roch, Francisco, & Unsal, Filiz (2020). *A Conceptual Model for the Integrated Policy Franmework*, IMF Working Paper 10/121.

Bianchi, Javier & Lorenzoni, Guido (2021). *The Prudential Use of Capital Controls and Foreign Currency Reserves*, NBER Working Paper 29476.

Bianchi, Javier & Sosa-Padilla, César (2020). *Reserve Accumulation, Macroeconomic Stabilization, and Sovereign Risk*, NBER Working Paper 27323.

Blanchard, Olivier (2017). *Macroeconomics*, Seventh edition, Pearson.

Byrialsen, Mikael R. & Raza, Hamid (2020). *An Empirical Stock-Flow Consistent Macroeconomic Model for Denmark*, Levy Economics Institute of Bard College Working Paper 942.

Caiani, Alessandro, Godin, Antoine, Caverzasi, Eugenio, Gallegati, Mauro, Kinsella, Stephen & Stiglitz, Joseph E. (2016). Agent based-stock flow consistent macroeconomics: Towards a benchmark model, *Journal of Economic Dynamics and Control*, Vol. 69, Issue C, pp. 375–408.

Calvo, Guillermo A. & Reinhart, Carmen M. (2002). Fear of floating, *Quarterly Journal of Economics*, Vol. 117, No. 2, pp. 379–408.

Central Bank of Brazil (2019). Reserves management and FX intervention, in *Reserve Management and FX Intervention*, BIS Papers, No. 104, pp. 75–86.

Cheung, Yin-Wong & Xingwang Qian (2009). Hoarding of international reserves: Mrs Machlup's wardrobe and the Joneses, *Review of International Economics*, Vol. 17, No. 4, pp. 824–843.

Chinn, Menzie D. & Ito, Hiro (2006). What matters for financial development? Capital controls, institutions, and interactions, *Journal of Development Economics*, Vol. 81, No. 1, pp. 163–192.

Danmarks Nationalbank (2021a). *Monetary and Exchange-Rate Policy*, Danmarks Nationalbank website, accessed on 27 December 2021: https://www.nationalbanken.dk/en/monetarypolicy/implementation/Pages/default.aspx

Danmarks Nationalbank (2021b). *Central Government Debt*, Danmarks Nationalbank website, accessed on 27 December 2021: https://www.nationalbanken.dk/en/governmentdebt/centralgovernment_debt/Pages/default.aspx

De Grauwe, Paul (1997). *The Economics of Monetary Integration*, Third Edition, Oxford University Press.

Domaç, Ilker & Mendoza, Alfonso (2004). *Is There Room for Foreign Exchange Interventions Under an Inflation Targeting Framework? Evidence from Mexico and Turkey*, World Bank Policy Research Working Paper 3288.

Dornbusch, Rudiger (1976). *Expectations and Exchange Rate Dynamics, Journal of Political Economy*, Vol. 84, pp. 1161–1176.

Dovonou, Vanessa O. (2021). *Trilemma Revisited with Dollar Dominance in Trade and Finance*, manuscript, University of Orléans, France.

Dutt, Devika (2021). *The Political Economy of the Cost of Foreign Exchange Intervention*, Doctoral Dissertations 2305, University of Massachusetts Amherst.

Fischer, Stanley (2001). Exchange rate regimes: is the bipolar view correct?. *Journal of Economic Perspectives*, 15(2), 3–24.

Fleming, J. Marcus (1962). Domestic financial policies under fixed and under flexible exchange rates, *IMF Staff Papers*, Vol. 8, No. 3, pp. 369–380.

Frenkel, Roberto (2007). The sustainability of monetary sterilization policies, *CEPAL Review*, No. 93, pp. 29–36.

Godin, Antoine & Yilmaz, S. Devrim (2020). *Modelling Small Open Developing Economies in a Financialized World: A Stock-Flow Consistent Prototype*, AFD Research Paper 125, Agence Française de Développment.

Godley, Wynne & Cripps, Francis (1983). *Macroeconomics*, Oxford University Press.

Godley, Wynne & Lavoie, Marc (2012). *Monetary Economics: An Integrated Approach to Credit, Money, Income, Production, and Wealth*, Second edition, Palgrave Macmillan.

Gopinath, Gita, Boz, Emine, Casas, Camila, Diez, Federico J., Gourinchas, Pierre-Olivier, & Plagborg-Møller, Mikkel (2020). Dominant currency paradigm, *American Economic Review*, Vol. 110, No. 3, pp. 677–719.

Gopinath, Gita & Itskokhi, Greg (2021). *Dominant Currency Paradigm: A Review*, NBER Working Paper 29556.

IMF (2009). *Balance of Payments and International Investment Position Manual*, Sixth edition, International Monetary Fund.

Krugman, Paul (1979). A model of balance-of-payments crises, *Journal of Money, Credit, and Banking*, Vol. 11, pp. 311–325.

Lavoie, Marc (2014). *Post-Keynesian Economics: New Foundations*, Edward Elgar, UK.

Ligonniere, Samuel (2018). Trilemma, dilemma and global players, *Journal of International Money and Finance*, Vol. 85, Issue C, pp. 20–39.

Machlup, Fritz (1966). *The Need for Monetary Reserves*, Princeton University Reprints in International Finance 5.

Mazier, Jacques (2020). *Global Imbalances and Financial Capitalism*, Routledge.

Miranda-Agrippino, Silvia & Rey, Hélène. (2015). *World Asset Markets and the Global Financial Cycle*, NBER Working Paper 21722.

Monetary Authority of Singapore (2021). *Monetary Policy*, Monetary Authority of Singapore website, accessed on 27 December 2021: https://www.mas.gov.sg/monetary-policy

Mundell, Robert A. (1963). Capital mobility and stabilization policy under fixed and flexible exchange rates, *Canadian Journal of Economic and Political Science*, Vol. 29, No. 4, pp. 475–485.

Obstfeld, Maurice (1984). Balance of payments crises and devaluation, *Journal of Money, Credit, and Banking*, Vol. 16, pp. 208–217.

Obstfeld, Maurice (2015). *Trilemmas and Trade-Offs: Living with Financial Globalisation*, BIS Working Paper 480.

Obstfeld, Maurice, Ostry, Jonathan D., & Qureshi, Mahvash S. (2017). *A Tie that Binds: Revisiting the Trilemma in Emerging Market Economies*, IMF Working Paper 17/130.

Passari, Evgenia & Rey, Hélène (2015). Financial flows and the international monetary system, *The Economic Journal*, Vol. 125, No. 584, pp. 675–698.

Patel, Nikhil & Cavallino, Paolo (2019). FX intervention: Goals, strategies and tactics, in *Reserve Management and FX Intervention*, BIS Papers, No. 104, pp. 25–44.

Raza, Hamid, Byrialsen, Mikael R., Gudmundsson, Bjorn R. & Zoega, Gylfi (2019). A post-Keynesian model of the balance of payments crisis, in: Jesper Jespersen & Finn Olesen (ed.), *Progressive Post-Keynesian Economics*, Edward Elgar Publishing, pp. 111–127.

Rey, Hélène (2013). Dilemma not trilemma: The global financial cycle and monetary policy independence, *Federal Reserve Bank of Kansas City Jackson Hole Economic Symposium Proceedings*, pp. 285–333.

Rey, Hélène (2016). International channels of transmission of monetary policy and the Mundellian trilemma, *IMF Economic Review*, Vol. 64, No. 1, pp. 6–35.

The People's Bank of China (2019). Reserves management and foreign exchange intervention, in *Reserve Management and FX Intervention*, BIS Papers, No. 104, pp. 99–102.

Valdecantos, Sebastian (2020). *Argentina's (Macroeconomic?) Trap: Some Insights from an Empirical Stock-Flow Consistent Model*, Levy Economics Institute of Bard College Working Paper 975.

Wray, L. Randall (2015). *Modern Money Theory: A Primer on Macroeconomics for Sovereign Monetary Systems*, Second edition, Palgrave Macmillan.

# 12 Sectoral balance analysis

## Evidence from Scandinavia

*Mikael Randrup Byrialsen, Robert Smith and Finn Olesen*

### 1 Introduction

The System of National Accounts (SNA) is the backbone of macroeconomic investigation; however, according to Bergman (2015), "A rather common view is that academics and other economic analysts do not fully comprehend the whole potential of the SNA … SNA is often not seen as the prevailing tool for economic analysis." As he emphasises, the information contained in the SNA can easily be reframed to provide alternative, highly insightful perspectives on the status of an economy.

The analysis in this chapter, which focuses on sectoral balances, is a particularly good example, as it requires that all constituent accounts are accurately reflected. The net lending or borrowing position of an aggregate sector is the cumulative effect of all income and expenditure activity of the participants of each sector.

We benefit from the fact that the SNA is a closed, dual-entry accounting system, and that the combined net lending positions of the institutional sectors are thus an accounting identity that by definition sum to zero. Since the sum of any imbalances is by definition zero, not all sectors of an economy can be net savers or net borrowers at the same time – when one sector is in surplus, at least one other sector must be in deficit. Both historically and in recent years, there has been a focus on identifying a general direction of correlation between deficit positions of the three main institutional sectors.

We break from this pattern, and, rather than providing point estimates, we present rolling short-run patterns of correlation, of progressively longer periods. We address the main institutional sectors, the government sector, the private sector and the rest of the world (ROW) sector, but also provide the estimates for the disaggregated private sector. That is, the household sector, the non-financial corporate sector and the financial corporate sector.

The main contribution is to illustrate the importance and power of the SNA to provide policy-relevant insights, as well as the benefit of persistent and accurate data collection.

The chapter is organised as follows: Section 2 provides a contracted historical review of various contributions to national accounts for the Scandinavian countries. Section 3 reviews some of the recent contributions to the

DOI: 10.4324/9781003253457-15

use of the sector balance analysis (SBA). Section 4 presents the data and method used, while Section 5 presents the results of the rolling-correlation analysis, and Section 6 concludes.

## 2 A brief history of the SNA in Scandinavia

As noted by van Ark (1995), the history on using national accounts concepts dates back many years. However, works on national accounting awaited the Keynesian Revolution before featuring significantly in macroeconomic works. Following the Great Depression, the need to be able to forecast the economic performance of modern Western economies became politically important, the aim of which was to identify the economic performance trajectory that was likely in the near future.

With a Keynesian strategy on economic policy matters, the need to introduce fiscal and monetary changes was, in general, a major priority on the political agenda. However, in order to make effective policy decisions, macroeconomists and politicians alike needed a tool, and that tool was found in developing macro-econometric models. However, to be able to do this, one needed to have the necessary data on relevant macroeconomic variables at hand. This triggered work that resulted in further data collection and eventually in the development of national account systems.

The British and American history of the standardised SNA employed today was driven largely by James Meade and Richard Stone from the UK, and Morris A. Copeland in the USA, who contributed greatly to the establishment of the 1953 United Nations System of National Accounts. As noted by Godley and Lavoie (2012, p. 24), the initial interest of Copeland in the 1940s was to investigate the financing requirements of economic activity between and across the national sectors.

As the demand for financial data increased, it led to the development of the flow-of-funds accounts, which is now an integrated part of the SNA. With the 1968 SNA standardisation, the financial balance sheet was added to the national account system. Adequate data for such a presentation of the financial side of the economy only became available in the 1970s and 1980s. It was, however, not before the implementation of SNA 93 guidelines that a fully specified system of financial accounts was established. These accounts were revised again in 2008, and for the European Union, the most recent version is the European regional and sector accounts 2010, which was published in the official law journal of the European Union in 2013.

The Scandinavian history pre-dates the efforts of Meade, Stone and Copeland by roughly 100 years. Christensen et al. (1995) surveyed the Nordic National Accounts from the 1880s. They dated the first attempts to calculate the national income in Denmark and Norway to the end of the 19th century and to the beginning of the 20th century for Sweden.

As they noted, the first Nordic estimate was for Finland, by K.E.F. Ignatius, for calculating estimated taxable and non-taxable household income in 1881, and national income from the production side in 1882. These were followed by rudimentary estimates by Professor W. Scharling for Denmark in 1885, and by A.N. Kiær for Norway in 1891. For Sweden, the first accounts mentioned were estimated by G. Siösteen in 1903, followed by K.-G. Hagström in the early 1920s. These efforts used an income statistical method based mainly on tax data.

Sweden had a somewhat later start that Denmark and Norway, and in the 1920s and the 1930s, a project titled "Wages, Cost of Living and National Income in Sweden, 1860–1930," was led by Erik Lindahl. This was described as either advanced commodity flow or basic input-output computation. Aside from the construction of historical national accounts, it was supplemented by series on wage data, cost of living indices and demographic data. According to Christensen et al. (1995, p. 33), this work was pioneering in an international context making "Sweden unique in the development of national income statistics" with national accounts dating back to the mid-19th century.

Danish statisticians, according to Christensen et al. (1995, p. 32), continued to work on national accounts. In contrast to the output-based statistics in Sweden, this began with the use of income-tax statistics. By the 1920s, the adaptation to the Swedish output method was overseen by H.N. Skade. Viggo Kampmann[1] ultimately secured national accounting as a core task for Statistics Denmark, further developing the output-statistical method though the 1930s – constructing input-output tables, use of input-output techniques and calculating series not only in current prices but also in constant prices.

Although initial estimates occurred very early for Norway, significant data collection activities only began in the 1930s with Ragnar Frisch emphasising the need to distinguish between real (goods and services) and financial aspects, a work by Frisch that was finally completed in the 1940s with his "Eco-circ System." However, as a pragmatic start, the less "imposing" output-based statistics of Lindahl and Kampmann were initially preferred in Norway, and a project was started in this tradition on National Income in Norway for the period 1935–1943. Despite the point made by Frisch of the importance of financial records, work on national accounts in this period hardly addressed financial accounts.[2]

Fløttum et al. (2012) present a thorough examination of the development of national accounts in Norway beyond 1930 where Norway is credited as one of the first countries, from 1952, to integrate input-output tables in their annual national accounts. By use of this tool, much analytical work on various aspects of national budgeting and macroeconomic planning was founded in the 1960s with the aim of developing better macroeconomic models of the Norwegian economy.

In Finland official calculations emerged in 1943 by Valter Lindberg, for the years 1926–1938, followed by Eino H. Laurila in 1950, for the late 1940s, and with the establishment of the official national accounts in 1949. Christensen et al. (1995) noted that

> The first input-output tables were for 1956 and were published in 1960. The so-called long-series of national accounts for 1948–1964 based on the SNA 1953 recommendation came out in 1968. The new 1968 SNA-based long series came out in 1981, covering the years 1960–1978.

As pointed out by Christensen et al. (1995), although the Nordic countries fully accepted the international guidelines, they also tried to stick to existing statistical traditions. In the 1960s initiatives were taken in Denmark, Norway and Sweden to extend the national account systems, and beyond the 1968 SNA revision the developments in the Nordic countries converged towards international standards.

Regarding the sectoral balances, two important aspects were thereafter taken into account. First, the institutional sectoral accounts were established, which separated the economy into five sectors (non-financial corporations, financial corporations, public sector, households and ROW). Second, the financial part of the national accounts was improved significantly.

Each of the statistical departments of the four countries has undergone the non-trivial full-scale revision of the historical records of national accounts several times, with revised annual data now available under the ESA2010 standard for Sweden from 1950, for Denmark from 1975, for Finland from 1980 and for Norway from 1978. It is these data that have been used in the analysis that follows; in all cases, financial accounts are available from 1995.

## 3 Sector balance analysis

The SBA as a tool for analysis provides an interesting perspective on economic policy and is based on the SNA.[3] It thus serves our purpose of illustrating the value of the long, consistent datasets that have been collected in recent decades.

The SBA approach could be described as a continuation of Copeland's goals (i.e. understanding the financing of economic activity) with the aid of modern technology. Wynne Godley is recognised by some (e.g. Bezemer [2010] and Fiebiger [2013]) as the instigating factor in the re-emergence of analysis of sector balances.

The earlier works emerged from applied work at the British treasury between 1956 and 1970, Godley and Lavoie (2012, p. xxxvi). These were subsequently developed in collaboration with Francis Cripps via the Cambridge Economic Policy Group, and later with several other collaborators. This was pioneering work in integrating the real and financial sides of the economy in a unified, stock-flow consistent macroeconomic modelling framework.

As highlighted by Tissot (2016), as a consequence of the global financial crisis of 2007–2009, the development of financial sectoral accounts has been high on the political agenda, as efforts to perform various financial stability analyses became a core concern of monetary authorities.

Despite the fact that sector balances are often discussed, surprisingly few empirical analyses can be found in the literature. However, in a recent paper, Glötzl and Rezai (2018) present an analysis that follows the work presented by Barbosa-Filho et al. (2006)[4] and Barbosa-Filho et al. (2008), where they use net lending to discuss possible causalities between the sectors. Additional, related analyses include Brink (1983), Krugman (2009), Bergman et al. (2010), Ali Abbas et al. (2011), Semieniuk et al. (2012) and Tissot (2016).

In Glötzl and Rezai (2018) the analysis covers 22 European countries using quarterly data from 1999 to 2013. The authors show how the net lending of the single sectors behave concerning the business cycles for the 22 countries focusing on which sectors lag or lead the business cycle, as proxied by the output gap.

Regarding Denmark, their analysis shows that the net lending of the household sector and financial corporations sector seems to lead the business cycle, while the net lending of the non-financial corporate sector and ROW seems to react as a response to the business cycle. The government sector shows no evidence of either lag or lead.

In Sweden, on the other hand, net lending of the government sector (and non-financial corporations) seems to lag the business cycle, whereas net lending of households seems to lead the business cycle. In both Denmark and Sweden, net borrowing of households and non-financial corporations is pro-cyclical, while net borrowing in the government sector is counter-cyclical. For Denmark, net lending of ROW is counter-cyclical and net lending of financial corporations is pro-cyclical, neither of which show significant patterns for Sweden.[5]

With regard to policy analysis, Semieniuk et al. (2012) conducted empirical analysis of the three-sector balances to discuss the possible outcomes of the European Stability Pact programme from 2011 to 2014. The authors use the approach to question the reliability of the predicted results from the European Commission of the Stability Pact.

Looking further back in time, Brink (1983) used arguments analogous to the present net lending discussions. He argued that the major reason for the persistent deficit on the public balance in Denmark during the 1970s and 1980s was low demand from abroad due to the global economic downturn and financial consolidation in the private sector. In accordance with this view of sector inter-relations, Krugman (2009) more recently noted that governmental deficits are often a consequence of the workings of the automatic stabilisers rather than as a result of expansionary fiscal policy changes – both apparently portraying the government balance as somewhat passive to changes in the other sectors.[6]

Tissot (2016) used the banking crisis in Sweden in the early 1990s as a case for highlighting the relevance of the approach. As a result of the crisis, the private sector in Sweden began to deleverage (reduce debt), which can be seen by the steep increase in net lending for the private sector in Sweden following the crisis. As a result of this deleveraging in the private sector, the government sector was massively affected. The lack of demand from the private sector is explained to have led to a deterioration of the government balance. After the initial phase the need for deleveraging in the private sector faded out, which coincided with a gradual improvement in the government balance.

Finally, Bergman et al. (2010) analysed the changes in balance sheets across the different sectors of the economy during 2008–2009, following the recent financial and economic crisis. Focusing on foreign debt, Bergman et al. (2010) linked the changes in balance sheet across time with net lending of ROW.

## 4 Empirical data and methods

### *4.1 Net lending*

In this section we present net lending formally. To understand the properties of net lending we start with the composition of GDP:

$$GDP = C + I_p + I_g + G + X - M \tag{12.1}$$

where $C$ is private consumption, $I_p$ is private investment, $I_g$ is government investment, $G$ is government consumption, $X$ is exports and $M$ is imports. By introducing transfer payments across sectors and including public investment in public consumption, $G$, the three-sector balance can be derived as

$$(S_p - I_p) + (NT - G) + (M - X - NIA) = 0 \tag{12.2}$$

where $S_p$ is private savings, $NT$ is tax payment received by the government, net of transfer payments and subsidies paid by government and $NIA$ is the net income and current transfers received from abroad. The first bracket expresses the sector balance for the private sector, the second bracket expresses the sector balance for the government and the third bracket represents the sector balance for ROW. Broadly speaking, changes in the net lending positions are driven by changes in either the incomes or the expenditures (including investment) of the sector in question.

From equation 12.2, an important property for the sum of the net lending across the three sectors can be seen in that

$$\sum NL = 0 \tag{12.3}$$

Following the method presented in Barbosa-Filho et al. (2006), a combination of national accounting and statistical properties can be used to provide information on net lending behaviour across the economy; in particular, how the net lending of different sectors co-moves. Since the sum of net lending across the different sectors is zero, the variance of this sum can be written as:

$$Var\left(\sum X_i\right) = 0 \tag{12.4}$$

where $X_i$ represents net lending of the single sector. Using the fact that

$$\sum_i Cov\left(X_i, X_j\right) = 0 \tag{12.5}$$

the result for a single variable can be written as

$$Cov\left(X_i, X_j\right) = Var\left(X_i\right) = -\sum_{i \neq j} Cov\left(X_i, X_j\right) \tag{12.6}$$

The variance in $X_i$ is therefore equal to the negative sum of the covariances between $X_i$ and the other variables. This property is used to investigate the decomposition of a change in net lending in one sector on net lending of other sectors.

This can be extended to test the behaviour of net lending of a single sector relative to the business cycle.

$$\sum_{i \neq j} Cov\left(X_i, Y\right) = 0 \tag{12.7}$$

where $Y$ represents the business cycle, while $X_i$ is the net lending of the single sector. If the covariance between net lending in a sector and the output gap is positive, net lending (net borrowing) of the sector is pro-cyclical (counter-cyclical), while a negative correlation can be interpreted as counter-cyclical net lending behaviour (pro-cyclical net borrowing behaviour). For example, if a sector's expenses exceed incomes for a given period where the output gap is positive, the sector will necessarily have negative net lending (positive net borrowing) and will have counter-cyclical net lending.

The test for possible lagged or leading co-variation between net lending of individual sectors and the business cycle implies that changes in the net lending of a sector might provide some information regarding general behaviour within the sector relative to economic expansions and contractions.

### *4.2 Data*

Unlike Glötzl and Rezai (2018), we chose to use annual data for the analysis, since annual data is available for a longer period of time, and it thus allows us to illustrate changes in relationships between the sectors over longer durations. Net lending data is sourced primarily from the Eurostat database, but for Denmark it is supplemented with data from the ADAM (Annual Danish Aggregate Model) databank, which is affiliated with Statistics Denmark. This data is all normalised by dividing each entry by GDP of the country in question for each year. In this way, we were able to get annual data starting in 1950 for Sweden, 1970 for Denmark, 1978 for Norway and 1980 for Finland.

The output gap data was available from the OECD database from 1985 for all three countries. It is calculated by estimating the potential level of GDP and calculating the proportionate difference between potential GDP and actual GDP. We replicated this data for each country using a Hodrick-Prescott (HP) Filter and used these series in our analyses.

## 5 Results and discussion

The empirical analysis comprises three main parts. The first part is a presentation of net lending against the output gap for all countries.

The second part is a replication of the analysis conducted by Glötzl and Rezai (2018), for five sectors (households, non-financial corporations, financial corporations, government and ROW). Our overall findings in this part of the analysis are similar to those of Glötzl and Rezai (2018), Barbosa-Filho et al. (2006) and Barbosa-Filho et al. (2008).

The third and most relevant part is the addition of rolling-period correlations. These are calculated for both the three- and five-sector scenarios for 4, 6, 8 or 12 years.[7]

In Figure 12.1 net lending for the five main institutional sectors of the four chosen economies can be seen together with the output gap.

As seen from Figure 12.1 both output gap (OGap) and net lending for the five main sectors fluctuate over time and no clear conclusion can be drawn directly from these four diagrams. In order to get further information, the statistical properties presented in Section 4.1 can be applied.

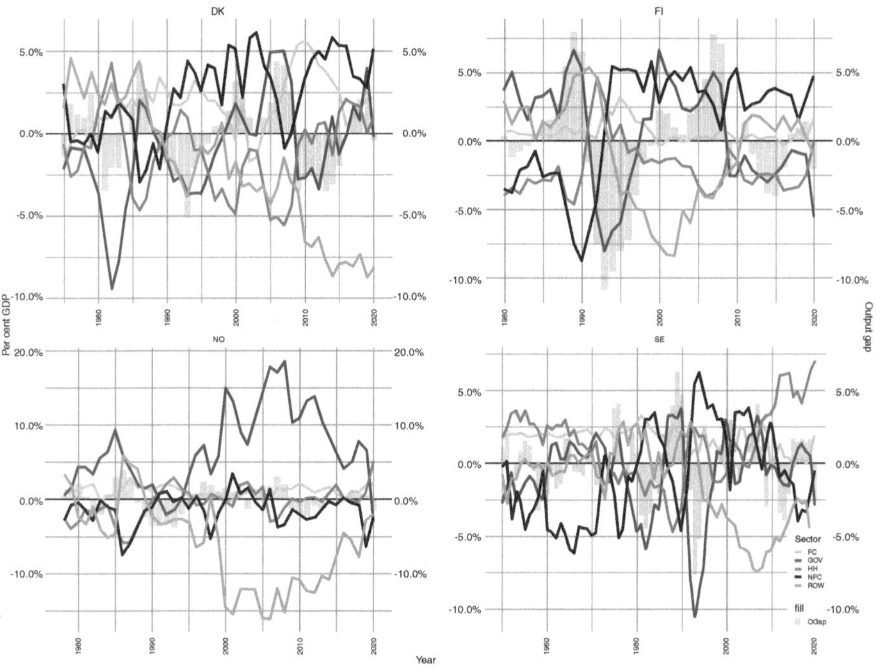


*Figure 12.1* Net lending for the five main sectors of Denmark (upper left), Finland (upper right), Norway (bottom left) and Sweden (bottom right).

Focusing on the correlation for the whole sample between net lending of the different sectors, the results diverge among the four countries. For Denmark, Norway and Sweden a negative correlation between ROW and the government (GOV) can be found, just as the private sector (PRI) as a whole is negatively correlated with both ROW and the government for Denmark, Finland and Sweden. Disaggregating the private sector into the three subsectors described previously provides additional information. For Denmark the negative relationship between ROW and the private sector is driven by a negative correlation between mainly corporations (non-financial corporations (NFC) and financial corporation (FC)), while the negative correlation between the private sector and the government is driven mainly by households (HH). In the case of Sweden, the negative relationship between ROW and the private sector is driven by a negative correlation between non-financial corporations and households, while the negative correlation between the private sector and the government is driven mainly by the non-financial corporations.

For all four countries, net lending of the government sector seems to be a pro-cyclical reaction to the business cycle, while the net lending of the private sector as a whole is counter-cyclical. The correlation between ROW and the business cycles is insignificant for all four countries.

Overall, our findings are similar to those presented in the empirical literature presented above. To add to this literature, we introduce rolling-correlation statistics for relationships between each sector and the output gap. In Figure 12.2, a 12-year rolling correlation with the output gap is presented, where each point on each line is the correlation statistic for the preceding 12 years. A positive correlation illustrates a tendency towards net lending (or to have a rising surplus) when the economy accelerates towards a boom phase, whereas a negative correlation suggests that the sector has a rising deficit under the same circumstances.

The point of most interest for us is whether these relationships remain relatively constant over time, and what the sign of the correlation coefficient is. The ROW net lending appears to have a declining correlation with the output gap for all countries around the same time, but while there is some evidence of similarity in the patterns for Denmark and Norway, the correlation coefficient seldom exceeds plus or minus 0.5.

The government sector, on the other hand, exhibits a strong counter-cyclical spending relationship for all countries except Norway. The

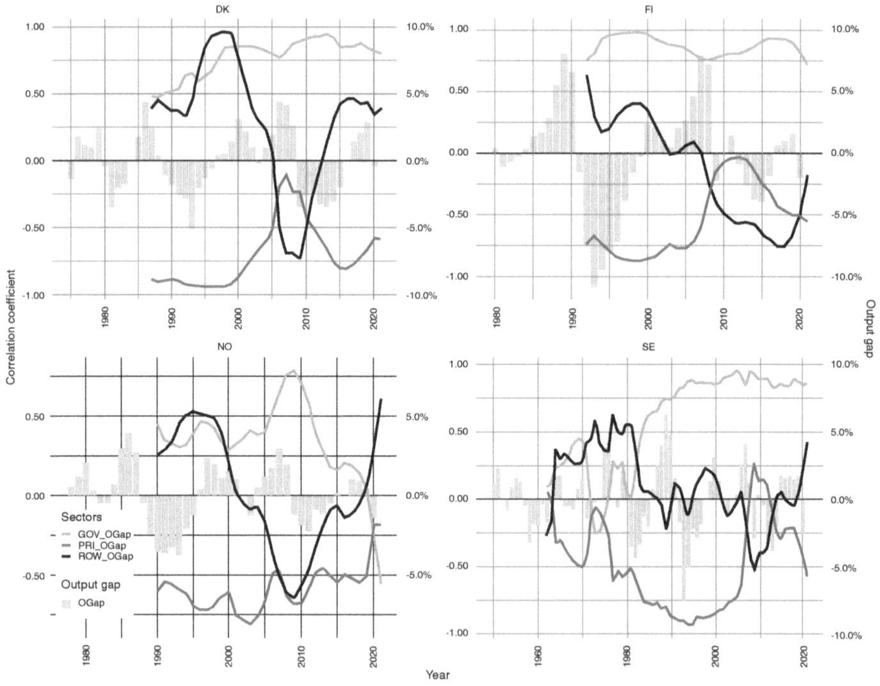


*Figure 12.2* Rolling correlations: 12 year lag, 3 sectors.

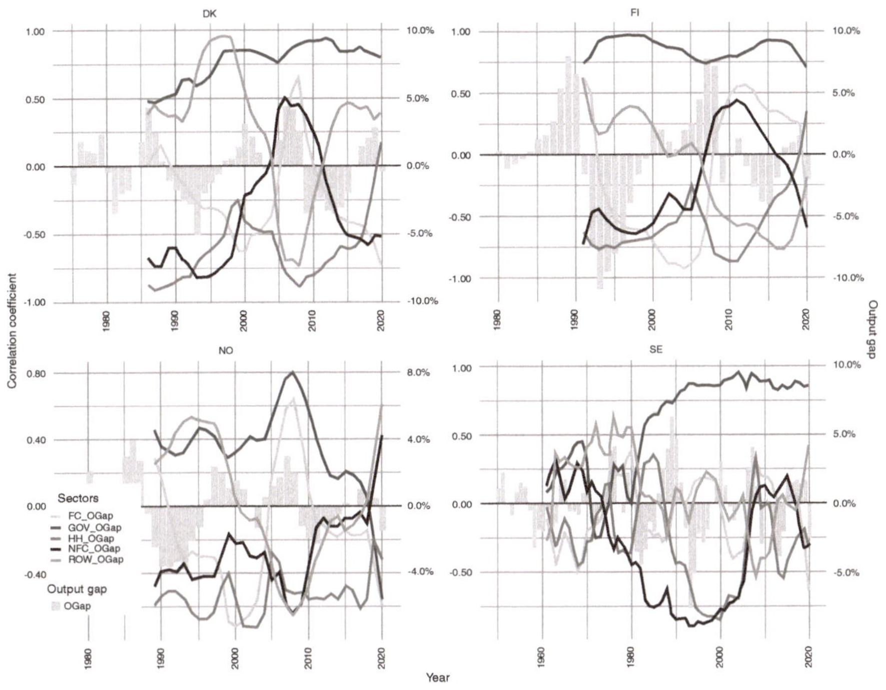


*Figure 12.3* Rolling correlations: 12 year lag, 5 sectors.

strong positive correlation between government net lending suggests that the government sector in each of the four countries has strong automatic stabilising policies, as should be expected for the four countries in this analysis.

For all four countries it is clear that for the year 1990 (i.e. for the 12 years from 1978 to 1990), the private sector had a persistent negative correlation, but that relationship gradually broke down in Denmark, Finland and Sweden as the rolling window approached the peak of the boom prior to the financial crisis in 2007–2008. In order to better understand the changes in the private sector, it can be disaggregated into the subsectors and seen in Figure 12.3:

If we consider Figure 12.3, we are better able to identify the cause of the breakdown of the negative correlation between private sector net lending and the output gap. In Denmark, Finland and Norway, households continued to exhibit pro-cyclical borrowing throughout the period, while non-financial corporations' net lending moved positively in Denmark, Finland and Sweden, and financial corporation net lending moved positively in all countries around the same time.

One possible explanation could be a lack of availability of credit for non-financial corporations following the financial crisis, or a consolidation of financial corporation balance sheets, but such conjectures would need further investigation. What is most interesting to us is that the nature of the relationship between net lending and the output gap changed in a very similar manner in all four countries for financial corporations, and for all excepting Norway for non-financial corporations. The inclusion of the last observations sees a sharp shift towards negative correlation for financial corporations in all countries, and the reverse for households in Denmark and Finland. The details of the drivers of each shift in the cyclical financing patterns of each sector are beyond the scope of this illustration, but that the pattern of these relationships change over time should not be in doubt.

What are the policy implications of our findings regarding net lending of the different sectors of an economy?

In this chapter we have focused mostly on correlation, which tells us very little about causality. As discussed in Byrialsen et al. (2021) information on causalities can identify which sector is the active and which passive, which might be very relevant for policymakers. In works by Krugman (2009), Glötzl and Rezai (2018) and Barbosa-Filho et al. (2006) it is suggested that the government sector is the accommodating sector, while the government sector is the active sector according to the standard hypotheses of Ricardian Equivalence and Twin Deficit presented in economic textbooks, where a negative net lending of the government sector leads to a positive net lending of the private sector (Ricardian Equivalence) or ROW (Twin Deficit).

This understanding of how actions initiated in one sector of the economy affect the behaviour in the rest of the economy is crucial in the application of economic analysis to policy. A recent illustration of this is the excessive focus on balance on the public budget (austerity) by the European Union after the global financial crisis as noted in Byrialsen et al. (2021). A policy with the purpose of reducing the public deficit (or debt-to-GDP ratio) under given circumstances (e.g. if the private sector net consolidates and ROW reduces demand for goods from the domestic economy) may increase domestic deficits (or debt-to-GDP ratio) by having the opposite effect than intended. Analysing the government sector in isolation, this reduction would improve the balance, but the result may be just the opposite, since it depends on the actions taking place in the other sectors.

Furthermore, one could ask, are the correlations of net lending between the different sectors of the economy stable and what are the possible implications of a shift in the correlations?

Focusing on the results presented above in the figures, several breaks from the estimated point estimates of correlation can be identified. The implication of this is that even the sign of the correlation between the net lending of a certain sector and the output gap might change over time, which makes economic analysis to policy much more complex. A sudden shift in the correlation can be for several reasons: a shift in the behaviour of a sector, like an increase in the degree of uncertainty in the economy following a crisis, easier access of credit or structural changes in the economy.

## 6 Conclusion

This chapter provides a brief introduction to the early contributors to the SNA for Denmark, Finland, Norway and Sweden, and an illustration of the usefulness of the national accounts to provide policy-relevant information.

The pioneers of national accounts in each country paved the way for us in 2022 to have access to over 40 years of standardised accounts. The accounting structures and definitions of the SNA (and European System of Accounts (ESA)) that emerged and have been implemented have, in addition, allowed us to draw insights from aggregate inter-sector flows.

Using the data available in the sectoral national accounts we investigate the statistical properties of the net lending of the different sectors of the four Nordic economies.

Our results regarding the correlation between net lending of the different sectors of the economy, together with the correlation between the net lending of the sectors and the different phases of the business cycle, confirm the results to be found in the scarce literature analysing the sectoral balances. Our contribution to this literature is the use of rolling correlations to establish a number of correlations instead of focusing on just one point estimate for the sample as a whole. This raises some concerns about the validity of point estimates over longer periods of time, and enables us to identify and discuss radical shifts in the correlation between net lending of a certain sector and, for example, the output gap, which might be explained by a change in the behaviour of economic agents, where a change in the behaviour of any broad group of economic agents might modify the effect of any economic policy.

## 7 Country-specific tables

*Table 12.1* Finland: correlation coefficients, 5 sectors: full sample: 1980–2020

| | *NFC* | *FC* | *GOV* | *HH* | *ROW* | *OGap* |
|---|---|---|---|---|---|---|
| NFC | NA | 0.08 | −0.39 ** | 0.12 | −0.74 *** | −0.34 ** |
| FC | 0.08 | NA | −0.47 *** | 0.42 *** | −0.03 | −0.52 *** |
| GOV | −0.39 ** | −0.47 *** | NA | −0.65 *** | −0.17 | 0.84 *** |
| HH | 0.12 | 0.42 *** | −0.65 *** | NA | −0.07 | −0.70 *** |
| ROW | −0.74 *** | −0.03 | −0.17 | −0.07 | NA | −0.04 |
| OGap | −0.34 ** | −0.52 *** | 0.84 *** | −0.70 *** | −0.04 | NA |

*Table 12.2* Denmark: correlation coefficients, 5 sectors: full sample: 1975–2020

| | *ROW* | *GOV* | *HH* | *FC* | *NFC* | *OGap* |
|---|---|---|---|---|---|---|
| ROW | NA | −0.33 ** | −0.23 | −0.38 *** | −0.71 *** | 0.24 |
| GOV | −0.33 ** | NA | −0.67 *** | −0.08 | 0 | 0.70 *** |
| HH | −0.23 | −0.67 *** | NA | 0.05 | 0.2 | −0.66 *** |
| FC | −0.38 *** | −0.08 | 0.05 | NA | −0.04 | −0.38 *** |
| NFC | −0.71 *** | 0 | 0.2 | −0.04 | NA | −0.35 ** |
| OGap | 0.24 | 0.70 *** | −0.66 *** | −0.38 *** | −0.35 ** | NA |

*Table 12.3* Norway: correlation coefficients, 5 sectors: full sample: 1978–2020

| | *NFC* | *FC* | *GOV* | *HH* | *ROW* | *OGap* |
|---|---|---|---|---|---|---|
| NFC | NA | −0.47 *** | 0.02 | 0.38 ** | −0.46 *** | −0.35 ** |
| FC | −0.47 *** | NA | −0.34 ** | −0.03 | 0.38 ** | −0.25 |
| GOV | 0.02 | −0.34 ** | NA | −0.17 | −0.82 *** | 0.45 *** |
| HH | 0.38 ** | −0.03 | −0.17 | NA | −0.35 ** | −0.55 *** |
| ROW | −0.46 *** | 0.38 ** | −0.82 *** | −0.35 ** | NA | −0.05 |
| OGap | −0.35 ** | −0.25 | 0.45 *** | −0.55 *** | −0.05 | NA |

*Table 12.4* Sweden: correlation coefficients, 5 sectors: full sample: 1950–2020

| | *NFC* | *FC* | *GOV* | *HH* | *ROW* | *OGap* |
|---|---|---|---|---|---|---|
| NFC | NA | −0.17 | −0.52 *** | −0.21 * | −0.37 *** | −0.40 *** |
| FC | −0.17 | NA | −0.06 | −0.40 *** | 0.33 *** | −0.03 |
| GOV | −0.52 *** | −0.06 | NA | −0.15 | −0.28 ** | 0.72 *** |
| HH | −0.21 * | −0.40 *** | −0.15 | NA | −0.41 *** | −0.28 ** |
| ROW | −0.37 *** | 0.33 *** | −0.28 ** | −0.41 *** | NA | −0.01 |
| OGap | −0.40 *** | −0.03 | 0.72 *** | −0.28 ** | −0.01 | NA |

## Notes

1 Minister of Finance in the 1950s as a Social Democrat, and later, Prime Minister of Denmark.

2 The lack of information on the financial side of the economy was not only a concern for Frisch, but also a concern for Copeland in the USA and Denitez in France. As expressed by Copeland (1949, p. 254), "When total purchases of our national product increase, where does the money come from to finance them? When purchases of our national product decline, what becomes of the money that is not spent?"

3 An early attempt to try to use a somewhat similar technique is given by Mishkin (1978).

4 Barbosa-Filho et al. (2006) presented a graphical illustration of net lending of the five institutional sectors for the USA, covering the period of 1947–2004, and a panel of developing countries, with data for the years 1980–2002, also to

investigate possible explanations for the link between the sectors, but unfortunately excluded the Scandinavian countries.

5 Norway is unfortunately not a part of the sample in any of the analysis presented here.

6 This, however, does not imply that discretionary policy changes have no effect on the sector balances, as policy changes directly affect the balances in private sector and rest of the world. In case of a lower propensity to import by the government relative to the private sector, an increase in governmen*t* consumption financed by an increase in taxes leads to an increase in net lending in private sector, while the net lending in rest of the world falls – that is, one would see an improvement on the current account.

7 The results for four, six and eight years can be provided upon request to the author.

## References


Ali Abbas, S. M. et al. 2011. Fiscal policy and the current account, *IMF Economic Review*, 59(4), pp. 603–629.

Barbosa-Filho, N. H. et al. 2006. Fiscal, foreign, and private net borrowing: Widely accepted theories don't closely fit the facts. *ANPEC – Associação Nacional dos Centros de ósgraduação em Economia [Brazilian Association of Graduate Programs in Economics]*.

Barbosa-Filho, N. H. et al. 2008. Cycles and trends in U.S. net borrowing flows, *Journal of Post Keynesian Economics*, 30(4), pp. 623–647.

Bergman, B. 2015. Balance-sheets. A financial/liability approach, in *A Concise Macro-Financial Framework: SNA Theory and Concepts Rapid Estimates of Market Valued Non-Financial Assets and National Wealth*.

Bergman, B. et al. 2010. *Tillgångar, skulder och kapitalvinster – Balansräkningens roll underskattas i statistik och analys.*, Stockholm, SCB, avdelningen för nationalärkenskaper.

Bezemer, D. J. 2010. Understanding financial crisis through accounting models, *Accounting, organizations and Society*, *35*(7), pp. 676–688.

Brink, H. 1983. *Statsbankerot?* Aalborg, Aalborg Universitetscenter.

Byrialsen, M. R. et al. 2021. Sektorbalanser förklarer offentliga finanser och bytesbalans i nordiska länder, *Ekonomiska Samfundets Tidskrift*, (1), pp. 2–19.

Christensen, J. P. et al. 1995. Nordic historical national accounts since the 1880s, *Scandinavian Economic History Review*, 43(1), pp. 30–52.

Copeland, M. A. 1949. Social accounting for money flows, *The Accounting Review*, 24(3), pp. 254–264.

Fiebiger, B. 2013. A constructive critique of the Levy sectoral financial balance approach, *Real-world Economics Review*, 64(1), pp. 59–80.

Fløttum, E. J. et al. 2012. *History of National Accounts in Norway: From Free Research to Statistics Regulated by Law*, Oslo/Kongsvinger, Statistics Norway.

Glötzl, F. and Rezai, A. 2018. A sectoral net lending perspective on Europe, *Cambridge Journal of Economics*, 42(3), pp. 779–795.

Godley, W. and Lavoie, M. 2012. *Monetary Economics: An Integrated Approach to Credit, Money, Income, Production and Wealth*, Basingstoke, UK, Palgrave Macmillan UK.

Krugman, P. 2009. Deficits saved the world – The New York Times, July 15th 2009.
Mishkin, F. S. 1978. The household balance sheet and the Great Depression, *The Journal of Economic History*, 38(4), pp. 918–937.
Semieniuk, G. et al. 2012. Nothing learned from the crisis? Some remarks on the stability programmes 2011–2014 of the Euro area governments, in *Keynes's General Theory for Today Contemporary Perspectives* edited by Jesper Jespersen and Mogens Ove Madsen, Edward Elgar, pp. 186–206. Cheltenham, UK.
Tissot, B. 2016. Development of financial sectoral accounts: New opportunities and challenges for supporting financial stability analysis, in *34th General Conference of the International Association for Research in Income and Wealth (IARIW), August 2016.*
van Ark, B. 1995. Towards European historical national accounts, *Scandinavian Economic History Review*, 43(1), pp. 3–16.

# 13 A new approach to financial instability

*Catherine Macaulay*

## 1 Introduction

The failure to predict the 2008 Financial Crisis using conventional economic approaches has inspired a quest to better understand, model and control instability. As a recognized component of recurrent instability, share market fluctuations have always presented theoretical challenges. However, key information regarding the nature of share markets, as determined by their origin, has been overlooked. It explains why they are intrinsically unstable, and predictive modelling is impossible. Furthermore, the 400-year history of share market development explains why instability will remain prevalent in capitalism while share markets are prominent in economic theory and policy. The widespread belief that 'No institution in our capitalist society is as venerable as the stock market' (Stiglitz 2013, 55) presumes that rogue traders ignorant of 'proper' market operations periodically spoil an essentially good system that could be better predicted and regulated with more realistic modelling. This is not supported by history. The gradual evolution of share markets, despite persistent instability, to become a respected pillar of capitalism and embedded in salary, pension and tax policies is found to be based on many misconceptions. Clarification of concepts, however, exposes new theoretical directions in the search for stability.

The share market's rise to prominence has been aided by confusing terminology. 'The share' evolved as a unique financial instrument so, for clarity, will not be called 'equity'. Their trading market will be called 'the share market' to distinguish it from other types of 'stock market'.

'The share', did not begin as, and never became, ownership equity that was traded. It evolved through a 1612 breach of contract when the Dutch East India Company compulsorily rolled over their ten-year bonds to avoid a statutory public audit that would reveal indebtedness and corruption. Fixing the bond capital created the new instrument. Its trading market was not carefully designed after considering consequences. It was opportunistic, exploiting the company register that facilitated trading by allowing ownership details simply to be altered after sale. This informal, volatile trading market neither instigated nor drove the Dutch Golden Age economy but

DOI: 10.4324/9781003253457-16

diverted capital into speculative trading, depleting the web of credit that funded business enterprise. General economic decline followed, in a pattern that recurred in industrializing Britain.

Understanding how trading the right to a share in the profits of a small and declining number of listed companies came to shape the global economy shines light on various intractable problems in economic theory. Economists facilitated share markets' ascent. Following Jevons' 1878 examination of share market data, Fisher and Keynes blended concepts of finance and economics, ushering share markets into economic theory. Ambiguity surrounding the definition of 'investment' permitted the conflation of productive investment activity and non-productive, secondary market transactions for rentier profit as 'investment', a category error that promoted the rise of share markets and confounded economic theory. Despite the 1929 Great Crash and 1970s downturns, economists and policymakers, again, assisted the share markets' return to prominence in the 1980s, introducing new conundrums for monetary policy and economic theory.

History demonstrates that share markets are not essential in highly productive, stable capitalist economies and that economists propelled their development. This suggests their extraction from economic theory is equally possible and potentially important for stability. It is proposed that, rather than increasing detail in models of the existing, unstable form of capitalism, establishing an unambiguous definition of productive 'investment' represents a theoretical starting point for promoting a more stable capitalist model. Clarifying the nature of 'the share' and 'investment', and reconsidering Fisher and Keynes' widely criticized fusion of the language of productive and rentier 'investment', could drive a paradigm shift. Relating 'investment' to productive activity and understanding share trading to be noninvestment transactions would alter the status of share markets and allow their re-positioning within capitalism. Rather than restricting share markets in the quest for stability, transitioning to a macroeconomic model based on productive investment could, instead, reposition them as an 'own risk' activity. Supporting small business' preference for internal or bank finance, directing pension savings towards investment in productive activity and confirming the original monetary policy goal of 'price stability', not the impossible goal of 'financial stability', would change economic objectives from stabilizing inherently unstable markets to building stable 'real' economies, returning economics to the study of productive economies.

## 2 The origin of 'the share' in the Dutch Golden Age

The Dutch Golden Age of technological advancement by merchants, farmers and craftsmen was evident in the 1540s, well before the world's first financial trading market began in Amsterdam in 1602. It was a capitalist economy featuring large numbers of small entrepreneurs funded by a varied, local network of credit linking households and enterprise. Entrepreneurial trading voyages, successfully financed as peer-funded partnerships, were a feature achieving annualized returns averaging 27% (Gelderblom, de Jong and Jonker 2010, 13).

The United East India Company (*Vereenigde Oost-Indische Compagnie* or VOC) was established through the Dutch government's compulsory amalgamation of six successful shipping companies following the 1601 departure of English East India Company ships. Voyages to the East Indies lasted several years, so an innovative company charter was devised: ten-year loan capital would be publicly raised, a dividend distributed when 5% of company capital was available and, after a publicized audit on maturity, a second ten-year bond would be sold. A register at East India house allowed investors to transfer ownership to a third party if funds were required earlier. Transferrable bond ownership using notaries was an established tradition but facilitating transfers was new. Rather than the usual handful of known investors, over 1,000 registered as the VOC's first bondholders in 1602.

The transfer arrangement was never used solely to recoup investment funds when necessary. Trading began immediately as investors saw potential in buying and selling, striking deals before changing the register at East India house. Market prices reacted to news, rumours, war and peace. Over five years, a third of the bonds changed hands in Amsterdam (Gelderblom and Jonker 2004).

With such active trading, few were earning dividends on bonds bought in 1602. Over the first century, returns on changing market prices averaged 3.75% pa, which was less than government bonds (Petram 2011, 8). For share

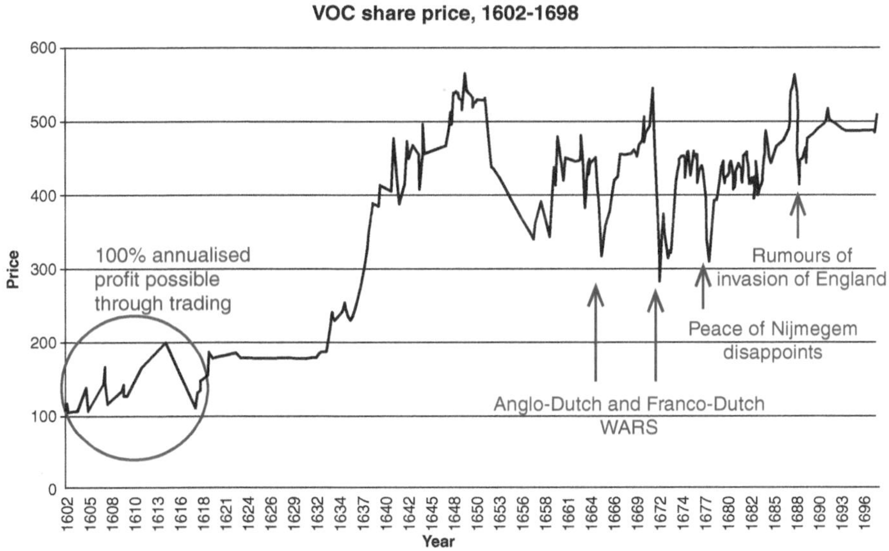


*Figure 13.1* Dutch East India share price.

traders, however, returns could yield significant, short-term gains or losses (Figure 13.1).

The company itself was indebted, debt averaging 10–12 million guilders from 1622 to 1700 (De Korte 2001). Cash flow problems have been attributed to the combined challenges of East India trade and government defence obligations, but there is also evidence of directors enriching themselves through commissions, personal lending to the company and direct expropriation. This made the ten-year public audit problematic. In a breach of contract, directors ensured the ten-year bonds were rolled over, arguing that the trading market allowed capital to be recouped at any time. Protesting shareholders were placated by a payment equivalent to the initial capital plus a return approximating prevailing interest rates, effectively matching the cost of honouring the original bond contract. This introduced the perennial burden of dividends with no new capital.

On maturity, the bonds were compulsorily rolled over again, becoming dividend-paying perpetual bonds or fixed, tradable shares, a new financial instrument. Shares were never the equivalent of ownership equity. They evolved from bonds as an opportunistic bet on the anticipated income accruing from dividends or sale to others. The desire to conceal accounts that could expose indebtedness and corruption helped create 'the share', pioneering the 'folly, negligence, and profusion' of management and promoting share trading, which Smith (1776, 312) specifically excluded as incompatible with the wealth of nations.

The listed company model was not an essential component of the Golden Age economy. Entrepreneurship remained funded by peer investment. Amsterdam's 1672 stock market crash, however, signalled the end of the era (Van Leeuwen and Van Zanden 2011). Occurring at a time of low interest rates, those with accumulated capital sent it abroad, seeking higher returns through innovative mutual funds and unit trusts. The absence of suitable investment capital stifled successful sectors like retail, textiles, brewing, distilling, glassmaking and diamond cutting and the domestic economy stalled, rendering financial development for rentier returns a plausible culprit in the Golden Age's demise.

## 3 Uptake of the listed company model

The VOC model was adopted unevenly. England's East India Company continued bond financing for over 50 years and hybrid models were eventually established in Denmark and Sweden (Figure 13.3). Danish Asiatisk Kompagni shareholders contributed to a transparent 'circulating fund' to pay costs and elected managers through democratic voting arrangements, while the Swedish Ostindiska Companiet provided no market structure for ownership transfers; that remained the responsibility of shareholders. In Germany, scepticism saw publicly traded shares avoided until 1820 when trading began in Frankfurt. National differences in the acceptance of share trading remain evident in varieties of capitalism.

### *3.1 History repeats: Britain's industrialization*

Victorian entrepreneurship is often associated with large, share-financed infrastructure projects, but listed companies did not instigate Britain's Industrial Revolution. Frenzied speculative trading in London's Exchange Alley, involving hundreds of ventures, became the target of the 'Bubble Act' (Wordsworth 1842, Appendix 2) two years before the South Sea Company bubble began in 1720. Listed companies other than those supported by Act of Parliament or royal charter were declared a 'public nuisance' with £500 fines for brokers trading their shares. Legal public listing was suddenly limited to the Bank of England, the East India and South Sea Companies and two insurance companies. The era of innovation and entrepreneurship began in the 1750s in 'a world in which equity markets were almost nonexistent' (Hutchinson and Dowd 2018). Burgeoning industrial enterprise was funded by family wealth, an informal capital market or county banks that provided short-term capital (Mokyr 1999).

The 1825 repeal of the Bubble Act revived share markets and financial instability. A crash before the next parliamentary sitting saw record bankruptcies, including over 80 county bank failures. A series of crashes followed. Following the 1837 crash, a speculative 'mania' almost doubled the railway share index. From 1844 to 1846, investors poured in almost half the value of British GDP, but by 1851 share prices had fallen by about a third. Repeating the Dutch pattern, Britain became a rentier nation, its industrial base undermined as capital was sent abroad seeking higher returns. After the 1873 Vienna stock market crash and international financial crisis, Britain experienced two decades of economic stagnation, losing 'First Industrial Nation' status as share market instability persisted (Figure 13.2).

### *3.2 Industrial development without share markets*

With different frameworks for financing the 'real' economy, America joined Germany in overtaking Britain as an industrial nation. The importance of share markets in financing America's canals and railways is a common misconception. The few that were share-financed drove Wall Street speculation in the 1830s. Bond finance was usual, often as Sterling bonds that drained capital from Britain's economy. Industrial capital networks developed to finance manufacturing and smaller enterprises, while America's share markets involved only the largest companies until the 20th century.

In Germany, creative entrepreneurs, not corporations, were recognized as primary economic drivers. Bonds and bank finance remained the preference. Banks supported the 'real' economy by diversifying into regions and

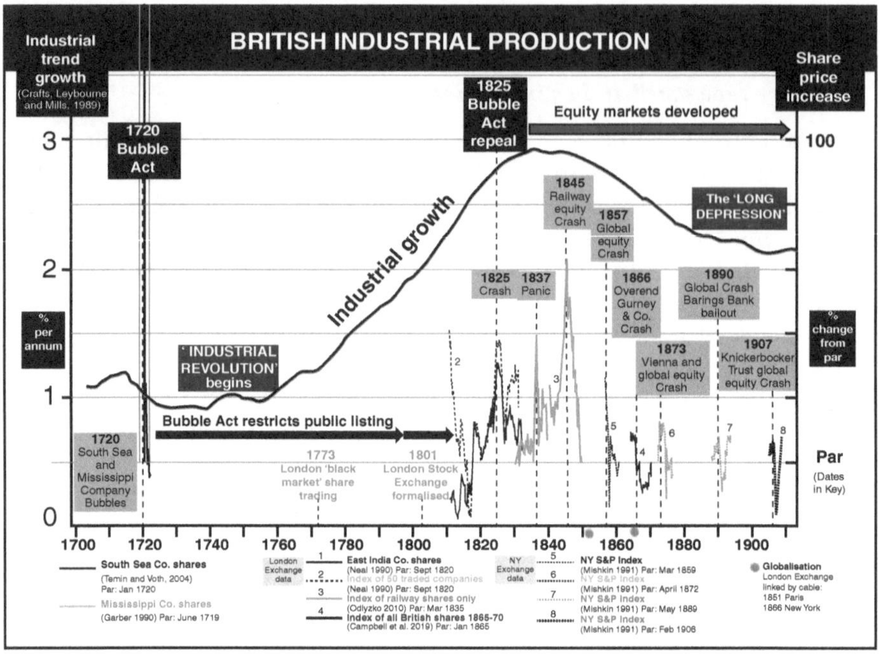


*Figure 13.2* British industrialization and stock market activity, 1700–1900.

offering financing alternatives to smaller interests. Germany's successful Mittelstand, with its unlisted, often family-owned businesses favouring internal or bank finance, is a continuation of the Dutch Golden Age economic model before the share market developed.

## 4 Introducing share markets into economic theory

When extolling the 'invisible hand' of free markets, Smith (1776) referred to primary markets, not share markets, which were vilified after the 1720 South Sea bubble. However, the idea that share markets could be modelled and controlled re-surfaced amidst the series of crashes following the 1825 Bubble Act repeal. Economists turned their attention to the 'the share' and its trading market (Figure 13.3).

Renowned statistician Mills (1867) had found 'commercial panics' recurred in 10.44-year cycles, proposing they resulted from 'the destruction of belief and hope in the minds of merchants and bankers' (Jevons [1878] 1884a, 215). Jevons rejected the idea of periodic change in human psychology. He sought explanations of share market crashes in the 'industrial environment', anticipating a decennial cycle complementing his 9–12-year

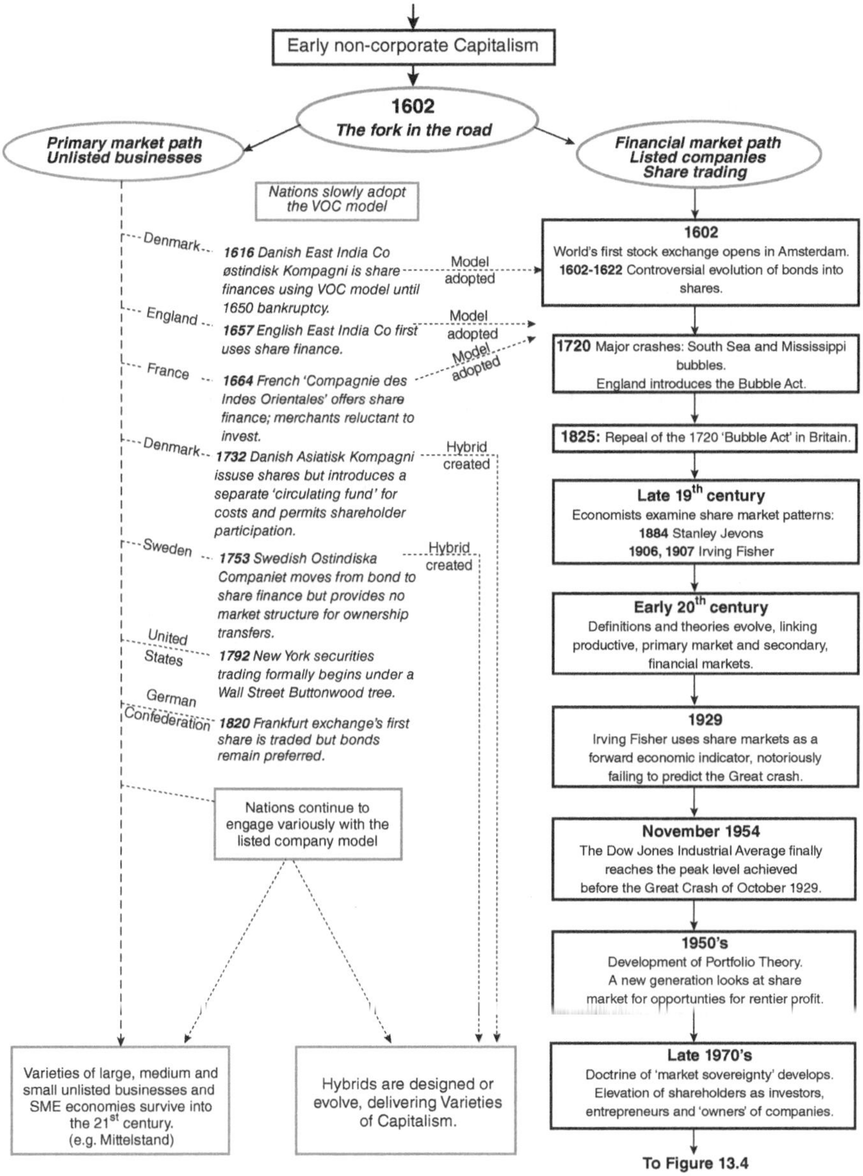


*Figure 13.3* Capitalism's two paths for capital: the productive economy and the financial sector.

commodity cycles and the recently reported 10.45-year period for sunspot activity. To reach his 10.466-year period for major 'commercial crises', Jevons ([1878] 1884a, 213) selectively chose famines in India, included some crises of 'doubtful existence' and justified discrepancies with Indian trade figures as reflecting significant, unrecorded smuggling. This established an 'almost perfect coincidence' with solar cycles and Jevons ([1878]1884b) confirmed a causal connection representing the 'missing link' that explained share market crashes. He recommended building meteorological observatories to prove 'cosmical variations' caused decennial speculative crises.

By 1900, Wall Street was recognizable but linked to 'business', not economic theory. Fisher (1907, 210) pioneered links between finance, economics and accounting through the application of a present value formula to 'any income stream whatever', including bonds and shares. This elevated the 'investment' activity of the trader/speculator/rentier. Fisher (1907, 42) disputed the claim that the 'productive' entrepreneur most deserved financial reward commending, instead, the 'sleeping partner' who 'does not lift a finger' for abstaining from consuming his capital. Veblen (1908) criticized Fisher's work as taxonomy for businessmen, but it began an ontological shift, blending economic and financial terminology.

Keynes intertwined terms further. He recognized share markets as disruptive institutions capable of disturbing economies, notoriously denigrated them as a casino, game of 'Old Maid', musical chairs or a beauty contest (Keynes 1936, 155) and akin to betting on horse races (Royal Commission 1932). However, for Keynes who 'loved any opportunity to have a gamble' (Harrod 1957, 695), examining the market became a lifelong morning ritual and it informed his economic thought. His 1909–1913 Cambridge lecture series, delivered from the age of 25, related to share market operations. Spending most of his early income on shares to ensure less than £100 remained in his bank (Kent 2012) reflected his conception of saving and 'investment' as 'different aspects of the same thing' (Keynes 1936, 74), with saving 'a mere residual' (1936, 65). Keynes was uneasy that this source of wealth was not 'derived from doing anything useful, from making anything' (Mini 1995, 55). His approach was rationalized, however, by distinguishing a 'love of money as a means to the enjoyments and realities of life' from the 'morbidity' of the love of money as a possession (Keynes [1931] 1972, 329).

By regarding share buyers as 'investors' or financial entrepreneurs with 'intelligence, determination and executive skill' (1936, 377), Keynes defined himself out of the categories of rentier or speculator. In advocating the 'euthanasia of the rentier', Keynes (1936) referred to those earning from land rent or interest-bearing securities, overlooking the possibility that share trading after the Initial Public Offering (IPO) was also 'functionless'. Despite deploring speculators' short-term trading as causing whirlpools, Keynes was an active trader within an increasingly 'buy and hold' approach. Only 5% of his share purchases for the King's College endowment fund were the IPOs that provide firms with new capital (Chambers and Dimson 2012, 28).

The rest were non-productive transactions, some undoubtedly speculative (Skidelsky 2009, 56).

In pre-General Theory correspondence with Hawtrey, Keynes ([1936] 1978, 629) rejected the criticism that his conception of investment insufficiently distinguished the shares of enterprises from capital goods, asserting: 'My intention is to apply to both indifferently. I do not see that, at the level of abstraction in which I am writing any different treatment is required'. His conception of 'investment', however, applies most appropriately to share markets. Windfall loss or gains 'due to unforeseen changes in market values' and their 'psychological influence' (1936, 57) on entrepreneurs considering what capital is available for spending describes shareholders watching the market daily better than the impact of changes in the value of a producer's machinery, to which the concept is extended. The idea that

> no one can save without acquiring an asset ...; and no one can acquire an asset which he did not previously possess, unless either an asset of equal value is newly produced or someone else parts with an asset of that value which he previously had
>
> (Keynes 1936, 81–82)

also relates better to share trading than to individuals saving 'for a rainy day' or entrepreneurs building factories.

Hawtrey (1931) accused Keynes of 'dictatorship of the vocabulary' but, despite criticism from less charismatic colleagues and his own lament that the share market was a 'casino', Keynes' rhetoric prevailed, and his new definition of investment ushered the casino into economic theory.

In 1929, Fisher was using the share market as a leading economic indicator: a rising index indicated a sound economy and future growth. A week before the 'Great Crash', the *Chicago Tribune* reported a recession in demand for steel and cars, key drivers of oil, gas, coal and construction industries (Mather 1929). Fisher, however, 'read the market' right up to the Crash, notoriously predicting further rises.

The Dow Jones index did not return to its 1929 peak until 1954. A new generation, seeing share market 'opportunities', developed theories of Portfolio Choice (Markowitz 1952, Roy 1952), reviving the focus on share market behaviour and optimizing rentier returns.

## 5 Introducing share markets into public policy

From the late 1970s, Keynes' share market 'casino' was embedded in policy globally after President Reagan followed recommendations of economic advisors, including deregulation exponents, Martin Feldstein, Arthur Laffer and Larry Kudlow, and directed government pension funds away from customary Treasury bonds and cash towards share markets. This paradigm shift fits within Keynes' (1936, 378) view of investment and his enigmatic policy recommendation of 'a somewhat comprehensive socialisation of investment'. However, the regular flow of funds into share markets drove up prices without stabilizing markets as Keynes ([1943] 1980, 322) anticipated.

The IMF simultaneously recommended divesting UK government shareholdings to reduce debt, inspiring the privatization movement and more accessible, deregulated share markets. Regarding them as economically beneficial, the IMF, World Bank and OECD embraced the Financial Market Theory of Development and, by 2005, 58 developing nations had opened new exchanges.

Economists' support helped share trading markets become a potent force in a complex new economic web (Figure 13.4). Shareholder value became a corporate purpose. A 1919 case brought by the Dodge Brothers against Ford after the 'Model T' profits were used to cut vehicle price, re-invest and increase wages had found corporations to be organized primarily for shareholder returns. Friedman (1970) promulgated this principle and it became ingrained after 1981 when General Electric's CEO confirmed that stock markets drive the economy, shareholders come first as company 'owners' and return on equity is the key financial measure. Perceived 'democratization' of company ownership saw shareholders press for greater reward at the expense of other stakeholders, the '1%' benefiting most as around $2 trillion was transferred to them in the 20-year Reagan/Thatcher bull market (Bogle 2005). Although Piketty (2014) did not emphasize them as a source of inequality, share markets have various de-stabilizing regressive mechanisms, including large financial sector salaries, executive bonuses paid in shares with buybacks aimed at raising their prices, tax benefits for pension funds and bonanzas for entrepreneurs of newly floated companies.

The view of share markets as beneficial helped legitimize active trading as 'investment', re-igniting debate on the line between investment and speculation. The term 'investment bank' no longer applied only to institutions like the European Investment Bank or the 19th-century Deutsche Bank that funded Edison's electrification projects but was extended to those 'investing' in shares and derivatives, like Goldman Sachs.

Including share markets in policy placed central banks in an invidious position. Share markets, constantly fed by pension contributions, provided optimistic feedback when a rising stock market was still considered a positive economic indicator. Pressure for central banks to support share markets increased, inducing moral hazard by diminishing the apparent need for prudence, conditions ideal for an unforeseen crash.

Central bankers remain in a wilderness of mirrors searching for appropriate supervisory, regulatory and macroprudential tools to contain constantly primed share markets, while mandates hover between 'price stability' and 'financial stability', something never achieved. As stimulus measures, some central banks bought shares, despite history demonstrating this does not stimulate economic activity, and many introduced Quantitative Easing,

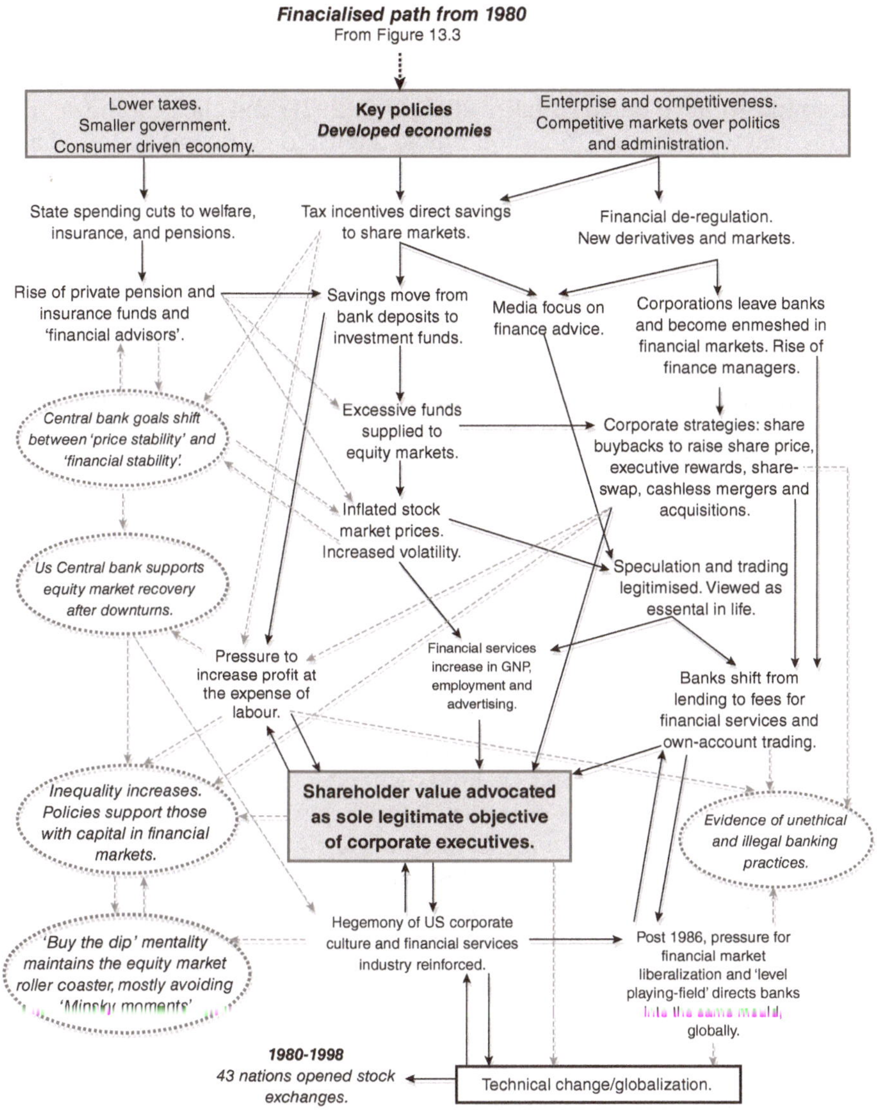


*Figure 13.4* 1980s: Publicly traded equity becomes enmeshed in the political economy of nations, globally.

which allowed fortuitous portfolio rebalancing, raising share prices with negligible economic stimulus. Following the expectation that maintaining a gentle bull market is both possible and the job of central banks, they remain at the centre of a conundrum relating monetary policy to moral hazard and asset bubbles, with considerable pension funds at stake.

The 1980s share market development institutionalized the processes that ended the Dutch Golden Age and British Industrial Revolution, attracting spare or borrowed capital to the detriment of productive investment and increasing inequality as wages stagnated. While the macroeconomics has been found to have failed (Stiglitz 2011, Dow 2021) and the search for stabilizing macroprudential tools continues, the listed company and its share market remain widely regarded as venerable. However, history exposes this view to be based on many misconceptions.

## 6 Misconceptions surrounding the listed company model

History does not support former US Federal Reserve Chairman Martin's (1955) contention that 'stock exchanges are designed to function so as to encourage growth in equity ownership rather than debt, with resulting benefit to the economy'. Exchanges were never 'designed', encouraging 'equity ownership' was not their purpose, the 'nonproduction transactions' of share trading do not contribute to GDP and history does not demonstrate unequivocal benefit to productive economies. Consistent with lessons from history, Pilkington (2013) concluded that speculative demand can drive up prices without increasing real incomes or output after considering the failure of pricing theories related to financial market speculation to capture reality.

### *6.1 Misconceptions surrounding 'the share'*

'The share' remains a unique instrument that puzzles legal academics (Ireland 1999). It did not develop as shared ownership equity made more liquid through trading. It conveys only the right to share in a company's profits at the directors' discretion and limited voting rights, far short of 'ownership' rights (Honoré 1961). The widespread belief that shareholders 'own' the company, which is run by directors, is not a legal certainty. Listed companies effectively have no owners, so IPOs cannot 'democratise ownership'.

### *6.2 Misconceptions surrounding listed companies*

If public listing is perceived as the ultimate stage in a firm's development (Figure 13.5), the small and declining number of listed companies and failure of eligible firms to 'go public' may seem a mystery. Unsophisticated business owners and underdeveloped markets are usually held responsible for this, not that it may be logical and reflect business preferences. Research has not found evidence relating low numbers to poor share market access (ECB 2010–2018). Most SMEs simply have no interest in adopting the listed model (Macaulay 2019). Even amongst the world's companies with revenue greater that $1 billion, 37% were privately owned in 2013 (Dobbs, et al. 2013). Unlisted companies like Aldi, Beretta, Bloomberg, Bose, Chanel, IKEA, Lego, Mars, Miele, New Balance and Rolex demonstrate that share funding is not essential for global companies.

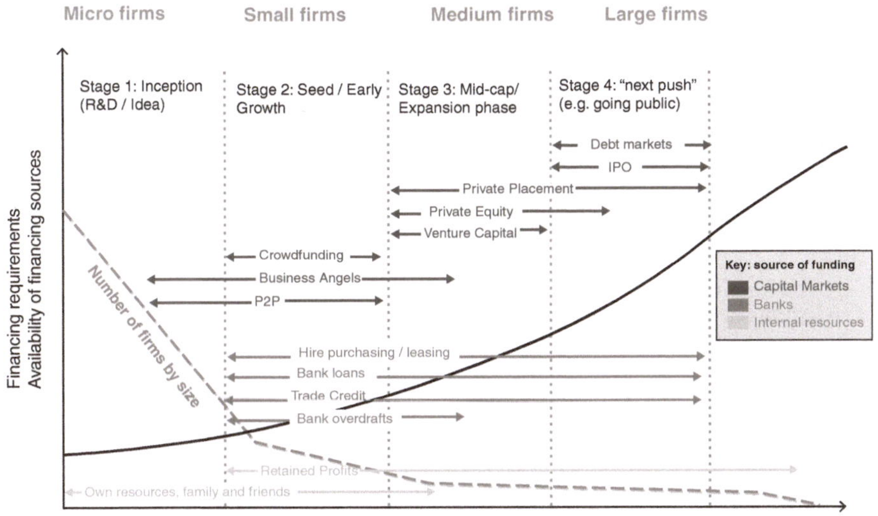


*Figure 13.5* Firm numbers at each stage of the corporate 'funding escalator' model.

### *6.3 Misconceptions surrounding 'investment'*

Keynes' deliberate alignment of share buying with productive investment was widely challenged. Like Hawtrey (1931), Kahn (1978, 549) declared: 'Keynes allowed himself to become confused by the two quite different meanings of the word "investment" – in securities and in new capital goods'. The unfamiliar meanings meant Keynes debated at cross purposes with colleagues. Kalecki ([1968] 1993, 260), whose investment analysis related to goods markets, past profits and business decisions that did not change frequently with subjective expectations, criticized the investment volatility, psychological emphasis and 'nebulous propensity to save' in Keynes' theory of investment, which better described share buyers reacting to daily market movements. Similarly, Hayek's (1945) markets were primary markets for labour and commodities like stationery, tools and tin, not secondary markets. He used the term 'stock exchange' rarely and pejoratively as representing 'paper profits' and 'pseudo-profits' (Hayek 1939, 133), and his painstaking analysis of Keynes' Treatise on Money found standard business practices becoming exceptions to the rule under definitions skewed towards share market 'investment' (Hayek 1931). Robinson (1960, 6) unequivocally declared: 'You are not investing when you buy a security; you are investing when you cause a house to be built' and 'investment does not mean buying a piece of paper, but making an addition to the stock of goods in existence'.

Keynes' recommendation that investors treat long-term holdings as series of short-term positions that can be changed with new information confusingly matches his conception of speculation as short-term whirlpools aimed at capital appreciation. Kaldor's theory of speculation (1939) embraced all purchases, from raw materials to shares, where the sole motivation is an expected price change. Compared with commodity markets that are logically impacted by weather and 'normal price' boundaries, he found share markets fundamentally speculative:

> The day-to-day movements on the Stock Exchange, where considerable changes in prices occur in accordance with the day's political news, could hardly be accounted for on any other ground but on the attempt of speculators to forecast the psychology of other speculators.

### *6.4 Misconceptions surrounding share markets*

Describing share markets as 'capital markets' suggests their purpose is raising capital for productive activity. However, productive capital is raised only at the IPO, so the perennial subsequent noninvestment transactions are, unavoidably, the main activity.

A company's 'market capitalisation' gives a false impression of value as it does not disaggregate uniformly. A single trading price never represents a value applicable to all shares, rendering a company's 'market capitalisation' illusory. All theories that incorporate share prices to better understand their movements, from Kaldor's and Tobin's ratios to the Efficient Market Hypothesis and Behavioural models, build on illusory company values.

Ultimately, there is no definitive formula behind share prices. The belief that they equal the present value of all future dividends involves sufficient unknowns to make it unreliable. Keynes (1936, 152) noted, 'all sorts of considerations enter into the market valuation which are in no way relevant to the prospective yield'. There is also no certain correlation between share prices and a company's underlying book value. When trading at $120 in 2008, Rio Tinto's book value was $17. The difference cannot be presumed to reflect the price expected in a takeover, resources still in the ground, future commodity prices or goodwill and other intangibles. It can be anything. 'Price discovery' relates to the exchange value of 'the share' at that moment, not a 'truer' company valuation. Changing information and circumstances ensure volatility, and a 'buy the dip' doctrine induces perpetual cycles.

If share markets are believed to efficiently reflect equilibrium prices, crashes inevitably surprise. Identifying unique triggers, often 'black swans', ex post cannot provide causal information relevant to the next downturn as all crashes are caused by shareholders simultaneously seeking to sell substantial numbers of shares, for *any* reason.

The 1929 Crash demonstrated share market fallibility as an indicator of economic health. Galbraith (1955, 93) later recognized share markets as a lagging indicator or one-way mirror: 'cause and effect run from the economy to the stock market, never the reverse'. While Galbraith's mirror, reflecting the reported 1929 industrial downturn, could have predicted the crash, Fisher's rising share market cannot. Their efficacy as an indicator was only declared 'murky' decades later, however (Stock and Watson 2001). Fed Chairman Greenspan, and Blanchard (2008) applied Fisher's reasoning and failed to predict the 2008 Financial Crisis. Galbraith's 'mirror', however, answers the Queens 2008 question of why the financial crisis was not predicted: like 1929, the stock market was wrongly used as a forward economic indicator.

Former Fed Chairman Greenspan still reads the market as an economic indicator (Li 2019) but the US Fed pivoted slightly to consider share markets as an 'economic driver' (Cieslak and Vissing-Jorgensen 2020). However, this still suggests buoyant share markets drive buoyant economies, and fails to recognise the vulnerability of all share markets to myriad unforeseeable triggers.

Share market regulation remains the favoured response to instability (Turner et al. 2010a, Blanchard and Summers 2019). However, restrictions cannot alter the market's speculative and, therefore, intrinsically unstable nature. The Glass Steagall Act, introduced following the 1929 Crash, was a successful defensive strategy separating licensed banking institutions from organizations involved in trading financial instruments, not a regulatory mechanism for stabilizing markets. That has never proven possible.

## 7 Implications for modelling, theory and policy

Seeking to promote stability through better share market prediction or regulation presumes that, despite responding to unknown future events, sentiment and contrarians' second guesses, a key to unlocking patterns exists. The internal logic that encourages analysts to surmise reasons for market movements is understood to imply that modellable cause-and-effect patterns exist. Developments in machine learning algorithms have rekindled the search and recent papers have claimed improved accuracy of new algorithms compared with conventional trend prediction models (Shen and Shafiq 2020, Tsai, et al. 2020). However, predictability requires unattainable knowledge of the aggregate share-buyer reaction to future events, about which we 'simply do not know' (Keynes 1936, 113).

Keynes' conflation of share buying and productive investment, now implicit in models of contemporary capitalism, confounds all theory and modelling. The conceptual twist supporting his accounting identity, S = I: 'Saving and Investment have been so defined that they are necessarily equal in amount' (Keynes 1936, 74), has generated controversial inferences. Robinson (1960, 10) answered her question 'How does it come about that, on balance, individuals always decide to save just as much as entrepreneurs have decided to invest?' with 'Saving is equal to investment, because investment ... causes incomes to be whatever is required to induce people to save at a rate equal to the rate of investment' and Lerner (1938, 301) concluded that individuals are not free to decide how much they are going to save and, as all saving is 'forced', 'free will is nothing but a pleasant illusion'.

As a useful accounting cross-check for copious data and heterogeneous components, however, Keynes' accounting identity has been accepted by mainstream and heterodox schools of economics. However, embracing share buying in the definition of investment meant it did not fit the National Accounting framework, where Kuznets had defined National income as excluding capital gains and non-productive transactions like share trading, and the problem of ordinarily unstable share prices has challenged the System of National Accounts since their introduction in 1968. Flawed assumptions have been needed to uphold the concept of share buying as investment. These have been imported into Stock Flow Consistent (SFC) modelling that strives to better integrate the 'real' economy and the financial sector. Shares are placed in the 'financial assets' category and, as if they are debt, their book value is used as if a corresponding liability is owed, which is untrue for shares. Companies owe no liability to shareholders other than residual claims in bankruptcy. Revaluation accounts incorporating share price changes over the accounting period are immediately out-of-date and add a false sense of value by mixing unrealised values with certain prices within the category.

Keynes' deliberate ambiguity placed the definition of investment in the eye of the beholder, opening a conceptual schism in SFC modelling. Moore's (2006, 156–170) Keynesian view of shares as 'investment' accepts unrealised share values as a realistic measure of 'wealth' and applies share revaluation data to present the S = I accounting identity as a measure of change in wealth. Closer to Kuznets' definition of investment, Lindner (2012, 22) sets aside the 'substantial economic implications' of a non-zero financial net worth, applies the flawed National Accounting premise of share book value as a company liability to ensure financial assets always sum to zero and finds non-financial asset production to be the only 'investment' that increases an economy's net worth. Keynes' ambiguous definition of investment underlies this divergence, inducing the flawed assumptions that make both approaches unrealistic. Clarification of the definition would promote more robust SFC modelling.

With no 'fact of the matter', economists are entitled to define terms as they wish (Sumner 2015). Robinson (1932) recommended definitions and assumptions be tractable and correspond with the real world. However, by including share buying as investment, Keynes' definition was so tractable it promoted a category error that has institutionalized instability and confounded economic theory. Re-assessment opens new theoretical directions, potentially driving a different form of capitalism.

Extracting share markets from the definition of investment, and recognizing them as speculative, does not necessitate restricting their operation. Share markets represent a long-standing freedom and restriction risks de-stabilization. However, building them into theory and policy, where they have been ascribed dubious roles as 'economic drivers' or markets for capital or 'wealth creation', has ensured their instability has become systemic. Reversing this is justified by history.

Returning the focus of economics to productive economic activity could drive a 'reset' more powerful than leaving share trading at the heart of capitalism and urging corporate responsibility to all stakeholders. Fortifying channels of internal finance and bank loans, the financing preferences of productive enterprise (Macaulay 2019), developing lending markets, investing pension funds in productive activity and isolating share trading as an 'own risk' activity (Macaulay 2015) represents a paradigm shift developing capitalism's productive path (Figure 13.3). This supports a paradigm akin to the early Dutch Golden Age model and still extant in Germany's Mittelstand, with its variety of banking and lending alternatives appropriate to all productive enterprise. Reducing share market prominence would not solve all capitalism's issues of power and purpose but would help ensure their instability is less systemic.

## 8 Conclusion

The differences between productive investment and noninvestment share market transactions have been diminished in economic theory and it is proposed that adding detail to models in which share markets are accepted as 'investment' builds on this flawed conception. Understanding the flaws and applying historic evidence of share markets as inherently unstable opens a new approach to instability, rather than more complex modelling of share trading ill-conceived as investment.

'The share' was not carefully designed. It was created through a breach of contract within a speculative market for trading Dutch East India Company bonds, becoming a puzzling tradable instrument with limited entitlements. Neither technology nor evolution has changed this structure. After the IPO, all share trades are non-productive transactions, reflecting speculation on their future price and/or dividends, in an inherently volatile market. Nowhere does history indicate that share markets can be tamed, or that poor regulation periodically spoils a good system. Instead, their 400-year history reveals they were unintended, opportunistic developments linked to instability and economic decline.

Share markets' ascendancy in capitalism was not inevitable but was assisted by politicians and economists, and misconceptions abound in every aspect of the model, from the share and its trading market to their importance to companies and the economy. From 1906, Fisher and Keynes altered the definition of investment to include share trading. Keynes deplored both speculation and rentier profiteers but legitimized share trading by categorizing it as investment by financial entrepreneurs, inviting what he recognized as a 'casino' into economics. The 1980s integration of share markets in the political economy, through sovereign funds, monetary policy, pension policy and development finance, cemented their central position in capitalist economies. While share market instability and the misconceptions surrounding the model were incorporated into economic theory and policy, the misconceptions have impeded attempts to model and stabilize the system.

There has been no better time to argue over definitions. Rather than lumping productive primary markets together with unstable, non-productive secondary markets in studies of 'markets', their separation in economic theory could be revolutionary, returning the focus of economics to productive economic activity. Share trading, though accepted as legitimate, would be removed from the heart of capitalism. Decreasing share market prominence would not solve all capitalism's issues but demoting a significant and contagious source of instability would improve overall stability. Reconsidering the spectrum of activity understood by economists, policymakers, business owners and consumers to be 'investment', and the subsequent choice of those given policy support, is a logical starting point for a new approach.

## References

Blanchard, O., & Summers, L. (2019). *Evolution or Revolution.* MIT Press.

Blanchard, O. J (2008). *The State of Macro.* MIT Department of Economics Working Paper No. 08–12.

Bogle, J. (2005). *The Battle for the Soul of Capitalism.* Yale University Press.

Chambers, D., & Dimson, E. (2012). *Keynes the Stock Market Investor.* Unpublished work.

Cieslak, A., & Vissing-Jorgensen, A. (2020). *The Economics of the Fed Put.* NBER Working Papers 26894, National Bureau of Economic Research, Inc.

De Korte, J. P. (2001). *The Annual Accounting in the VOC, Dutch East India Company.* Aksant Academic Publishers.

Dobbs, R., Remes, J., Smit, S., Maniya, J., Woetzel, J., & Agyenim-Boateng, Y. (2013). *Urban World: The Shifting Global Business Landscape.* McKinsey Global Insttitute.

Dow, S. (2021, Feb. 1). *The Future of Macroeconomics.* Retrieved Feb 10, 2021, from https://www.ineteconomics.org/research/experts/sdow

ECB. (2010–2018). Survey on the Access to Finance of Enterprises in the Euro Area (SAFE). *ECB Eurosystem.*

Fisher, I. (1907). *The Nature of Capital and Income.* New York: Macmillan Company.

Friedman, M. (1970, Sept 13). The Social Responsibility of Business is to Increase its Profits. *New York Times Magazine.*

Galbraith, J. (1955). *The Great Crash 1929.* Houghton Mifflin.

Gelderblom, O., & Jonker, J. (2004). Completing a Financial Revolution: The Finance of the Dutch East India Trade and the Rise of the Amsterdam Capital Market 1595–1612. *The Journal of Economic History, 6*, 641–672.

Gelderblom, O., de Jong, A., & Jonker, J. (2010). *An Admiralty for Asia. Isaac Le Maire and Conflicting Conceptions about the Corporate Governance of the VOC.* ERIM Report Series ERS 2010–026-F&A.

Harrod, R. (1957). Clive Bell on Keynes. *The Economic Journal, 67 (December)*, 692–9.

Hawtrey, R. (1931). Reviews of Statistical and Economic Books. *Journal of the Royal Statistical Society*, vol XCIV pp. 618–623.

Hayek, F. A. (1931). Reflections on the Pure Theory of Money of Mr. J.M. Keynes. *Economica*, 270–295.

Hayek, F. A. (1939). *Profits, Interest and Investment and Other Essays on the Theory of Industrial Fluctuations*. New York: Augustus M Kelley.

Hayek, F. A. (1945). The Use of Knowledge in Society. *American Economic Review*, *35*, 619–630.

Honoré, A. M. (1961). Ownership. *The Nature of Property and the Value of Justice*, 370–375.

Hutchinson, M., & Dowd, K. (2018). The Apotheosis of the Rentier: How Napoleonic War Finance Kick-Started the Industrial Revolution Martin Hutchinson and Kevin Dowd. *Cato Journal*, 655–678.

Ireland, P. (1999). Company Law and the Myth of Shareholder Ownership. *Modern Law Review*, *62*, 32–57.

Jevons, W. S. ([1878] 1884a). The Periodicity of Commercial Crises and its Physical Explanation from the British Association conference and published in *Journal of the Statistical and Social Society of Ireland*, *7*, 1878, 334–342. In W. S. Jevons, *Investigations in Currency and Finance* (pp. 206–220). London: Macmillan and Co.

Jevons, W. S. ([1878]1884b). Commercial Crises and Sun-Spots-from *'Nature'* journal, *6*, 1878, 33–37. In *Investigations in Currency and Finance* (pp. 221–243). London: Macmillan and Co.

Kahn, R. (1978). Some Aspects of the Development of Keynes' Thought. *Journal of Economic Literature*, *June*, 16(2), 545–559.

Kaldor, N. (1939). Speculation and Economic Stability. *The Review of Economic Studies*, *7*(1), 1–27.

Kalecki, M. ([1968] 1993). Contribution to the Debate on 'The Main Problems of Political Economy and Teaching It', In J. Osiatynsky. (Ed.), *Collected Works of Michal Kalecki Vol. IV.* OUP.

Kent, R. J. (2012). Keynes's Investment Activities While in the Treasury During World War I. *History of Economics Review*, *56*(1), 1–13.

Keynes, J. M. ([1931] 1972). *Essays in Persuasion Volume 9 (Johnson and Moggridge Eds).* London: Macmillan.

Keynes, J. M. (1936). *The General Theory of Employment, Interest and Money.* Cambridge University Press.

Keynes, J. M. ([1936] 1978). *The Collected Writings of John Maynard Keynes Volume 13 The General Theory and After: Part I. Preparation (Johnson and Moggridge, Eds).* Cambridge University Press.

Keynes, J. M. ([1943] 1980). *The Collected Writings of John Maynard Keynes Volume 27 Activities 1940–1946: Shaping the Post-War World Employment (Moggridge Ed.).* London: Macmillan.

Lerner, A. (1938). Saving Equals Investment. *The Quarterly Journal of Economics*, *52*(2), 297–309.

Li, Y. (2019, Sept. 4). *Greenspan Says the Stock Market will Determine Whether There's a Recession.* Retrieved Dec 16, 2020, from CNBC: https://www.cnbc.com/2019/09/04/greenspan-says-whether-there-is-a-recession-or-not-could-depend-on-the-stock-market.html

Lindner, F. (2012). *Saving does not Finance Investment: Accounting as an Indispensable Guide to Economic Theory.* Institut für Makroökonomie und Konjunkturforschung.

Macaulay, C. R. (2015). Futures Capitalism's Renaissance? The Potential of Repositioning the Financial 'Meta-Economy'. *Futures, 68*, 5–18.

Macaulay, C. R. (2019). Smaller Firms and Public Equity: New Platforms with Old Problems. *International Journal of Globalisation and Small Business, 10*(3), 248–277.

Markowitz, H. (1952). Portfolio Selection. *The Journal of Finance, 7*, 77–91.

Martin, W. M. (1955, Mar. 14). The Study of the Stock Market. *Statement of William, McChesney Martin, Jr, Chairman, Board of Governors of the Federal Reserve System, at hearings on the study of the stock market before the Senate Committee on Banking and Currency, Monday, March 14, 1955.* Senate Committee on Banking and Currency.

Mather, O. (1929, Oct. 17). Note Recession in Demand for Steel, Autos. *Chicago Tribune*, p. Finance Section.

Mills, J. (1867). On Credit Cycles, and the Origin of Commercial Panics. *Transactions of the Manchester Statistical Society*, 5–10.

Mini, P. (1995). Keynes' Investments: Their Relation to the General Theory. *The American Journal of Sociology, 54*(1), 47–56.

Moore, B. (2006). *Shaking the Invisible Hand: Complexity, Endogenous Money and Exogenous Interest Rates.* Palgrave macmillan.

Mokyr, J. (1999). Eurocentricity triumphant. *The American Historical Review*, 104(4), 1241–1246.

Petram, L. O. (2011). The World's First Stock Exchange. http://www.worldsfirst-stockexchange.com/phd- thesis.html.

Piketty, T. (2014). *Capital in the Twenty-First Century.* Bellnap Press.

Pilkington, P. (2013). *A Stock-Flow Approach to a General Theory of Pricing.* Levy Economics Institute.

Robinson, J. (1932). *Economics is a Serious Subject: The Apologia of an Economist to the Mathematician, the Scientist and the Plain Man.* W. Heffer & Sons.

Robinson, J. (1960). *Introduction to the Theory of Employment.* Macmillan.

Roy, A. (1952). Safety-First and the Holding of Assets. *Econometrica, 20*, 431–449.

Royal Commission. (1932). *Royal Commission on Lotteries and betting.* XXVIII.

Shen, J., & Shafiq, M. O. (2020). Short-Term Stock Market Price Trend Prediction Using a Comprehensive Deep Learning System, *Journal of Big Data*, 66.

Skidelsky. (2009). *Keynes The Return of the Master.* Allen Lane.

Smith, A. (1776). *An Inquiry into the Nature and Causes of Wealth of Nations.*

Stiglitz, J. E. (2011). The Failure of Macroeconomics in America. *China & World Economy, 19*(5), 17–30.

Stiglitz, J. E. (2013). Applications to Capital, Labor, and Product Markets. In *Selected Works of Joseph E. Stiglitz: Volume II: Information and Economic Analysis.* Oxford: OUP.

Stock, J. H., & Watson, M. W. (2001). *Forecasting Output and Inflation: The Role of Asset Prices.* Conference paper: June 2000 Sveriges Riksbank Conference on Asset Markets and Monetary Policy.

Sumner, S. (2015, Feb. 14). *There's No Point in Arguing Over Definitions.* Retrieved Nov 16, 2021, from https://www.econlib.org/archives/2015/02/theres_no_point.html

Tsai, M., Cheng, C., Tsai, M., & Shiu, H. (2020). Forecasting Leading Industry Stock Prices Based on a Hybrid Time-Series Forecast Model. *PLoS ONE, 13(12).*

Turner, A., Haldane, A., Woolley, P., Wadhwani, S., Goodhart, C., Smithers, A.,... Layard, R. (2010a). *The Future of Finance.* London: The London School of Economics and Political Science.

Van Leeuwen, B., & Van Zanden, J. (2011). *The Character of Growth before 'Modern Economic Growth'? The GDP of Holland between 1347 and 1807.* CGEH Paper 4.

Veblen, T. (1908). Fisher's Capital and Income. *Political Science Quarterly, 23,* 112–128.

Wordsworth, C. F. (1842). *The Law of Joint Stock Companies.* London: Saunders and Benning.

# Index

Note: Bold page numbers refer to tables; italic page numbers refer to figures and page numbers followed by “n” denote endnotes.